FLOWERS

selecting . arranging . caring

GREGORY MILNER

WOODSLANE
PRESS

Woodslane Press Pty Ltd
10 Apollo Street
Warriewood, NSW 2102
Email: info@woodslane.com.au
Tel: 02 8445 2300 Website: www.woodslane.com.au

First published in Australia as 'Fresh Cut Flowers' in 2009 by JoJo Pulishing
This revised edition, entitled 'Flowers', published in Australia in 2017 by Woodslane Press
© 2017 Woodslane Press, text and images variously © 2017 iStockphoto, Gregory Milner and as
specified (see image credits, page 342 for details)

The information in this publication is based upon the current state of commercial and industry
practice and the general circumstances as at the date of publication. Every effort has been made to
obtain permissions relating to information reproduced in this publication. The publisher makes no
representations as to the accuracy, reliability or completeness of the information contained in this
publication. To the extent permitted by law, the publisher excludes all conditions, warranties and
other obligations in relation to the supply of this publication and otherwise limits its liability to the
recommended retail price. In no circumstances will the publisher be liable to any third party for any
consequential loss or damage suffered by any person resulting in any way from the use or reliance on
this publication or any part of it. Any opinions and advice contained in the publication are offered
solely in pursuance of the author's and publisher's intention to provide information, and have not been
specifically sought.

National Library of Australia
Cataloguing-in-Publication entry
Creator: Milner, Gregory, author.
Title: Flowers : selecting arranging caring / Gregory Milner.
Edition: 2nd edition.
ISBN: 9781925403596 (hardback)
Notes: Includes index.
Subjects: Cut flowers.
Cut foliage.
Flower arrangement.
Flowers--Collection and preservation.

Printed in China by APOL
Cover page: Gregory Milner and Nicole Gibson, photographed by Hayden Golder
Book design by: Rob Ryan
Illustrator: Chris Dent and Rob Ryan

Dedication

This book is dedicated to two great women: Norma Schifferle and the late Mietta O'Donnell. Both have led fascinating lives and my own life became entwined with theirs through flowers.

Norma Schifferle is affectionately known as the Grand Duchess Norma. This is partly due to her associations in England. She has dedicated her life to her love of flowers and the knowledge and constant source of pleasure she receives from flowers, especially from her own garden, is a great inspiration to me. I am yet to meet anyone who can make a garden posy of mixed flowers and foliages as beautifully as Norma can. They are an absolute joy to receive.

Norma was a dear friend of my late mother, Marjorie Milner, and she is a dear friend to my wife Vicky and myself. I wish to sincerely thank Norma for her advice and the benefit of her endless knowledge that has assisted me with this book.

Mietta O'Donnell was passionate about flowers – her famous Melbourne restaurant was always adorned with them. I was Mietta's florist for over ten years and our flowers decorated tables for royalty and prime ministers as well as grand weddings and numerous functions. I have such fond memories of so many occasions and events through my association and friendship with Mietta.

Contents

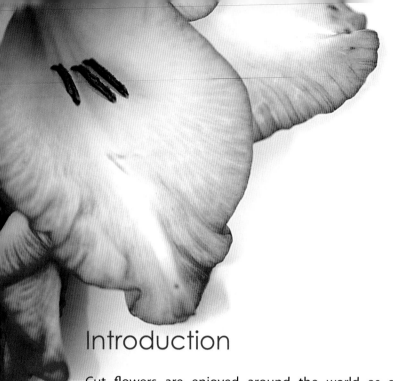

Introduction

Cut flowers are enjoyed around the world as a visual source of beauty and pleasure and a wonder of nature. They play an important role in cultural ceremonies and social expression, and are given as tokens of love, friendship, apology, condolence and celebration.

The joy of giving, receiving and using cut flowers is always enhanced by their beauty, freshness, and quality. These are attributes that can be controlled by the grower, the commercial florist and the general consumer. Whether cut from the home garden or purchased commercially, all flowers need to be handled and treated carefully to ensure that they last for their maximum life span.

Gregory Milner's Flowers is the all-in-one guide to selecting, preparing and caring for cut flowers. In this book you will learn how to identify the freshness and quality of flowers, how to look after your flowers once they are cut from the garden or purchased commercially, and most importantly, all the secret tips and tricks to help them last as long as possible. Also learn about the common pitfalls for the buyer, both wholesale and retail, the common causes of damage to cut flowers, and how to revive flowers that have wilted unexpectedly.

For readers with a creative streak, learn how to create basic arrangements using flowers, vases and floral sundry products such as wire and floral sprays. For professional florists and floral artists there are hints and tips for running a florist business and working with corporate and wedding clients.

The A-Z directory is a complete guide to all commercially available flowers that can last for five or more days as cut flowers. The directory contains comprehensive advice about care and handling, general use and wedding and corporate use for each flower variety. Topics such as cut flower life span, colour availability, growing conditions and history are also covered. Remember that months of availability will vary depending on climatic conditions.

All flowers in the A–Z directory are listed by their botanical names. To find a flower by its common name, refer to the common names index on page 336.

About the author

Gregory Milner is considered to be one of Australia's most respected and admired florists and educators. A third generation floristry expert, he has spent his working life teaching others about the joy of flowers. Today, he is the principal of the nationally accredited Registered Training Organisation, Marjorie Milner College (founded by his late mother, Marjorie Milner in 1946).

Gregory has judged numerous national and international floristry competitions. He has taught, demonstrated and judged across Australia as well as in Japan on numerous occasions. In 2001 he was invited to judge in Nagoya, Japan in the presence of their Imperial Highnesses, the Imperial Prince and Princess of Japan. He has received invitations to demonstrate at the Fine Arts Museum in San Francisco as well as in England.

Gregory is a past chairman of Interflora Victoria/ Tasmania and is a National Judge for Interflora. He has taught for TAFE Tasmania and for RMIT, and has designed and produced 24 training DVD's which are distributed around the world (<www.flowersdvd.com>).

Gregory was inducted into the Floristry Hall of Fame in 1999, following his mother's induction in 1992. He and his family have run florist shops over three generations and he is working harder than ever to ensure that Marjorie Milner College is the industry leader in floristry training. The College has grown to become Australia's largest floristry industry-based trainer, with

Gregory and his team of floristry experts training the floristry industry of both Victoria and Tasmania, as well as students from all across the world with the College's study in Australia' pathways programs.

Gregory was educated at Trinity Grammar School, Kew, and holds a Masters Degree in Education from the University of Melbourne as well as a Degree in Education Technical, a Diploma of Technical Teaching, a Trained Trade Instructors Certificate and a Floristry Tradesman's Certificate. He is dedicated to floral education and is one of the most highly qualified professional florists in the world. The students at Marjorie Milner College win more industry competitions than any other Floristry training provider in Australia.

Gregory wrote his first book in 1984, titled *The Art of Flower Arrangement*. His later books include *Wedding Flowers* and *The Complete Book of Flower Arrangement*, which is a suggested reference on the Australian National Curriculum for Floristry. This book, *Flowers*, also meets the requirements of the National Floristry Training Package.

For more information about Gregory or Marjorie Milner College please visit the College's website.

Marjorie Milner College
Excellence in Education Since 1946
www.marjoriemilner.edu.au

Acknowledgments

I would like to thank my mentor, the late Marjorie Milner, my mother.

I would also like to thank the following people for their help in producing this book: my wife Vicky Milner, for her ongoing support and encouragement; my daughter Lauren and son James for their photography and support; Norma Schifferle for her advice; Nicole Gibson for all her efforts and photography.; David and team at Woodslane Press for their enthusiasm in re-releasing this book.; Charlotte Strong for her thorough editing skill and expertise as well as Riima Daher and Louise Treyvaud; Rob Ryan for his fabulous graphic design and photography; Australian Association of Floral Designers; Fusion Flowers; APACK for their supply of floral sundries and their dedicated support of floral education; Oasis Australia; www.flowergoss.com floristry forum for promotion of this book; Lyndell Parker and the support of all the staff at Marjorie Milner College.

Gregory Milner

Glossary

Air emboli	Air bubbles that are drawn up the stem after cutting
Bacteria	Small living organisms
Bent neck	Heads that fall just under the flower head
Botrytis	Air-borne fungal disease
Callus	The healing tissue of a healing plant
Calyx	The outer whorl of flowers with a composition of separate or united sepals
Desiccation	Drying out, usually the petals
Disbud	The top flower that develops when lower buds are removed
Emboli	The process of air bubbles forming in the xylem vessels of a flower stem
Embolism	An air blockage in a flower stem
Ethylene	A hormone produced by decaying plants which speeds the maturity of the flower.
Fungi	Living organisms that attach to flowers, foliage and stems
Panicle	A flower head that is loose-branched with a number of flowers
PH	Level of acidity or alkalinity in a substance
Plugging	When the xylem vessels become blocked
Physiological plugging	When flowers seal over to prevent penetration of microbes
Preservative	A flower preservative that contains sugar, germicide and an acidifier
Sepals	Found directly under the petals
Sleeves	Clear polyethylene sheathe enveloping flowers
Spadix	The central spike of certain flowers surrounded by the spathe
Spathe	A fused petal or broad bract that surrounds the spadix
Spray	A grouping of flower heads all of similar size
STS	Silver thiosulphate solution. A spray used by growers to prevent ethylene damage
Transpiration	The loss of water from leaves and flowers to the atmosphere
Turgid	Fully hydrated, not wilted
Xylem Vessels	Fine tubes in the stems of flowers that carry moisture/food

UNDERSTANDING PLANTS AND FLOWERS

The structure and function of plants

To appreciate cut flower care, the structure and functions of a plant should be considered.

There are five main parts to a plant:

- roots
- stems
- leaves
- flowers
- fruit

Each part of the plant has important functions. If any part becomes diseased or damaged, the plant cannot grow to its full capacity.

The roots have two functions:

- to absorb moisture from the ground and dissolve nutrients
- to anchor the plant in the ground.

The stem has two functions:

- to carry water and food
- to provide support for the leaves.

The main function for the leaves is to provide food. This process is achieved through *photosynthesis*. The main function of the flower is to provide seeds by sexual reproductive means. The main function of the fruit is to protect the seeds and aid in the distribution of the seeds.

Photosynthesis

Photosynthesis is the process by which chlorophyll (the green pigment in plants) uses light energy to convert carbon dioxide and water into carbohydrates, made up of oxygen and hydrogen. Plants use most of the hydrogen, combining it with other chemicals. The oxygen is released into the atmosphere (see *Respiration* below). The most important part of photosynthesis is how it produces oxygen, which is vital to the survival to all forms of life on this earth.

Respiration

The chemically controlled release of energy in plants is called respiration. It is important not to confuse respiration with breathing. Breathing in humans or animals is an exchange of gases. Humans breathe in oxygen and breathe out carbon dioxide. Plants take in carbon dioxide and release oxygen when they photosynthesise.

Respiration takes place 24 hours a day for every living plant. With cut flowers, if you mix preservative into the vase water it will act as a food source during respiration.

The parts of a plant

flowers

leaves

stems

fruit

roots

2

The parts of a flower

The structure and function of flowers

Flower shapes

Tubulate

Salverform

Calceolate

Campanulate

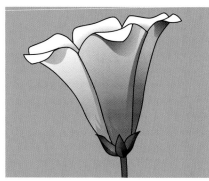

Funnelform

Umbela

Papilionate

Urceolate

Cyathiform

Saccate

Labiate

Crateriform

Rotate

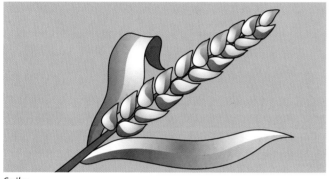

Spike

Stellate

Pannicle

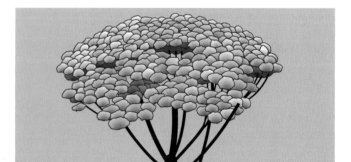

Corymbs

Radiate

Spathiate

Male and female parts

The majority of flowers are made up of both male and female parts. The male parts are collectively known as *stamens*, which are made up of filaments and anthers. The filaments are fine hair-like stalks that the anthers sit on top of. The anthers produce and contain the pollen. Some flowers, such as Longifoliums, Asiatics and Regale Lillies, have very prominent anthers. In other flowers the anthers are hard to see. The number of stamen in each flower is usually equal to the number of petals the flower has.

The female parts are collectively known as the *pistil*, which is made up of a stigma, a style and an ovary. The stigma is the sticky bulb that you can see in the centre of the flower. The style is the long stalk that the stigma sits on top of. The ovary is at the base of the flower, and contains an ovule, which is the part of the ovary that becomes the seed when the flower is fertilised.

Petals and sepals

The petals and sepals surround and protect the reproductive parts. The petals are the brightly coloured parts. Some flowers have petals that form distinct and different shapes. Orchids are a good example. Be aware that some flowers do not have any petals at all. Banksias, Proteas and Leucadendrons have coloured parts known as *bracts*, instead of petals.

The sepals are found directly under the petals and are often green. They control the opening of the flower and protect the petals when the flower is in bud form. You can look at the position of the sepals on a flower to determine the flower's age. For example, the sepals on a rose face upwards when the rose is in bud, outwards at various angles as the rose is opening, and downwards, near to the stem, when the rose is fully open. The further downwards they face, the older the rose.

Some flowers, such as Leucadendrons, have separate male and female flowers.

The petals of Campanulas are an example of flowers where the petals fuse to form a tube. This tube is known as a 'corolla'.

Above: *Campanulas*
Left: *Leucadendron*

Flowers and reproduction

A flower's purpose is to attract a pollinator to fertilise it. Pollinators (birds, bees, wasps, flies and other insects) are attracted to the flower's bright colours, as well as its pollen or nectar (the food that makes the flower irresistible to the pollinator). Fertilised flowers turn into fruit or seed, which enables the plant to reproduce.

Pollination and fertilisation

Pollination and fertilisation are two separate processes. Pollination is the transfer of pollen from the flower's male parts to its female parts (i.e. when a pollinator brushes pollen from a flower's anthers on to its stigma). The pollen then germinates and a pollen tube grows from the germinated grain, down the style and into the ovary. The male nucleus of the pollen grain then passes along the pollen tube and joins with the female nucleus of the ovule. This is when fertilisation occurs.

After fertilisation, the female parts of the flower develop into a fruit. The ovules become seeds and the ovary wall becomes the rest of the fruit. This fruit separates from its parent plant and grows into a new plant.

Plant and flower life cycles

Flowers in the garden are a source of great pleasure and can also be enjoyed as cut flowers.

Annuals

Annuals are plants that basically have a life cycle of one year. The cycle is from seed to bloom and returning to seed. If you remove the spent flowers during the blooming cycle you will prolong the blooming cycle. Many annuals will re-seed themselves. Annual plant seeds are readily available to purchase and they are a fabulous way of giving your garden that extra surge of colour in late spring and summer.

Biennials

These plants have a cycle that takes two years to complete. In the first year the plant grows roots, stems and leaves and often it will be dormant over the winter period. Usually the stem remains short and the leaf formation is low to the ground. These form a rosette. The colder period is needed for the plant to vernalise before it will flower. The following spring the plant will surge in growth and produce flowers. In an ongoing cold climate, some biennials will take the form of annuals.

Perennials

These plants return year after year, growing in size and strength until they reach maturity. Many perennials will become straggly after three to four years and need to be replaced. Most perennials are grown from cuttings or can be divided. They can also be grown from seeds.

It is very important to prepare the ground before planting perennials. This allows nutrients as well as the root formation to grow and spread more rapidly.

Does your local florist always seem to have the same tired, old stock? A seller who turns their perishable stock quickly is best!

PURCHASING CUT FLOWERS

Everybody loves cut flowers! There's no better feeling than bringing home a gorgeous bunch of flowers, fresh from the market or local florist, and displaying them in your favourite room. However, not all flower sellers are the same, and it's important to make sure that the flowers you purchase have been handled correctly by the seller.

An astute buyer of cut flowers will be very observant. Likewise, a successful seller of cut flowers should be equally astute and observant. The seller should have professional training, but unfortunately some do not, or they have fallen into sloppy habits. There are retailers who do not treat their cut flowers correctly. For example, some flower sellers put their stock out into the shop during the day and then into a cool room during the night (then back into the shop the following day). These continual changes in temperature and conditions shorten the life span of the flowers.

There are ways to tell if retail flowers have been treated correctly. Follow the advice in this chapter and you'll never bring home a bad bunch of flowers again!

Ethylene gas

Ethylene gas is an odourless, colourless, natural plant hormone. It is also a by-product of man-made processes such as combustion. Ethylene gas speeds up deterioration in sensitive flowers and can even kill them.

In the natural environment, ethylene is emitted by ripe fruit as well as dead or damaged flowers and foliage. In the man-made world, it is emitted by cigarette smoke, motor vehicle exhausts and closed storage environments such as refrigerators and shipping containers.

Certain varieties of flowers are more sensitive to ethylene gas than others. Flowers that have been adversely affected by ethylene will usually show signs of leaf and flower drop, as well as wilting. Petal drop or petal curl are also signs. You can see this in Stock, Gypsophila, Sweet William, Carnations and Liliums. Alstroemeria, Freesias and Roses may fail to open if exposed to ethylene. However, don't confuse natural petal drop with that caused by ethylene – some flowers, such as Delphinium and Larkspur, will drop petals easily, so ethylene exposure may not be the cause.

To counteract the effects in sensitive flowers, some growers treat these flowers with *Silver Thiosulphate Solution*, or STS. Flowers treated with STS will become resilient to ethylene. For example, STS-treated Delphiniums can last up to three weeks with no petal drop at all.

Flowers treated with STS are more costly to purchase. Ask your florist if the flowers have been STS treated. If you are a seller, always point this out to a client. The spray is not harmful to the consumer but the process has strict controls by the grower.

To find out which flowers are highly sensitive to ethylene gas, see the A – Z directory of cut flowers in Chapter 6.

What to look out for when purchasing cut flowers

Where is the stock located?

- Avoid buying flowers that are outside. They are prone to wind, heat and cool, not to mention possible knocking by passers-by. They are also exposed to ethylene gas emitted by car exhausts. This will shorten their life span, in some cases, dramatically.

- Do not buy flowers from service stations as the effects of ethylene gas on the flowers are likely to be severe, and generally speaking, these flowers are substandard in quality.

- Do not buy flowers stored with fruit (such as at a green grocer). Ripened fruit emits ethylene gas and this shortens the life span of cut flowers.

- Do not buy flowers from supermarkets – this stock usually presents badly, and is always in airconditioning or heating.

Without wanting to criticise green grocers, service station owners or roadside sellers, I do strongly urge you to only buy flowers from reputable florist shops. Buy your fruit and veg from the local green grocer and your petrol from the service station, but if you want quality flowers that will last the distance, purchase them from a professional.

How is the stock handled?

Look at how the flowers are handled by the seller. Are they showing care and training for the product?

Many flowers are damaged in the way they are placed on a surface area. For example, Lilies, Gerberas and most open flowers will be damaged if they are placed directly onto a bench, as the side petals bearing the flower weight will crease and therefore bruise (see Figure 1). If the seller slides their hand under the flowers, the petals are protected as they are laid down (see Figure 2).

Also watch the seller as they carry bunches of flowers from the containers over to the counter. Do they allow the water from the stems to drip over other flowers in the store? This is bad practice – water drips may cause damage to the other flowers or expose them to fungal infection.

What can the seller tell you?

A good florist will be happy to give you advice about everything from cut flower care to what varieties are available, so take advantage of their knowledge and ask them questions! At the very least, each time you buy flowers you should ask the seller when the flowers were picked and how long they should last, if cared for properly.

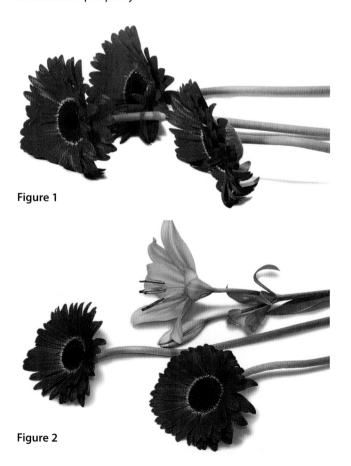

Figure 1

Figure 2

What do the flowers look like?

Stems

- Stems should be strong and crisp looking.
- Look at the stem end. Is there a dark mark? If so, this may indicate fungal infection.
- Check that there isn't a filmy substance over the area of the stem that's under water. This indicates they have been sitting in the same water for an extended period of time.
- Feel the stems. Are they cold? If they have come straight from a cool room they will be cold and therefore they may not be fresh stock.
- Flowers that have nodules or nodes on their stems, such as carnations, should be checked for stem strength and any signs of rust on the nodes.

Leaves

- Have leaves been removed above the waterline? If so, buy with caution. The leaves would have been removed because the plant has suffered air blockage and has deteriorated.
- Check the foliage. Is it strong in colour and undamaged?

Flowers

- Look at the centres of the flowers. Any visible pollination is usually a sign of age. Gerberas are a clear example. The centres should be really tight with no sign of any yellow pollination. If you can see between the little anthers of pollen, then the flowers aren't young and fresh as they should be.
- With multi-flowered stems, check that all flowers are perfect.
- Open blooms are advanced in their life span. If you want flowers to last longer, buy in bud formation.
- 'Field flowers' (flowers grown outdoors) carry more bacteria than those grown under controlled conditions. You will find with many of these flowers, if they are bunched tightly or left in sleeves without sufficient airflow, they will deteriorate quickly. Many will grow mould if left compacted or placed in a cool room for days. Check for signs of health when buying field flowers.

Opposite
Top: *a healthy flower*
Bottom: *an unhealthy flower*

What about the packaging?

- At the shop, check that both the container and the water the flowers are sitting in are spotlessly clean.

- Do not buy cut flowers that are sitting in the shop in plastic sleeves or other types of wrapping.

- Flowers displayed in glass containers gives you the clearest view of the stock and water. Buying from buckets gives you the reverse.

- Most flowers should be sold with a water source. Usually this is a small plastic bag with water inside (sometimes also with wet tissue) attached to the base of the flower bunch with an elastic band, raffia or twine. Roses are usually sold with individual water vials attached to each stem. Ask for this if it is not supplied.

- Ask for sachets of flower preservative. Some sellers include these in the cost of the flowers and others sell the preservative separately. A trained seller will have this product available at all times or give you advice about how to make your own.

- If the seller tries to wrap your flowers in plastic or cellophane, stop them. Ask for paper wrapping (flowers may sweat in plastic, causing bacteria to grow).

Top: *a water vial*
Above: *a bag-style water source*

If you notice
white sediment in
the base of your
vase, be aware
that it's probably
not undissolved
preservative, but
lime from the
water. Change
the water and
add more
perservative.

CARING FOR CUT FLOWERS

What to do when you bring your flowers home

Cut flowers, stems and leaves all have bacteria and fungi on them. The bacteria and fungi will multiply in water and as time continues in the cut flower life span, the flower stems will become blocked. This is a natural process, but there are things you can do that will slow it down and almost stop it altogether, ensuring that your flowers stay fresher for longer.

Packaging and handling

When you purchase cut flowers they will often be wrapped in paper or plastic sleeves. To the remove flowers from the packaging, simply cut vertically down the side of the sleeve and remove the flowers carefully.

As a buyer, consider your movement in the carrying of cut flowers. If you place flowers on the backseat of your car on a warm day and you stop for coffee or continue shopping, the life span of your flowers will be adversely affected. Always buy your flowers at the end of your shopping trip and go straight home to prepare them for display.

Recutting stems

Why do we need to recut stems?

When a flower stem is first cut from its mother plant and exposed to air, it draws up air bubbles through its xylem vessels (the internal tubes in the stem which carry food to the flower), causing a blockage to the stem. This air blockage is called an embolism, and the process is called emboli. The longer a flower is out of water after being picked, the harder it becomes for it to draw moisture past the embolism. In some flowers, emboli is a quick process and in others it can take hours to occur. By recutting the stems of a flower with an embolism, you 'clear the path' in the stem, enabling the flower to eat and drink properly again.

Is recutting necessary for all flowers?

Emboli occurs in all cut flowers, with varying degrees of severity. So, yes, it is important to recut all flowers when you bring them home.

Recutting stems under water

It is best to recut stems under water because this is one place where air bubbles cannot form! Cutting under water is more difficult but by far the best practice.

Use a wide-mouthed container or a deep square or rectangular receptacle, such as the kitchen or laundry sink. Make sure it is spotlessly clean before filling it with water. Also make sure that your hands and cutting tools are clean, so that you don't introduce bacteria to the water.

Hold the stem about 5–6 centimetres underwater and cut off the end of the stem at an angle, to create the largest possible surface area for water to be taken up into the stem. Place the flower into your display vase as soon as you've cut it. This is important – you should never leave flowers sitting out of water.

Tools for recutting stems

A sharp knife or a pair of snippers or cutters is best for recutting fleshy stems. Use sharp secateurs for woody stems. Woody stems can also be gently crushed (see page 27 for more information). All tools should be cleaned daily to prevent bacteria build-up.

Cutting above the blockage

Some flowers, such as hothouse or glasshouse Chrysanthemums, develop embolisms very quickly after being picked. You can place Chrysanthemums into a vase and the next day they will have wilted even though you have recut them and they are sitting in fresh water with preservative. If you have recut the stems then how can this happen?

The most likely explanation is that the embolism has travelled higher up the stem than where you cut it. The best way to ensure that you've cut above the embolism is to check the stem end after cutting. Does it look dried out? If so, then cut a bit more off, until the stem end looks fresh and moist.

There are many people who have received beautiful roses and placed them into a vase of clean water only to find the next morning the heads have drooped. This is usually due to air blockage in the xylem vessels. The roses can be saved.

(see page 29)

Above: *recutting stems with secateurs*
Right: *recutting stems under water*

Vases should be
filled with water
to a 75% capacity
(3/4 full).

Some flowers have very thin stems, which makes it difficult to see if the stem ends are dry or not after recutting. In these cases the best thing to do is recut the flowers as usual and arrange them in the vase. Keep an eye on them for the next day or two, and if you see the lower leaves starting to droop, then you'll know that the embolisms are still in the stems, and that you need to recut them again. With flowers such as Roses, glasshouse Chrysanthemums, Sunflowers and Snap Dragons, drooping lower leaves are a sure sign that the stems are blocked and need to be recut.

Removing leaves

To avoid a build-up of bacteria, all leaves that will be below the waterline in your vase should be removed. If the leaves remain and are submerged, water contamination will occur and in many cases the foliage will not only foul the water but will also smell.

It is best to remove the leaves underwater at the same time as you recut the stems. To remove the leaves from the stem, simply snip them off or run your hand firmly down the stem, stripping the leaves as you go.

Removing leaves and thorns from Roses

Obviously, running your hand down the stem is not an option with Roses! There are special plastic or metal Rose strippers available that clamp onto the stem, and as you pull down, the leaves and thorns are removed. This is practical for speed, but the process damages the outer fibres of the stem and this allows bacteria to penetrate the stem and shorten the life span of the flower.

With Roses, it's best to use snippers to cut the foliage from the stem and leave the thorns alone. However, keeping the thorns can make handling the Roses difficult. If you must remove the thorns, use gloves and a hand towel. Pull the towel down the stem to remove the thorns and leaves. This method

will not damage the outer fibres of the stem. Another option is to use a product called 'The Flower Stripper' made by Oasis. You do need to be aware that the stem is still prone to bacteria entry where the thorns have been removed. However, if you change the water regularly then the life span of your Roses will only be slightly shortened.

Top: *The best way to remove leaves and thorns from Roses is with a towel*
Bottom: *Oasis product: The Flowers Stripper*

Water and preservative

Tap water

There's no need to waste money on expensive bottled water for use in the vase if you have access to clean, good quality tap water. The average temperature of tap water (10–15 degrees Celsius) is actually perfect for cut flowers. If the tap water is of high quality, you may not need to use additional preservatives or flower food (but you'll still need to add bleach to fight bacteria – about one capful per average-sized vase).

Keeping the water clean

What causes turbid water in vases and containers?

Micro-organisms such as fungi and bacteria are the main causes of turbid (dirty) water. Bacillus, Pseudomonas and Enterobacter are the most common forms of bacteria in vases. They also occur in the stems where they cause vascular blockages. If your vase water looks dirty, the best thing to do is cut 5–10 centimetres from the stem ends and replace the water and preservative.

What flowers foul the water?

Some flowers are prone to fouling the water. Matthiola (also known as Stock) will foul the water if the leaves under the waterline are left on. If the water remains unchanged for several days then it will become like soup. Iberus (also known as Candy Tuft) will also foul the water badly, as will Ageratum, Aster, Calendula, Cornflower, Gypsophila, Mignonette, Queen Anne's Lace, Ranunculus, Snapdragon and Statice. The leaves that will sit below the waterline must be removed before the flowers are placed in the vase and the water must be changed regularly. Add bleach to the water for these varieties, as it fights bacteria and helps the water to remain clear.

Adding sugar or bleach

Sugar

Sugar breeds bacteria in the water quickly which severely affects a flower's life span, however, sugar added to vase water can help flowers to 'open up', if the flowers' petals have not yet done so. Lemonade added to vase water has the same effect. If you need to open flowers, put them into luke-warm water with 1 tablespoon of sugar or half a cup of lemonade. You can then put them in direct sunlight to help speed up the process.

Remember, adding sugar or lemonade should only be done if you need blooms to open for a wedding or other upcoming occasion where the flowers' life span beyond the event is not a consideration.

Sugar can only be used as a preservative when mixed with other ingredients (see the recipe opposite). The only exception to this rule is with Kangaroo Paw – sugar added to the vase, without other ingredients, can be used as a preservative in this case.

Bleach

Bleach can help keep vase water clear and therefore assist in fighting bacteria. Some people find that bleach works as a good preservative for some varieties, if the water is of good quality to begin with. Poor quality water needs a proper preservative.

Using preservative (or 'flower food')

When flowers are growing, the leaves provide all the food they need. Carbohydrates, produced in the leaves (by photosynthesis), provide flower food in the form of sugar. When a flower is cut from the plant the water supply and food supply are also cut off. The use of flower preservative in vase water takes the place of the natural food supply. It also absorbs organic substances produced by cut flowers.

You can make up your own preservative or use a commercial one. For home-made preservative, cane sugar (sucrose) is most suited to cut flowers and should be used together with vinegar or citric acid and bleach or swimming pool chlorine (see the recipe right).

There are many commercial brands of preservative (known as Bactericides) in sachet, granular or liquid form. These are graded in quality and can be purchased in commercial as well as domestic quantities. Obviously it's best to go for the highest quality that you can afford – you will find White King bleach used on its own to be far more effective than a no-name brand.

Some of the more popular quality brands include Chrysal, Floral Life and Florish. There are also preservatives that are structured to specific flowers, such as bulb flowers, Narcissus specialty, Lilium and Alstroemeria specialty, Syringa, Mimisa, Chrysanthemeum, Tulip, Bouvardia and Rose. These types of preservatives are mainly available in sachet form.

When using preservative, always use the correct amount for the container size and water volume. Check the instructions on the packet.

If Lily-of-the-Valley wilts it can be quickly revived by placing it on ice.

Preservative recipe

Here is an easy recipe to make your own preservative:

- 5ml (1 teaspoon) of citric acid or vinegar
- 4g (3/4 teaspoon) of slow release chlorine (from florists' suppliers or pool shops)
- 5g (1 teaspoon) of sugar
- 5 litres of water

Mix all the ingredients together and use it as your vase water (do not add to existing vase water).

Using a conditioning solution

If flowers have been out of water for a while, it's a good idea to stand them in a conditioning solution before you recut the stems and put them into a vase.

Conditioning solution recipe

Here is an easy recipe to make your own conditioning solution:

- 1.25 ml (1/4 teaspoon) of citric acid or white vinegar
- 1/4 capful of bleach
- 5 litres of warm water

Do not use sugar at this stage. Leave the flower stems in the conditioning solution for up to 24 hours, then recut and place them in a vase with clean water and preservative.

This preservative is friendly to the environment and can be used as grey water for the garden.

Changing the water and preservative

Whenever possible, use the same preservative brand or type when you change the water. In the first five days the preservative is important as a food source but after that you can ease back to clean water with bleach added.

Late spring, summer and early autumn heat

For most flower varieties, it is best to change the vase water every second day in dry heat. Keep an eye on the water level, as some varieties will drink more than others and may need a water change every day. Also check that the water is clean, and replace if it isn't.

Humidity

Tropical flowers grow naturally in humid conditions, so a light misting throughout the day is adequate to keep them healthy. With other varieties, if they are exposed to extended periods of humidity, it is best to change the vase water up to three times a day.

Native flowers

Native flowers will drink heavily in vase water. Banksias and Proteas can drink a large vase dry in two days! Make sure you check water levels and choose a sensible vase.

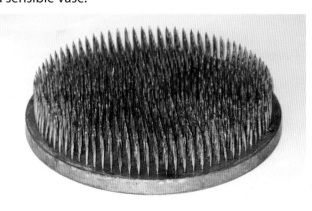

Above: *Pin holder*

Vases and containers

Choosing a vase

The choice of vase is very important. If you want to arrange flowers in a traditional style, the best container shape is the 'hourglass shape'. This allows for the stems to be spiralled in the vase and the lip allows the formation to broaden out around the vase. Tall thin vases suit vertical, upright designs. Squat round vases suit posies and short flower stems. A narrow base will help to hold the stems in place as you have arranged them.

Glass vases

Glass vases are a good choice. They are hard and smooth and there is no reaction between the vase water and the glass. Glass vases do not easily scratch on the inside and they are easy to clean.

Crystal vases

Older crystal vases may have small pores, in which micro-organisms can accumulate. This will affect the life span of your flowers. Antique crystal vases may also have high lead content, so it's best to avoid these. New crystal vases do not have this problem.

Metal containers

These should be avoided, as the acid produced from cut flowers and preservative may react with the metal irons in the vase water. This is toxic to cut flowers and will cause leaves to burn and flowers to develop brown tips. If you must use a metal vase or container, always use a plastic liner inside it.

Ceramic containers

Unglazed ceramics should not be used as they are hard to clean properly and micro-organisms can accumulate in the ceramic. Any chips or crazing are breeding grounds for bacteria. Glazed ceramic containers are fine to use.

Plastic containers

High quality plastic containers that are made of acid-resistant material are fine to use. Avoid plastic containers that scratch easily – this is an indicator of poor quality plastic.

The need for clean containers

The need for clean containers cannot be overstated. Nothing will kill a flower faster than the bacteria caused by dirty water or detergent residue! To prevent this happening, follow these steps:

- Always rinse a vase before you use it.
- Always store vases upside down. If they have been standing upright dust may settle inside them and this can cause bacteria in the water.
- If you wash vases using dishwashing detergent make sure you rinse thoroughly to remove any residue.
- Use bleach to clean your vases. Bleach that contains at least four per cent chlorine is best. Simply place the vases in a bucket with one capful of bleach per litre of water. Wear protection for your clothes when using bleach.
- Use vase-cleaning tablets whenever possible. These will clear your vase water of any micro-organisms that may affect the flowers.
- Wash cut flower stems to remove extra particles of dirt, before placing them in the vase.
- Change the vase water regularly – fungi and microscopic bacteria can grow in even the cleanest of vases.

Displaying your flowers

There are certain spots in your home where flowers will not be happy! Areas to avoid include:

- draughty areas, such as near open doors or windows
- underneath or next to overhead or upright fans – these dry the flowers out. If you need to use a fan, then remove the flowers from the room
- near heaters or airconditioners – flowers will lose moisture much faster when the air is dry
- in direct sunlight.

Flowers look great when placed on a hall table, or in an area where they will be seen as soon as you enter the house. Just be careful to put them in a spot where children, pets or guests won't knock them over!

Pin Holders, also known by the name **kenzan** are used to hold flowers steady in the vase. The best ones to use are brass but the newer ones are plastic with weights attached under their base. Always make sure these are thoroughly cleaned after each use.

What to do when flowers wilt

If a flower needs revival it has already suffered and therefore the life span of the flower has already been affected. However, if you take steps to revive the flower as soon as you notice that it has wilted, there's a good chance that you can keep it alive and healthy for days to come.

Recutting stems again

Flowers wilt for a variety of reasons, namely bad handling and care. However, a lack of nutrients can also contribute to a flower's deterioration. Lack of nutrients is generally caused by blocked air vessels (embolisms) in the flower's stem. Symptoms include:

- limited bud and flower development
- limited or lack of scent development
- limited flower development on the spike
- droopy heads and leaves
- faded colours.

Recutting stems when you bring your flowers home was covered earlier in this chapter. However, if you've recut the stems and days later the flowers are showing signs of ill-health, you'll need to recut them again, making sure that you cut above the embolisms. See page 16 for instructions on how to recut stems properly.

Opposite
Top left: *Crystal vase*
Top centre: *Glass vase*
Top right: *Crystal vase*
Bottom left: *Metal vase*
Bottom centre: *Glass vase*
Bottom right: *Porcelain vase*

Certain flowers need scalding after they've been cut to prevent them leaking a milky sap known as latex. Dahlia, Poppy and Helleborus are usually scalded by the grower just after they're cut from the plant. You can tell if this has been done by looking at the stem – if it has been scaldered, the stem will be darker. Years ago florists were also taught to sear the end of the stem over a flame if they cut the stem above the scald line. These days it's generally thought that searing is not necessary unless the stem has been recut quickly after being scalded.

Orchids should not be soaked for longer than fifteen minutes.

Scalding

Some cut flowers, such as Sunflowers, Roses and Delphiniums, can be scalded if they need to be revived. By scalding the stem ends, you are forcing out the air bubbles that caused the embolism in the stem.

To scald a stem, you will need boiling water and some conditioning solution. Support the flower heads so that they sit upright and place the stem ends in boiling water for about one minute. Transfer the stem ends immediately to conditioning solution made up with warm water. Always observe Occupational Health and Safety when handling boiling water.

Scalding stems will considerably shorten the life span of a cut flower, but sometimes it's the only way to prevent it from dying then and there. Scalding is a great way to 'save the day' if the flowers are needed for a special function or event and are starting to wilt.

Misting

Tropical flowers enjoy light misting, as it increases the humidity in their immediate environment. Misting makes the blooms look freshly picked, but also helps to revive them when they get a bit weary.

Heliconias, as a cut flower, have very little uptake of water and misting assists in moisture on the surface area of the flower and foliage. Heliconia flowers will outlast its foliage.

Some flowers, such as Boronia and Violets, require misting to survive after being picked, but be careful of misting where moisture can be caught in the flower, such as with Hyacinths, Stephanotis and Singapore orchids.

Soaking

There are a number of cut flowers and foliages that will benefit from soaking, namely flowers that drink through their surface area instead of through their stem. Many tropical flowers fall into this category.

Helleborus, Thrytomene, Boronia, Violets, Lily-of-the-Valley, Anthuriums, Ginger, Heliconias, Singapore orchids and Hydrangea all benefit from a good soaking.

Soaking can revive a wilted flower by helping it to regain its stem strength, which in turn will stop it from bending at the stem and developing blockages. Soaking can also be beneficial for flowers that don't look crisp and firm when you first bring them home.

To soak flowers, you will need a large container, bath or basin (a receptacle that's big enough to accommodate the size of your flowers). Make sure the receptacle is clean and free from detergents and soap scum. Fill it with tap water and gently lay the flowers in the water. Leave them to soak for around 30 minutes. If they have not revived after this time, leave them to soak for a little longer, but no more than two hours.

When the flowers are ready to be taken out of their bath, gently shake off any excess water and arrange them in the vase as you normally would.

Crushing stems

Some horticulturalists advise against this practice because they believe crushing damages the stem tissue and therefore shortens the life span of the flower. My research of growers and florists of many years' experience clearly shows that this practice is beneficial to the life of woody-stemmed cut flowers and foliage.

Autumn leaves or cut flowers with yellow or grey foliage should not be soaked. Yellow foliage will turn brown if it is soaked in cold water.

When crushing a stem, make sure you don't crush too hard. Use a hammer or other heavy object to do the crushing, but don't smash the stem, just gently grind it until it splits.

The process of crushing can lead to fungal infection if your vase water is not scrupulously clean.

Above
Top: *Helleborus*
Middle: *Anthurium*
Bottom: *Orchids*

For the conditioning solution, warm water is best as it travels up the stem more rapidly than cold water. It is also best to use rainwater, if possible, because tap water has a higher oxygen content. Gerberas in particular will perform better in rainwater as they dislike chloride.

The wilted Rose

Of all flowers, there's no worse sight than a vase full of wilted Roses! Many times I have heard people say they had joyfully been given a bunch of Roses, only to wake the next day and find them wilted and droopy.

The cause of this is usually air embolisms in the stems of the Roses. As with other varieties, the best thing to do is recut the stem above the embolism. This may mean cutting 6–8 centimetres off the stem, but it's better to have healthy roses with short stems than sick Roses with long ones.

If recutting the stems doesn't work, you can try standing the Roses in a conditioning solution. To do this, lay them across a large sheet of paper, straightening the wilted heads out from the stem. Wrap the paper up tightly so that the heads are forced to stand, and secure with sticky tape. Pour some conditioning solution made up with warm water into a vase, and place the wrapped Roses in the vase (see the recipe for conditioning solution on page 21). Leave for six hours, then take them out of the vase and unwrap. In most cases your Roses will have revived. If not, try the process again. After this, your Roses will not last their maximum life span, but you should get another three to five days out of them.

Sunflowers and hothouse or glasshouse Chrysanthemums can also be treated this way to revive them.

If wrapping doesn't work, you can try soaking the flowers. See the instructions for soaking on page 34.

Your last resort, if the Rose heads do not revive, is to tightly wrap the Roses in paper, with the heads forced to stand straight, and place the stem ends in boiling water. Leave them for thirty seconds and then place them in a vase with lukewarm water. This process will release the oxygen in the stem, but the life span of the Roses will be shortened.

THE BASICS OF FLOWER ARRANGEMENT

Flower arranging is a magnificent art form, celebrated all around the world in cultural exhibitions, competitions and festivals. Although it takes many years of training and a high level of creative skill to be a professional flower arranger, you can, in your own home or office, create beautiful arrangements with just a little bit of know-how and an appreciation of aesthetics.

In this chapter you will learn how to arrange a simple bunch of flowers using the spiral method, as well as learning the basic elements and principles of design. With a little practise, you can learn to create beautiful arrangements using mixed flower varieties, foliage, floral foam and wire support.

The elements and principles of design

The elements and principles of design should be considered when creating flower arrangements.

The five elements of design are:

- form
- space
- texture
- colour
- line

The principles of design make the elements work. The seven principles of design are:

- balance
- proportion
- scale
- harmony
- contrast
- rhythm
- dominance

Every arrangement that you make uses the elements. You have *form* in the flower, foliage, accessory and container sizes. There is *space* throughout your design including the space between petals and foliage fronds. There is *texture and line* in every component used, and *colour* is a feature in every arrangement.

Understanding the principles

Balance

There should be balance in the spacing of the flowers. If you have ten blooms that you want to arrange, draw a large circle (representing the mouth of the vase) and then draw ten smaller circles within it (representing the flowers, or 'blooms'). There should be one bloom in the centre, three around the centre and six around the circle's edge. If there is equal space between the blooms and they are all of the same size, you will have balance.

There also needs to be balance between the flower sizes, known as forms. If there is a sizing difference between your flowers, place the largest bloom in the centre. Then surround it with flowers the next size down, followed by the smallest blooms around the edges. It works the same in reverse, i.e. if most of the blooms are large, place a smaller one in the centre, then surround it with the next size up, and so on.

The final balance consideration is colour balance. When you mix colours it is harder to balance the design. Draw the circle again. If there are five of one colour and five of another, colour-in the circles to see how the colours will balance. You may need to try this a few times to get it right … this is where the skill and creativity of the arranger will develop.

Proportion

When you choose a vase or container, it's size must be in proportion to the mass or amount of flowers that will fill it. For example, don't use a small, squat vase for a big bunch of Banksias, and don't use a large, wide-rimmed vase for a small bunch of Forget-me-nots!

Scale

The scale of flowers and foliages refers to how these relate to each other. For example, King Proteas (flower) and tiny Scillas are not a good match, because they are out of scale (or size) with each other. Choose foliage that complements the flowers.

Harmony

Harmony is when all elements of the design are compatible and work well together.

Contrast

Contrast refers to opposites working together in colour, form, texture and space. It means mixing dark and light colours, large and small blooms, smooth and rough textures and large and small gaps within the arrangement. Contrast is important when working with several varieties of flowers in the one arrangement.

Rhythm

Rhythm is the visual movement throughout a design. When a design has rhythm, it has a 'pattern' or 'flow' within it, created by the various other elements of design.

Dominance

Dominance refers to the flower or flowers that attract the eye first. This can be achieved by size, colour or prominence in a design. In a vase of flowers the most dominant flower is usually in the centre.

A simple vase of flowers

Sometimes simplicity can be the most beautiful aspect of floral design! A simple and attractive floral design can be achieved by *spiralling* the flowers, so that all stems flow in the same direction. All it takes is a fresh and healthy bunch of flowers (of single variety) and the right vase.

As a general rule, the height of the vase should be one third of the height of the flowers you wish to arrange. Prepare the flower stems as per the advice in chapter 3. Fill the vase with water so that it's about three quarters full, and mix in some preservative.

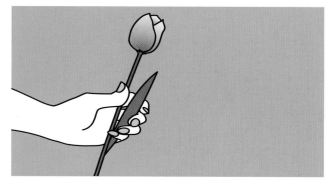

1   Begin by picking up the flower you want to place in the centre.

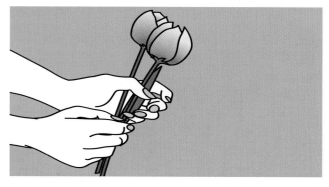

2   Holding this stem in your hand, gather the next stem and place it next to the centre stem, but in a slighter lower position.

3   Add another stem, then another, while rotating the bunch in your hand, always in the same direction.

4   When you get back to your starting position after a full rotation, place the next round of stems slightly lower than the round before. By lowering the height of the flower heads with each new rotation, you'll be creating a slightly domed effect.

5   When all the stems have been added to the bunch, carefully place them into the vase, and in one gentle motion, spread your hands out so that the flowers fall naturally.

6   This should result in a beautifully balanced arrangement, with the stems sitting in a spiral pattern at the base of the vase. This looks particularly attractive if you're using a clear glass vase.

If one side of the vase looks more crowded than the other, carefully rearrange the stems to achieve the right balance. Spiralling is something that might take a bit of practise, but keep trying until you get it right – the results are worth it!

Using extra foliage

In most floral arrangements, extra foliage can be used to 'anchor' the flowers in position. The foliage should be placed at the mouth of the vase, higher in the centre (inner perimeter) and lower around the edges of the vase (outer perimeter). To check if you've arranged the foliage correctly, look down on the vase and see if the foliage is in a round formation. If you want to mix different foliages, use heavier foliage in the centre and lighter foliage around the edges. Always remember to spiral the stems.

Foliage can be used as a base or added with the flowers when arranged in the hand or placed directly into a vase.

Planning your flower placements

You must have balance in the forms, and colours of the flowers from one side of the axis to the other. If the axis is off centre – so is the entire balance of the hand-tied item. For example, an iris or asiatic lily rarely look straight upwards therefore, unless wire supported, they are unsuitable as the focal bloom. Some florists advocate the one-three-five-eight rule and this pattern works well when working with a single colour (you can use different varieties of flowers in this one colour). When you select blooms of more than one colour and you want to intersperse these colours within the one level, you must select an even number for the level otherwise the colour will not balance. This is demonstrated in the diagrams on page 38 which show the dispersion of pink and white blooms within a round hand-tied design.

Even if you are making an informal item of mixed flowers, rather than a formal piece, you must still consider visual balance of forms and colour distribution. Always consider the form (shape and size) of the foliage pieces. They must have a shape to suit the item or be discarded and used in another floristry item.

Size and Spacing of Blooms

When selecting blooms for a hand-tied item, their size is very important. Single headed blooms are the most desirable however clusters of blooms may be used if they are of a consistent size. Traditionally, the largest bloom is placed in the centre (or conversely it can also be the smallest). The sequence that follows is to place flowers around the central bloom with the final smallest blooms around the edges. Likewise, if the smallest bloom is central, the largest blooms are placed around the perimeter.

For example, if you were to open a fresh bunch of yellow roses and you intend to make a round bouquet, you need to first spread them all out on your bench top and work out what sizes of blooms you have. If you found that you had three blooms in bud, one open bloom and the rest half open, you would need to decide on how you were to place these within the bouquet. There is only one sensible option. You start by placing the open rose in the centre, use the three bud roses evenly spaced one level down, then the next lower level would use six of the half open roses to complete the bouquet.

Be careful of four blooms around a central bloom as these can visually form a square or diamond rather than three or five blooms which creates a circle. A more advanced florist would take this advice and may decide to use groups of flowers (also termed 'groupings' within the industry).

The use of space also greatly impacts on the placement balance. Equal spacing needs to be used when using flowers of a consistent size or grading the flowers. Additionally, if foliage is visible it too should have an even placement.

Colour Balance

Traditional colour balance is comparative to the grading of flower sizes. Either the strongest colour is placed to the centre and blooms then grade to lighter and smaller towards the edges (or the exact reverse). It is vital in all round hand-tied items that there is a balance of colour from one side of the axis to the other. The size of blooms also impacts on the colour balance of a design.

The distribution of colour is another consideration. For a visually appealing and balanced distribution, an appropriate use of space between flowers and colours is vital. Consider a combination of tuberoses, (centre), pale pink roses, white asters and pink spray carnations or another selection, such as Dutch iris, (centre) yellow roses, yellow tulips and cornflowers.

Hand-tied Construction

When making your selection for a mixed hand tied you should select materials based on the following and will need to plan the following techniques/equipment:

- Round compact flowers
- Single flowers including focal or choice flowers
- Spray flowers, multi-headed flowers – transitional flowers
- Spike shaped flowers like heliconias, strelitzia, etc.
- Stems that will bend and curve
- A selection of foliage (keep in mind tall, short, bushy, curved and pendulous)
- Larger leaves which may be used to form a collar on completion
- Having a budding knife, cutters, necessary wire, parafilm and embellishing materials on hand.
- Possible stem support techniques
- How you will spiral the stems in construction
- The plan of placements prior to construction

Before you start the construction of any item, you must have your workbench prepared and have a water source for your blooms. Once you are ready, prepare the flowers by removing bruised petals. Lay your flowers (carefully to avoid bruising) on the workbench and look at the size (form) of the heads and stem lengths (all stems must be able to reach the water). Look at the colours of your blooms. Plan where you will use them as their distribution needs to balance equally throughout the design. Put the flowers back in water and use from the bucket during construction. When removing foliage from your blooms, do not remove the foliage from above the tie-point (unless it is damaged or diseased). This will help you to give body to the bouquet and means you will not need to use as much added foliage.

Above
Top: *A trailing hand tied design with cymbidium orchids*
Bottom: *A hand-tied, mixed flower posy with flowering broom trails*

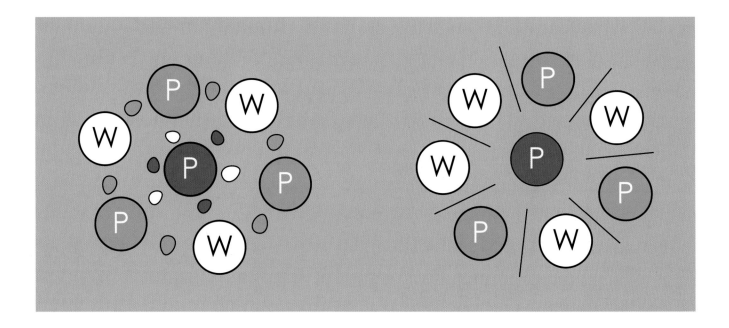

Start at the centre and build around the axis or focal bloom. This should either be the best bud formation or the most open bloom. Continue evenly placing around the central flower. Add foliage evenly as required. Always consider the space between the blooms and whether it is consistent.

Checklist for construction

- Is it round?
- Is the space consistent?
- If it has layers, is each one consistent?
- Does it have a domed shape? Remember you can choose the height of the dome.
- Is one side higher than the other? You will have a balance problem if it is.
- Is it to be wire supported?

A round hand-tied item should be round, domed with a consistent use of space. Space may vary in layers but each one must have consistency. For example, all layers may be even in placement or the centre may be tighter in space between the blooms and have a little more space as you progress outwards towards the edges. You must choose the height of the dome. If one side is higher than the other you have a visual balance problem. If wire support is required refer to flower preparation.

Finishing Techniques

Ribbons and half bows can be used as a finishing tool for a round hand-tied. If using a bow it is best to use a turned loop style as these loops sit flatter to the surround. Half circle bows are very effective and are normally made from a No. 5 width ribbon (22mm) for posies and No. 9 or 16 for bouquets and fastened to the hand-tied using wire. These are then placed evenly around the item except if only using a single half bow. The wire(s) must be placed into the centre of the tie-point so no wires are visible amongst the stems. This is so it looks professionally finished. This is done to create a 'frontal view' of the posy or bouquet and gives some direction when in a vase.

Round hand-tied items can also be placed into an attractive carry bag. There are many types available such as jute bags, Harmonica Bags and Eden Bags. A Salim holder is another suitable finish (refer to an Apack Sundry House brochure to see the range of carry bags available).

Above:
The design on the left is correct.
The design on the right has correct form and space but incorrect colour balance.

Using floral foam

Floral foam is used to keep flowers steady in the vase or container that you've arranged them in. It is ideal for more complicated designs, where the flowers must sit at different angles and heights.

There are a number of floral foams available, however the most recognised (and recommended) brand is Smithers Oasis.

Floral foam should not be stored in warm areas as it will discolour and won't absorb water properly. If the foam exudes an orange/brown colour when it's soaking, this means it has gone off and should not be used.

Preparation

Ensure that your flowers are kept in water while you're preparing the foam. Start by soaking it in a clean container of cold water, following the manufacturer's instructions. If the brand of foam you're using does not have preservative in it, add some to the water prior to soaking.

The best way to soak the foam (as advised by the manufacturers) is to gently place the foam brick into water and let it sink so that the water is level with the top of the foam. Make sure that the foam brick is placed into the water the right way up – this is to ensure that the vertical fibres in the foam can absorb the moisture. You can tell which surface is the 'top' by looking for the brand name – it should be imprinted on the top of the foam brick. Do not push the foam down into the water or you may create air pockets in the foam – if a flower is inserted into an air pocket then it will die.

Floral foam should not be reused as it will not fully absorb water again.

Using the foam

Place the soaked, shaped foam with the imprint writing facing up, into your vase, then fill the vase with water to 75% capacity. The foam should be wedged in firmly. If you need to extend stems outwards (horizontally) or downwards the foam will need to be raised above the lip of the container.

When you insert the foam, make sure you leave enough space to re-fill the vase with water under the foam level. If you're using a solid vase where you can't see the water level from the outside, it's a good idea to shave off a triangular section from the back corner of the foam – this way you'll be able to check the water level from above and re-fill when necessary.

Cut the flower stems on an angle and insert them firmly into the foam. Be careful when inserting the stems not to pull upwards slightly and then press down again. This may cause air pockets in the foam when the water level drops.

Always place the stems evenly in the foam. Do not overcrowd one section, especially at the front of the container.

As the flowers drink their fill and the water level drops, the foam will dry out from the top and any flower stems that sit above the water level will have their life span minimised. So, watch out for low water levels and fill up when needed.

Three simple rules for floral foam

- Do not overcrowd the vase with foam
- Never let the foam dry out
- Leave watering space

Basic arrangements

Many people are frustrated because they feel their arrangements of flowers never look quite right. There are basic rules you can follow that will always give you an attractive result, however simple your materials are. A quick arrangement to construct is made with three – seven main flowers and a simple numbers of leaves.

First, it is important to choose a suitable vase for the flowers. One with too narrow a neck will mean the flower stems will be jammed together and the arrangement will look tight and stiff. A tall, narrow container suits a tall narrow design. A squat, round container is best for a round low arrangement such as for a round table. See Using the foam on page 39 for details of how to fill your container with floral foam. Second, in an arrangement using floral foam it is important how space is used. If flowers are closer together they attract the eye as they become a larger shape and more colour. Spacing is a rule that guides the placement of blooms. Third, you should always strive to place the focal blooms (the most important) towards the base and this/these are usually the largest. The highest one, which is furthest away from the base, is placed towards the top and it is usually the smallest flower. Quite simply, the further a flower extends away from the base (container) the smaller it becomes. This is called gradation where flowers grade from smaller towards the top and step down in size to the largest at the base. This will make all the difference to the arrangement.

However basic your design, you should always prepare your flowers correctly; make sure the stems are clear of foliage below the waterline. Cut on an angle and remove 2-3 centimetres (1-2in) off before using, to remove any air blockages. This will prolong the life of the flower.

Combining flowers and foliage

The next step in arranging flowers in a container is to combine flowers and foliage. A good start is selecting two kinds of foliage, a straight, finer variety to give structure and height, then a more flowing variety, such as fern to provide movement, plus the basic numbers of flowers. Choose a container suitable to the number of stems and height of the arrangement – the height will be the dependent on the taller foliage variety.

Special Tips on foliage selection

1. Look at the shape of the foliage. If the foliage has a slight curve, select a second piece that follows the same curve or direction.

2. If a foliage curves it is usual to face the curve to the central axis, not away from it (face the curve inwards).

3. Wide foliage, with multiple branches, is the most difficult to use as the eye follows all those shapes and lines. Slim foliage shapes are much easier to use.

Solid leaves are excellent as a base cover in arrangements, particularly the philodendron varieties, aralia (also known as fatsia by gardeners) saxifrage, large ivy, fig and croton. If you prefer to use finer, flowing foliage you will achieve a cascading look, but you will need to use a higher container.

Simple Gerbera Arrangement

This arrangement uses just a few stems to create an interesting design. You will need: a flat or shallow container complementing the gerbera's colour (if in doubt use a dark container), one third of a brick of florist's foam; two aralia leaves; three stem of agapanthus, flowers removed or (three stems of papyrus); three gerberas and some moss.

Preparation

Cut the soaked foam to a shape to suit the container, with a 2cm-(1in) lip above the container. Make a second cut across the back corner of the foam to allow for watering. Cut off all the flowers of the agapanthus and trim the edges of the head to three varied sizes (you can also use them dried) See diagram. This also controls the size you want to use. Note: If you use papyrus cut the edges of the head in your hand so you can trim the edges more easily.

Gerberas will turn towards the light after they have been arranged, so they need to be wire supported or internally wired. Wiring does not affect the lifespan of the bloom (see diagram bottom right page 49). To recap over wiring select a .90 (20) gauge wire and insert the wire internally up the lumen of the stem. Make sure the wire does not protrude through the flower. If internal wiring is difficult insert the wire into the base of the head and run the wire down the back of the stem (hold the wire and the stem together as you insert into the foam).

Construction

Step 1

Cut the aralia stems to 3cm (1.4in) long. Insert the first stem near the centre of the foam, and push the leaf flat to the foam. Then place the second leaf to cover the other half of the foam, slightly overlapping over the first.

Note: if your container is large you may need three leaves to cover all the base.

Step 2

Choose the agapanthus stem with the smallest head. Cut to approximately 60cm (24in) on a sharp angle. Hold the stem near its base and place it through the aralia leaf near the back of the foam in the centre. The stem should look vertical from the front but incline slightly backwards from the back of the container. If you look at the container side on the flower should be level with the back of the container.

Step 3

Cut the second largest piece of a agapanthus, with the middle-sized head, to approximately 20cm (8in) long and insert through the aralia a little in front of the first agapanthus stem.

Step 4

Cut the third, largest, agapanthus stem very short and insert slightly in front of the second stem. It will sit slightly above the aralia leaf, like a flat, open hand. You already have an interesting design.

Step 5

Take the smallest gerbera bloom and cut its stem so it is a little shorter than the tallest agapanthus grass. Place it in front of the grass, with the head looking upwards.

Step 6

Cut the second, slightly larger gerbera so it is a little shorter than the second agapanthus and place a little to the side of it. The third, largest gerbera sits on the base agapanthus grass. All the heads should look upwards.

Step 7

(Optional) You may spray leaf shine on the aralia leaves to give a glowing look.

You can simplify this arrangement even more by replacing the aralia leaves with moss to cover the foam. Alternatively, use moss with the leaves to cover any foam showing. The moss is secured using prongs made from wires 4cm long shaped like hairpins.

Look at your arrangement from the side. It should only have gradual steps forward

Upright Line arrangement

If you have success with the first design, try this one. It is similar but with a few more components. This arrangement steps forward very gradually. Fill with florist's foam and the top of the foam should be two centimetres above the lip of the vase

Construction

Step 1

Select two brown bamboo poles. Cut them on an angle using secateurs or a small saw. They can be fresh or dried. The brown bamboo poles give the structural stability to the design. They form the central axis and each one is placed into the foam near to the back of the container.

Step 2

Select six roses and make sure any bruised petals are removed (pinch out the petal at the base using your index finger and thumb). The leaves are removed as the stem becomes a feature with the taller blooms. Cut on an angle and insert near the bamboo. Slightly step forward with each flower as you place into the foam. The three roses at the base are placed close together and looking upwards.

Step 3

Cut the flowers off five stems of agapanthus and place the longest and smallest behind the bamboo in the centre line. Place the next dropping down slightly and continue stepping down to the base next to the roses. Each agapanthus is slightly forward of the previous one if you look from the side.

Step 4

Two stems of dendrobium (Singapore orchids) are chosen. Choose upright flowers on each stem. If the flowers are wide you can tighten the loose fall of the orchids using a fine .4 (26) gauge wire. The wire

is wound around the orchid flowers to form them more tightly. You must be gentle doing this so as not to bruise the orchids. Place the orchids one longer one shorter to the left side of the arrangement. The tips of each stems faces the centre line.

Step 5 (optional)

Six fronds of date palm seeds are placed into the foam. Two to the left side curving to the centre and four to the right side angling down to the base of the container.

Step 6

Use moss to cover any foam showing. The moss is secured using prongs made from wires 4cm long shaped like hairpins. Another line arrangement also known as a linear design

Special Advice

A general rule in arranging is one third of the content to the top half and two thirds of the content to the base half.

Arrangements

The strong line of this design, (photograph top left) created by the agapanthus (flowers removed) and green leucadendron's, is placed of centre to the left.

These are counter-balanced by the content on the right, being the umbrella fern. The strong leaf to the front is monstria. The remaining flowers in this design are Singapore orchids, leather fern, stachy's (dusty miller), carnations, bound spear grass, willow (nearly all leaves removed) and lithrope (these are the two leaves near the top, one arching over the top agapanthus).

The right hand photograph above features an arrangement in a tall, brown, rippled ceramic container. It has bleached bamboo to give it height. Heliconia's are placed, one towards the top in the central line (smallest) with a second stepping down the centre line. Two are placed to the lower left. You will see two burgundy/red anthuriums placed to the right. These counter balance the left placements. One anthurium looks up in the centre. You will also see a line of leaucadendrons starting below the second heliconia and working down to the base next to a cluster of roses.

Layered leather fern is placed on the left at the base and lime amaranthus flows downwards from the rose cluster. The foliage is anthurium leaves. Finally, the feature at the front is bleached cane. This is optional and it is criss-crossed over and under forming a grid.

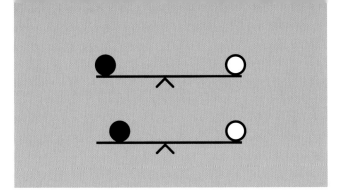

Top: *Incorrect* **Bottom:** *Correct*

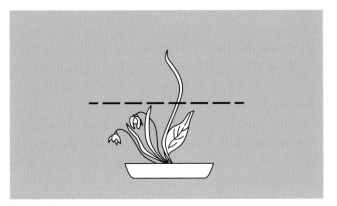

Bottom Heavy

Lopsided, too much visual weight on the left

Top heavy

Balance Advice

The see-saw shows how you should use balance in an arrangement. The darker cirles are heavier and must move closer to the central axis point to balance. Therefore, heavier flowers are placed closer to the axis (centre base) of an arrangement and the lighter are further away from the axis either horizontally or vertically or angular.

Groupings

This arrangement (photograph above) features groupings where the foliage and flowers are in sections of the design. If you want to substute hyacinths in groups please note following advice hyacinths in florist's foam can bend with the weight of the blooms. They need to be internally wired using a 1.25 (18) gauge wire that is inserted up the middle of the stem. Make a hole in the foam first before you insert the hyacinth stem.

Round Table centre

Flowers crown a dining table. The size and shape of the table determines the type and shape of the arrangement. A circular table usually has a circular arrangement. A rectangular table will usually have an extended table centre that is extended lengthways along the table.

When arranging flowers for a dinner table, place them either above eye level (for example set on a high centrepiece) or below eye level, so that they don't obstruct peoples view across the table. For an arrangement below eye level, the container is usually a low bowl. Make sure the bowl holds sufficient water for the number of flowers you are intending to use. A posy bowl is ideal for coffee tables and reception areas where it will be viewed from all sides. A round table centre or a posy bowl/box is literally a posy made into florists' foam. The principles of construction are the same.

A posy bowl can be low, medium or high as a gift item as well as small or large. Make sure you have a plan of placement before you begin construction. Work out how many flowers you have and how many you can use around the perimeter, the middle and the top. If you have more than one colour you will need to balance the colours within the circle base. Plan this carefully as it will distinguish your work as a success or a failure.

Many florists consider the ratio of eight, five, three, one works well. This would mean eight flowers around the perimeter, (if there were two colours four and four), then five on the next layer followed by three and then the top bloom.

Above:
Top: *The base of foliage and flowers*
Middle: *The completed round arrangement*
Bottom: *An aerial view of placements*

These steps outline how to make a round design:

Step 1

If you start at the base (optional) you can make a circle of foliage. Always cut foliage on an angle and cut away from your hand. If you use two varieties of foliage place evenly and alternating around the perimeter. Angle foliage slightly downwards. You can also place foliage into the centre of the foam. It must look upwards as this is the axis of the design. The selected piece must be equal each side of the axis. You can place foliage between the central foliage and the outer edge, creating a stepped design and a domed shape. A foliage base should be the exact shape of the completed design (round).

Step 2

Place flowers evenly around the edge and slightly downwards. These flowers may be longer, equal with or shorter than the base foliage. If the flowers are two colours make sure they work evenly around the base and have a pleasing harmony. You cannot have two of the same colour meeting or there will be a colour imbalance around the perimeter.

Step 3

Place the top focal bloom, it must look upwards. Be careful if you use iris as these can look to one side. As this is the axis it must be straight and central or the balance is lost.

Step 4

Place flowers down from the focal bloom stepping out, but not as far as the base flowers. To check - work back upwards in steps from the outer base blooms. You must distribute form (size) and colour with fairly equal amounts of space between.

Step 5

If you want to add more flowers you will need to place these in-between the flowers already arranged. Remember that the largest sizes are placed to the base.

Study the steps in the diagram shown below should read Study the steps in the diagram shown on the opposite page. This is constructed with the central rose first, then three to four roses making the desired dome shape. Foliage is inserted and then the rest of the roses are placed to complete the design.

Check your work by looking at it from above. Ask yourself these questions:

- Is it round?
- If you halved the design, do you have equal balance on each side? This will include sizes of blooms and colour distribution.
- Can you see all blooms?
- Is foliage evenly distributed?

Round table centres can be made larger by using a more open shape. These shapes can be constructed on a raised stand for tables. Another form of round construction for tables is the wreath frame base (refer to the wreath notes in this unit for construction details).

A round centre is seen from all angels, rotate the design to make sure it is pleasing from every direction

Wire support

Some flowers need to be wired for support, whether it's for a bouquet, a design set in floral foam or simply for the vase.

Floral wires come in different gauges (or widths), generally ranging from 18 to 26 gauge (the higher the gauge, the thinner the wire). The wire must be able to support the weight of the flowers, so it's important to choose the correct gauge for the flowers you're using.

Floral wires are available as green or black painted, fabric covered or plain metal. Multi-coloured wires are also available. They can be purchased online from floral sundry stores and from some craft stores.

Most flowers should be wired externally (with the wire running down the outside of the stem). However some flowers, including Zinnias, Shasta Daisies, Hyacinths and Gerberas can be wired internally. Only painted wires should be used for internal wiring, as unpainted wires may oxidise in water and infect the internal stem of the flower.

Wiring methods

Pierce and mount

This method is mainly used for wired bridal work. It is done by piercing the wire through the top of the stem (calyx) and bending the short wire that has come through the other side down the stem (this is mounting the wire). Both sides of the wire are then fastened and air-locked to the stem with binding tape.

Hairpin

With this method, the wire is arched into a tight bend (or hairpin) and inserted down the throat of the flower. It is fastened with binding tape.

Cross wiring

This method of wiring is used mainly for Camellias and Azaleas in wired bouquet work. Remove the calyx from the flower (if it has not already dropped off by itself) and wire through the side of the flower. Place a second wire at a right angle to the first. This forms an 'X' through the base of the bloom. Pull the wires down and fasten using binding tape. This method works for berries and moss as well.

Support wiring

Some flowers need wire support if their heads are heavy or their stems are weak. With support wiring, the wire is inserted up into the calyx and returned down the flower stem.

When using floral foam, hold the wire to the stem as you insert it into the foam. A handy tip is to leave the wire a centimetre or two longer than the stem end. This gives more grab into the foam.

To wire roses (to stop head droop or for stem support) use a 22 gauge wire and insert into the base of the head, then run the wire down the stem. Never insert into the petals or you will see bruising when the flower opens.

Imperial to Metric conversions

Although Australia uses the Metric system for measurements, in the floral industry wire gauges are often still referred to in Imperial measurements. Here are the conversions:

Imperial	Metric
18	1.25
20	.90
22	.71
24	.56
26	.45

Opposite
Top left: *pierce and mount wiring*
Top right: *hairpin wiring*
Bottom left: *cross wiring*
Bottom right: *support wiring*

Bouquets

Fully wired bouquets

Fully wired bouquets are a popular arrangement choice for floral designers who want to manipulate or shape flowers using the wire. It's essential that all flowers are in peak condition before wiring.

In a fully wired bouquet the flowers are cut and wired onto a central axis.

The wired flowers are sealed with strips of binding tape, which fastens the bloom to the wire and airlocks the stem so that the food source is trapped inside the stem and sepal area. (The flower will die when this source is depleted but usually this will take two or three days.)

A more modern version of the fully wired bouquet is to feature. This means that the flower heads and stems are wire supported. The wires sit at the back of the stems so that they're not visible. Generally fewer flowers are used in this kind of bouquet as the texture and line of the stems need to stand out as a feature of the bouquet.

Fully wired bouquets are the most expensive of all bouquet types, as they are the most time consuming to make. In decades past nearly all bouquets were fully wired.

Natural stemmed bouquets

Natural stemmed bouquets have become very popular in recent years. They are made up of flowers arranged in a spiralled pattern of placement, with wire support for some flowers. When wire support is needed, the wires should never extend below the tie point on the stems.

The skill in making these bouquets is in the selection of flowers and the colour dispersion, as well as the form (or sizes) of the flowers. They must balance across the axis and a trained designer will analyse the elements and principles of design so that the space, size and colour of the design works properly. Natural stemmed bouquets can feature a trailing cascade. This must be considered by the designer when spiralling the flowers for the bouquet, to prevent the cascade from being too stiff.

Natural stemmed bouquets are tied and bound with ribbon or fabric around the stems for ease of holding and a professional finish.

Bouquet holder designs

An alternative to a fully wired or natural stemmed bouquet is to create a bouquet with a partially pre-soaked bouquet holder as the internal structure. Bouquet holders are made from plastic and water absorbent foam and are ideal for designs that need a constant water source (see further description on page 50). Bouquets made with holders are also faster to construct than fully wired bouquets.

To construct bouquets with a holder, fasten the guard to the base using wire or cold glue. Then wire-support each flower by piercing up into the calyx, and while holding the natural stem and painted wire together, insert the stem end into the pre-soaked foam. Oasis cold glue can be applied to the side of the stem for extra hold in the foam. The flowers should be placed into the foam from the base upwards, finishing in the centre. Remember the elements and principles of design for balance of form, colour and space between the blooms and foliage.

For trailing bouquets, the wire support should extend further down the stem and be fastened with binding tape. (Do not tape over the stem ends or else they won't be able to drink from the water in the foam.) Start with construction of the trail. Insert the wire at the base of the foam holder right through the foam to the other side, making sure the natural stem is in the foam. Bend the wire over the guard and fasten with glue. The centre of the bouquet can then be constructed as per the instructions above.

Bouquet holders can be finished with tulle, ribbon, cord and Abaca (a natural fibre). Leaves can be wired and placed in the spaces at the back of the holder to disguise the plastic and foam. The tilt head can be carried with the handle facing up or down, depending on whether the carrier wants to hold the bouquet against her bodice or her hip.

Wiring leaves using the stitch and mount method

A leaf is wired using a stitch and mount method. You thread the wire mid-leaf like using a needle and thread. The wire is returned and this is known as the mount. For use on a bouquet holder the wire is returned to be equal each side. Parafilm to the end of the short leaf stem and place into the foam of the holder. Cold glue a can be applied to the wire for extra strength.

Opposite left: *a fully wired bouquet*
Opposite right: *a natural stemmed bouquet*
Above left: *view of a bouquet holder from the back*
Above right: *a design made with a bouquet holder*

Products and tools for flower arranging

Bouquet holders

Bouquet holders are commonly used for wedding bouquets. A traditional bouquet holder looks a bit like a lollipop, with a bulbous head on top of a thin plastic stalk. The head contains water-absorbent foam held in place by a plastic guard. There are various shapes available – some with flat, squat heads and others with angled heads. The *Oasis Grande* is the most popular in the market.

Bouquet holders are great for warmer weather, when the flowers in the bouquet need a water source. Soak the bouquet holder before use by placing the head of the foam into water. This should be done the day before the bouquet is required. Once the bouquet has been made up, you can lightly spray water onto the foam to add more moisture if needed.

Glue

Floral cold glue (Oasis Floral Adhesive) can be used to hold flowers in position in floral foam or in bouquet holders.

To use in foam, apply a small amount of glue on the side of the stem before you insert it in the foam. It sets in about a minute and will hold very strongly. For bouquet holders, the glue can be used to secure the plastic guard over the foam. The guard should be glued to the base of the bouquet holder so that it can't dislodge.

Never use glue on the end of a flower stem, as this will block the flower's water source.

Preservative sprays

Preservative sprays are used to slow the respiration of a flower. The most popular brand in the market is Clear Life (made by the American floral sundry company Design Master).

Clear Life should be sprayed on the surface area of the flower as well as underneath it, to produce a film over the flower (you may need to airbrush the flower several times). This prevents air being drawn from the flower and therefore preserves it in its current state.

This product should only be used on good quality flowers as it will not repair or preserve old flowers. It should also only be used on lighter coloured blooms as the film is visible on dark colours. Do not mist the flowers with water when you use this product as this will break down the product's effectiveness.

Floral colour sprays

Floral colour sprays can be used to enhance the colour of flowers. They can also be used to change a flowers colour, as long as the flower is white or cream to begin with. When using spray colours it's best to lightly mist or airbrush the flowers several times instead of heavily spraying them only once or twice. These sprays affect the life span of the flowers.

The company Design Master have a wide range of flower spray colours available.

Moss balls

A small moss ball is a filling product, designed to fill out the base of a bouquet and look great as well. A moss ball is made up from a bunch of moss gathered together with two wires crossed over and returned underneath it. For use in a bouquet holder, make sure the wires are locked together under the moss ball, with two forked feet that can be fastened into the holder. For use in wired bouquets, use Parafilm to join the wires together and make a single wire, before the bouquet construction begins. Moss balls are excellent fillers if there are spaces at the base of your bouquet.

Binding tape

Binding tape is used to secure and disguise wiring in floral bouquets. It holds the wire to the stem and air-locks the flower, keeping the moisture locked inside. It is generally available in green, white and brown, but other colours can also be purchased.

There are several different brands of binding tape available, including Flora Tape and Stemtex. These tapes bind only and have no stretch, unlike the industry favourite Parafilm, which can be twisted and stretched and is very strong. It is plastic based and works like kitchen plastic wrap.

Binding tape should be kept in an airtight container so as not to become brittle.

Glycerine for foliages

If you want to include foliage in your bouquets or arrangements, the use of glycerine can be advantageous as it may preserve the foliage for months.

Mix one part glycerine with two parts hot water. Hammer the stem ends of the foliage branches and stand them in 4–6 centimetres of the glycerine/water mixture. Remove them as the water cools. Hang the branches in a well-ventilated area for three weeks and you will see if the method has taken. The leaves should be pliable and not dry. Foliages such as Copper Beech and Tri-colour Beech generally react very well to glycerine preservation.

Overleaf left
Top left: *A simple orchid trail falling from the wrist.*
Top right: *A ball of flowers held by in the palm of the hand.*
Bottom left : *A trailing orchid bouquet*
Bottom right: *A trailer bouquet attached to a slender handbag.*

Overleaf right: *Winning designs by Gregory Milner and Nicole Gibson displayed at the Melbourne International Flower and Garden Show*

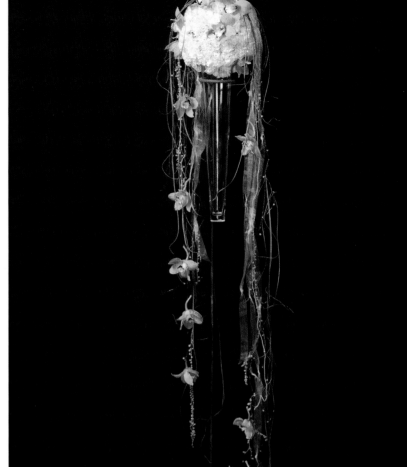

FLOWER RETAIL, WEDDINGS AND CORPORATE DECORATING

The retailing of cut flowers

The term 'Florist'

The term 'florist' first came about in the seventeenth and eighteenth centuries, when societies that competitively produced and displayed new floral varieties sprang up in England, and later across Europe. These were known as florist's societies and they were devoted to eight categories of flowers: Anemones, Auriculas, Carnations, Hyacinths, Pinks, Polyanthus, Tulips and Ranunculus. The term 'florist' referred to someone who raised and developed new floral varieties.

Today, the term florist is used to describe a professional flower retailer or floral designer.

Flower retailing

These days cut flowers are sold through many different retail outlets. Apart from florist shops, flowers are sold at service stations, milk bars, roadside sellers, supermarkets, fruit shops, chemists and many other retail stores. Unfortunately, in many cases the seller's knowledge of floristry is minimal or in some cases non-existent.

Training

There is a lack of training across the Australian floral industry. In Australia anyone can open a florist shop, regardless of whether or not they possess qualifications or industry experience. There are a number of untrained and unqualified 'florists' in business who use poor care and handling techniques, which impacts on the quality and presentation of the cut flowers sold in these outlets and also on the reputation of the florist industry as a whole.

To rectify this situation it is imperative that flower retailers get the right training. Vital areas of training include learning and understanding how flowers are grown, how to handle them, what they need, how they should be used and flower hygiene.

It's also important that florists train their employees and support any staff who are undertaking floristry traineeships/apprenticeships.

To find out more about training courses in Australia, visit the National Training Information Service website <www.ntis.gov.au> and search for 'floristry'.

Knowledge of product

Knowing your product is essential for any retail business, and in floristry this means having a comprehensive understanding of flower varieties and their natural seasons of growth. Although many flowers are now available all year round (due to hothouse production), knowing the natural seasons of growth for all flower varieties is important, as this knowledge will assist the florist in understanding the care and handling requirements for each flower. For example, flowers that grow in warm climates generally should not be placed in a cool room.

Florists should visit gardens and markets and especially growers to develop an appreciation of the growing and treatment conditions for all flower varieties.

Wholesale markets

Most florists purchase their stock (at wholesale prices) from flower markets. The way this is done today differs from how it was done in the past, and this has resulted in changes in how cut flowers are retailed.

Up until the early 1990s, growers would bring their produce to the market (enough for one day's trade) and then leave when all the stock had sold. The florists would buy their stock from the market (enough for one day's trade) and return to their shops to sell it, and their aim was the same as the growers' – sell out and go home. Therefore a customer entering a florist shop late in the day would be greeted with a very limited selection, as the day's stock would have nearly sold out.

This provided the best rotation method for fresh stock. It should be remembered that *cut flowers are one of the most perishable products that a customer can buy.*

The way in which flowers are sold at the market today has impacted greatly on the way florists now sell the product. Many of the small growers that sold their flowers at market no longer do so. Often these growers sold their flowers at one given crop season or they specialised in one or two types of flowers only. Their product is now purchased by dealers or larger growers.

Cut flower stock is now delivered to market in refrigerated vans and most markets have refrigerated display areas or at least some form of refrigeration on site. Whatever is not sold on the first day is returned to the cool room to be displayed for sale again the next day, or at the next market, so the stock that ends up in the florist's shop is not always as fresh as it should

be. Alternatively a florist may buy fresh stock from the market, display at their shop and whatever stock is not sold that day is placed in the cool room and returned to the footpath the following day. Again, the stock is not as fresh as it should be.

The buying public will no longer accept limited selections at the end of the day and often associate the size and quality of a retailer by the variety of stock on hand. But we are referring to perishable stock and the consumer gains the best product from the freshest stock. This is a complex issue for retailers, who must choose whether to replenish their stock from the markets on a daily basis and therefore have limited stock available late in the day, or only visit the markets a couple of times a week and have plenty of stock to sell at all times, but perhaps of a lesser quality.

As a florist, regardless of how quickly you replenish your stock it is absolutely essential that you identify the quality of the stock that you're buying. You should ask the growers when the stock was picked and examine the product to ensure it is fresh and healthy.

You should also ensure that the stock you purchase from the market is correctly transported to your shop. At the market, place your purchased flowers into clean buckets filled with clean water, then transport these containers to the van, which should also be clean. The van should be driven to the shop with all windows closed, to prevent ethylene gas contamination from the surrounding traffic.

Flower storage

When professional flower growers place cut flowers in temperatures of 1–4 degrees Celsius to retard their respiration, this is called 'storage'. The flowers can be stored from a few days to a few weeks, and the result is that their development is essentially stunted, so that when they are removed from storage they look

Highly perfumed Lilies will react badly with Roses, Gladiolus and Carnations when they're all in the cool room together. The strong perfume of the Lily can cause petal curl in the other flowers.

exactly as they would if they were freshly cut. The storing method is used when flower growers need to prolong the life span of their stock in order to meet client demand.

The downside to storing cut flowers is that although they look fresh and healthy when removed from storage, they usually deteriorate very quickly and have nowhere near the regular life span that they would have had if unstored.

Roses, Carnations, Iris, Tulips, Chrysanthemums and Gypsophlia can all be stored but they will open very quickly when exposed to room temperature and roses will be prone to head droop. Gerberas, Lisianthus, Stephanotis, Alstroemeria, Anemone and Marigold should never be exposed to storage temperatures.

Storing cut flowers is something that should only be attempted by flower growers or professional horticulturalists. *A retail florist should never store cut flowers in these temperatures.*

Cool rooms and display refrigeration

In retail florist shops it's best to keep flowers at room temperature if possible, as they acclimatise and handle delivery and weather exposure better if they haven't been refrigerated. It is recommended that florists and flower sellers keep their perishable stock turning over rather than keeping it in a cool room or display refrigerator, as the cooling process can create an illusion with how fresh the stock actually is. Cooled cut flowers may look good when they're first taken out of the cool room, but they won't last very long once the customer takes them home.

If refrigeration is needed, moderate temperatures of 6–8 degrees Celsius is recommended for most flowers.

Tropical flowers should never be placed into a cool room or a refrigerated display cabinet. They require a temperature that is not below 12 degrees Celsius. This includes Ginger, Heliconia, Gloriosa Lily, Orchid varieties, Poinsettia, Euphorbia, Strelitzia and Anthiriums.

Top: *Rose*
Bottom: *Carnation*

Cool rooms and special occasion flowers

Cool rooms can assist with temporarily keeping flowers at a certain stage in their life span, in preparation for a special occasion such as a wedding or funeral, where the life span of the flower beyond the day of the occasion is not a consideration. On the actual day that the flowers are to be used, they should be at their peak of beauty and therefore three quarters through their life span. For example, for a casket tribute of roses, the blooms should be three quarters open to look their best for the service. The skill of the florist is to buy, prepare and anticipate the opening process of the flower. The use of a cool room can assist this process.

For special occasion flowers, weather conditions are a very important part of the planning process. If a floral arrangement was placed in a cool room and then removed for delivery and the anticipated delivery time was half an hour on a hot day, plus there was a chance that the flowers would sit for another couple of hours in heat, then of course the flowers may start to wilt. The key here is to plan ahead, choose appropriate flowers for the arrangement and be careful with how you utilise the cool room.

Handling stock

When you place bunches of flowers into buckets, tubs or vases, hold the stem ends together to avoid them catching the rim of the container. This also applies to single stems in a vase. It's best to group the stems, spiralling them together, and place them into the vase as one unit rather than as individual stems.

If you place them individually you increase the risk of breaking the stems.

Always place your hand under the flowers as you place them onto a table or bench. This will help to avoid bruising of the petals.

If your flowers have been in cool storage then placing them in ice water for about 30 minutes will help them to recover. In storage, the flowers' respiration is slowed by temperature. Air bubbles clog the vascular bundles and this decreases water absorption. Ice water dissolves these bubbles and the flowers will drink.

Packaging

Plastic sleeves around flower bunches were introduced by growers in the 1980s. They were designed to protect the flowers from damage during their transportation from the grower to the market, and then from the market to the florist shop. However, they also cause the flowers to develop mould, especially if the flowers are kept in a cool room, and for this reason plastic sleeves should be avoided.

The other reason to avoid plastic sleeves is that they make it difficult for the florist (when buying from the market) to see any damage to the flower stems or any bent, crushed or broken leaves. If a bunch of flowers is kept in a plastic sleeve from the time it leaves the grower to the time it's taken home by the consumer, then it is the consumer who will open the bunch of flowers only to discover damaged and mouldy leaves and stems. This obviously is not good for business! So, avoid buying wholesale stock that's packaged in plastic, or remove it quickly, and never use plastic in your own florist shop. Paper is a much better option for wrapping up your customer's purchase.

Helping the customer

Professional flower retailers should focus on helping the customer select the right flowers for their requirements. To do this, the flower seller should ask the customer the following questions:

- What do they intend to do with the flowers?
- How long do they need the flowers to last?
- What kind of vases do they have to put the flowers in?
- Do they require stems of varying lengths for floral arrangement?

When a customer wishes to purchase a variety of flowers and foliages, the flower seller should assist them in selecting blooms with complementary colours and sizes, and flowers and foliages with similar life spans.

Customer expectation

As with any other retail business, the most important aspect of retail floristry is to keep your customers happy. This means always having fresh stock, knowing how to care for, handle and package the stock, being able to pass on your knowledge to the customer and ensuring that you meet the customer's needs. If your customers are impressed by the quality of your product and can be confident that the flowers they purchase from you will last five or more days, then you are on the right path to building a reputable floristry business.

Tips for successful retailing of cut flowers

- Keep detailed records of stock buying and sales so that you can accurately determine your stock requirements.
- For field flowers, forecast possible shortages due to weather and drought conditions, and plan your purchase of stock accordingly.
- Avoid displaying your stock in outdoor areas, especially if your shopfront is on a road with lots of traffic.
- Make sure that your stock is kept cool and always out of direct sunlight and draughts.
- Change the water regularly and use bleach and/or preservative where required.
- Most cut flower varieties should be sold with a water source (either a water-filled plastic bag attached to the base of the flower bunch, or individual water vials). A responsible flower seller will provide this, free of charge, to ensure that their product remains fresh and healthy, even after leaving their shop. Roses in particular should never be sold without a water source.

As a floral retailer, you might want to consider offering your customers a printed 'floral care' guide that they can refer to at home.

As a general rule, a bride should allow 10 to 20% of the cost of her wedding dress for her bridal bouquet. Remember, the bouquet is held in front of the gown and should therefore measure up in quality.

Wedding flowers

Weddings are an exciting (and lucrative) area for floral designers to work in. Not only do you get to create beautiful, memorable designs, but you also get to contribute to the magic and romance of a couple's big day. However, wedding orders are not for the inexperienced. For wedding flowers to be a success, every detail must be carefully planned and coordinated. If you are involved in wedding bouquet construction or service and reception flowers, knowledge of flower care as well as all design aspects is vital. Creativity is only part of it – there's a lot of hard work involved too, not to mention the responsibility of getting everything just right for the big day.

Types of wedding flower arrangements

Wired bouquets have been favoured in floristry for over 150 years and are still popular with brides and their entourages. Bouquet holders are used especially for summer weddings where the flowers need a constant water source. Hand-held natural stemmed bouquets are also very popular for weddings.

Most other wedding flower arrangements also require wiring and construction. These include hairpieces, corsages, handbag and wrist corsages, cake top and sprays, pew ends, circlets, tiaras, garlands, trail bouquets, posies, shower bouquets, crescents, drop showers and arm sheaves.

See chapter 4 for detailed instructions on basic wiring methods.

Wedding flower planning and preparation

Know your market

Be aware of current wedding trends. Visit bridal houses and exhibitions and use bridal magazines and websites to research current styles of gowns and accessories as well as flowers.

As well as keeping abreast of current trends, it's important to understand the basics. First, know your fabrics, as the texture of a bridal gown will suit some flowers more than others. For example, Phalaenopsis Orchids have a curved edge and this can suit scalloping on a gown.

Second, know your colours, and how they will contrast with the other decorations and designs in the wedding. For example, white Roses may look cream when held against a white satin gown.

You also need to have a solid understanding of which bouquet styles complement which gowns and how the bouquets should be held by the bride. For example, if the bodice of a gown is very ornate, the bride would be best advised to hold the bouquet lower, against the hip. The size and height of the bride is also a consideration. A very tall, thin bride holding a tiny posy looks out of proportion.

The initial consultation

The initial consultation with your potential client (most often the bride or a wedding planner) should be scheduled at a time when you can give them your undivided attention. Most bridal consultations take at least one hour, so plan this into your day and perhaps even suggest an after-hours consultation if this will work better for you.

Remember that at this stage, your client is not yet your client – they're meeting with you to ascertain whether you're the best person for the job, and as such you'll need to impress them. Show them examples of your designs (an album containing photographs of other bridal work you've done, with written recommendations from the clients). Explain how you can work within their budget and in accordance with the style of their wedding. If you've had lots of bridal clients then emphasise your expertise and experience, and if you're just starting out then emphasise your competency, creativity and any non-bridal floral design experience you have (i.e. corporate decorating).

During the initial consultation you should ask your potential client the following questions:

- When is the wedding? (date and time)
- Where is the service taking place?
- Where is the reception taking place?
- What is the style of the wedding?
- What will the bride be wearing? (fabric and style of gown)
- How many people are in the bridal party?
- What clothing styles and colours will the bridal party be wearing and what are their heights, builds and hair and skin colourings?
- What hairstyles and hair adornments will the bride and bridesmaids have? (this is only relevant if floral hairpieces are required)

You also need to ascertain very early on, what floral items the bride and groom have in mind. You may suggest the following:

- buttonholes for groom, groomsmen, fathers and grandfathers of the bride and groom, ushers, master of ceremonies and special guests
- corsages for mothers and grandmothers of the bride and groom and special guests
- service flowers, including large arrangements, pew decorations and altar flowers
- reception venue decorations, including table centerpieces, foyer arrangements and even rest room flowers
- flowers for the wedding cake
- flowers for the home (especially for photographs)

- flowers for wedding car decoration
- an arch of flowers usually for an outdoor wedding

Once you have the answers to these questions you can begin to plan the designs and the work/cost involved. The bride and groom will most likely have an allocated budget, but you may find that if what they want doesn't fit within their budget, they'll extend the budget accordingly!

The creative collaboration

Some brides (and grooms) will come to you with a strong idea of which flower varieties, colours and designs they want. Others will have only a vague idea of what they want, and some will come to you with no ideas at all. The skill of the floral designer is to work with the client to achieve the best possible results. If what your client wants is simply not possible, then suggest alternatives that fit with their original vision (or budget). Help your client visualise the flowers and designs that will fit the style of the wedding. Many established wedding florists have a wide range of sample silk bouquets for the bride to see and hold – these assist greatly with helping the bride to visualise what bouquet will suit her best.

Ordering and handling stock

When ordering the required stock, do not give instructions to your supplier of what stage (visually) you want your flowers to be. Instead, have fresh stock delivered several days (or for some flowers a whole week) in advance and control the opening of the blooms yourself.

When the stock has been delivered, remove it from the plastic sleeves immediately, then recut the stems and place them into clean water with conditioning solution.

To speed up the opening of blooms, use sugar in the water or place the stems into lukewarm water.

You can also refrigerate the flowers at eight degrees Celsius, but in most cases this should be avoided as flowers that are exposed to room temperature after being kept in the cool room may deteriorate very quickly after opening.

Correct preparation and treatment of wedding flowers is vital. There is nothing worse than wilted flowers in a bridal bouquet!

Care and handling of popular wedding flowers

Lilies

Lilies (one of the most popular wedding flowers) should be delivered to you a week prior to the wedding. Let them open naturally. You can slow down their development by placing them in a cool room if needed but make sure they are removed 24 hours before you start making up the arrangements so that they have time to acclimatise in room temperature. Remove the anthers from the Lilies as they open to avoid any staining on the flower.

Never leave Lilies out of water as they can drop and wilt within two hours. This is especially important if they are to be wired in a bouquet. When the bouquet is made up, the binding tape seals the stem end so the air cannot dry out the flower but if the bloom has been left out of water it has little food left to draw on and will collapse. For wired bouquets, damp cotton wool can be placed at the base of the Lily stem and taped against the stem. For hot weather weddings, this is an ideal way to ensure that the Lily has a constant water source.

Tulips

Tulips look beautiful in wedding bouquets but they can be difficult to prepare. Not only can they continue to grow as a cut flower (sometimes up to 20 centimetres in height), they will also turn to the light. To retard their growth, pierce the top of the stem with a pin (this allows air to enter the stem). To stop them turning to the light, cover them in black plastic and keep them in a dark room. In a wired bouquet the stem is shorter and they are air-locked with binding tape. This will keep growth to a minimum. In bouquet holders they will grow as they have a constant water source. Don't wire into the bloom as the tulips can grow off the wires. Make a small loop at the top of the stem with the wire and this will allow for the growth but still give support.

Be aware that Tulips can be delivered by the supplier in green bud form, particularly in winter. As they grow their colour continues to form, even as a cut flower. Don't be caught out by this – check with your supplier and if the buds are tight, get the stock into your premises as soon as possible and put them in conditioning solution.

A Tulip's development as a cut flower is best controlled by you, not the supplier.

Roses

Depending on weather conditions, Roses may be delivered to you five days prior to the wedding (i.e. on Tuesday for a Saturday wedding). You will need to control them carefully to ensure that they look their best on the wedding day, and you will find some Rose varieties will be stronger than others. The outside layer of petals are usually removed to make sure the flower looks perfect. Never use Roses that have blemishes, and if you can see the veins in the petals (same with Orchids) it means that the Rose is too old. The petal surface area should be smooth and their centres should not be visible.

If Roses have been kept in a cool room, check them for Botrytis (a fungus that is caused by the flowers being covered in damp conditions) as this can cause the heads to rot and fall off.

Orchids

Orchids can also be tricky wedding flowers, as they can develop air embolisms while still attached to their main stem, but show no symptoms of this until a day later when they begin to wilt. If you are using Orchids in a wired bouquet, you can prevent this problem by cutting the Orchids from their main stems and inserting the flowers on their short stems into a shallow dish filled with cotton wool and clean water. Insert the stem through the cotton wool into the water.

This preservation method can be used for most flower varieties, but is particularly effective for Frangipanis, Gardenias, Helebors and Stephanotis.

Storing of bouquets

Bouquets that are kept in a cool room should be covered in tissue and plastic and with all lights turned off. This will help to prevent the blooms from opening any further, and will also stop the cool room fans from drying them out.

If you choose to keep the bouquets in room temperature then there will be less shock to the blooms, particularly in summer, but remember that the blooms will continue to open in their natural growth pattern. Allow for this in the planning stage by making up the bouquets a little earlier. Do a trial run with excess stock if you are unsure how to time this.

Opposite
Top Row: *Nymphaea, Azalea, Bracteantha*
Middle Row: *Liliums, Gerberas Tulips,*
Bottom Row: *Freesia, Anthurium, Hyacinth*

Suitable cut flowers for bridal bouquets and wedding accessories

The following is a list of flowers that are suitable for wedding use. They are listed alphabetically by common name and where their botanical name is different, this is listed after the common name in brackets.

For more information about using these flowers for weddings, see the sub-heading 'Wedding flower use' on the individual flower listings in chapter 6. Also see chapter 4 for instructions on wiring methods and basic wedding bouquet arrangements.

Agapanthus

Ageratum

Allium

Alstroemeria

Amaranthus

Andromeda

Anemone

Anthurium

Arab's Eye (Ornithogalum)

Arum and Calla Lily
(Zantedeschia)

Aster and Easter Daisy
(Callistephus)

Astilbe

Azalea

Baby's Breath (Gypsophila)

Banksia

Belladonna (Amaryllis)

Berzelia

Bird of Paradise (Strelitzia)

Blushing Bride (Seruria)

Boronia

Bottlebrush (Callistemon)

Bouvardia

Broom (Cytisus)

Broom (Genista)

Bush Rose (Dryandra)

Camellia

Carnations (Dianthus)

Chincherinchee
(Ornithogalum)

Chrysanthemum

Clivea

Cockscomb (Celosia)

Cornflower (Centaurea)

Cosmos

Cyclamen

Dahlia

Daphne

Delphinium

Dogwood (Cornus)

Flannel Flower (Actinotis)

Frangipani (Plumeria)

Freesia

Gardenia

Garrya

Geraldton Wax
(Chamelaucium)

Gerbera

Gladiolus

Globe Thistle (Echinops)

Gloriosa Lily

Godetia (Clarkia)

Granny's Bonnett
(Aquilegia)

Grape Hyacinth (Muscari)

Heliconia

Helleborus

Hyacinth (Hyacinthus)

Hydrangea

Hypericum

Golden Rod (Solidago)

Iceland Poppy (Papaver)

Iris

Isopogen

Ixia

Kalmia

Kangaroo Paw
(Anigozanthos)

Knautia

Lambs Tail (Lachnostachys)

Larkspur (Consolida)

Lavender (Lavandula)

Leucadendron

Liatris

Lilac (Syringa)

Lilium

Lily of the Valley Tree (Clethra)

Lily of the Valley (Convallaria)

Lisianthus (Eustoma)

Lotus Pods (Nelumbo)

Marguerite Daisy (Argyrranthemum)

Marigold (Calendula)

Monks Hood (Aconitum)

Mignonette

Molucca Balm (Molucella)

Narcissus

Nerine

Oncidium

Orchid

Oyster Plant (Acanthus)

Pampas Grass (Cortaderia)

Peony Rose (Paeonia)

Pin Cushion (Leucospermum)

Pineapple Lily (Eucomis)

Protea

Queen Anne's Lace (Ammi)

Red-hot Pokers and Torch Lily (Kniphofia)

Rose (Rosa)

Scabiosa

Scilla

Shasta Daisy (Leucanthemum)

Shell Heath (Erica)

Smoke Bush (Conospermum)

Snap Dragon (Antirrhinum)

Soloman's Seal (Polygonatus)

South Australian Daisy (Ixodia)

Statice (Limonium)

Stock (Matthiola)

Straw Flower (Bracteantha)

Sweet Alice (Alyssum)

Sweet Pea (Lathyrus)

Teasels (Dipsacus)

Thryptomene

Tuberose (Polianthes)

Tulips (Tulipa)

Water Lily (Nymphaea)

Waxflower (Stephanotis)

Zephyr Lilies (Zephyranthes)

Zinnia

Corporate and business decorating

As a florist, having repeat-business corporate clients is a wonderful acknowledgment of the success of your business and can also be quite lucrative. However, it's not as easy as preparing a lovely floral arrangement and dropping it off at the office – you also have to factor in maintenance, administration time and occasional disaster when someone in the office turns the heating up high! Despite the time and energy involved, decorating offices, restaurants and other business environments is a great thing for a florist to do, for both creative expression and forming connections with others in the business community.

Practical considerations
Location and environment

The location of floral arrangements within the corporate environment is an important consideration. In offices, flowers are often placed in reception areas where there is strong overhead lighting and multiple

heating and airconditioning ducts. Airconditioning or heating will dry flowers and foliage rapidly. Heating or cooling that is on all day but turned off during the night, then turned on again the next morning, places enormous stress on flowers as their environment temperature is constantly changing. This combination, along with doors opening and closing all the time, will shorten the flowers' life span considerably. For office decoration, choose tough flowers that can withstand unnatural lighting and temperatures.

In restaurants, flowers are often placed near entrances or foyers, where there's a lot of human traffic and doors opening to the street outside. Again, it's important to choose hardy flowers that won't wilt or bruise easily when exposed to sudden changes in temperature or people brushing up against them.

It's important to choose flowers that will look attractive throughout the week. After all, this is the purpose of floral arrangements in businesses!

Quality and handling of blooms

Flowers must be fresh! Do not take them straight from a cool room into an office as the temperature difference will immediately send the flowers into shock. Instead, help the flowers to acclimatise by keeping them in room temperature prior to delivering them to the business.

Always ensure that the arrangements are looking their best before they're delivered. The stems should be fresh and strong and there shouldn't be any sign of pollination in the flowers.

Transportation

If bunches have been prepared in the hand make sure they are transported in water. Many flowers will air block if they are left out of water. An airconditioned van is best in the summer months.

Vases and containers

For an office or business floral arrangement, use a sensible vase that holds a quantity of water that will supply the flowers and foliages for a week. There should be no overcrowding or stems crushed together. If you use floral foam, a wide dish vase with sides that are equal to the height of the foam is most appropriate as the water level can be seen and the foam will remain nearly immersed. Use stones if camouflage is needed, but make sure they're washed first so as not to breed bacteria. Remember, as the water level drops, the water in the foam will fall and flowers not firmly placed down into the foam are susceptible to drying out.

Recording weekly details

Florists who cater for businesses should record the details of the flowers used in each floral arrangement. Most businesses do not want to receive the same flowers or colours each week. Set up a database and record the selection of flowers and foliages used in

each arrangement, as well as the accessories used, the times of delivery and whether or not the vase has been supplied by the client. This database can also assist in costing your items by recording the exact value of all components.

Variety in designs

It's a good idea to alternate flowers in a vase with flowers in foam every second week. Also use props to add interest to the designs. Bamboo is a useful prop – it consists of sections, and by using a saw you can cut above a natural join in the bamboo, which will allow you to use the bamboo as a vase. This also allows you to create height for orchids or other thin-stemmed flowers within your design.

Accessories like paper bark, stones, fungi, twigs, (use Pussy Willow with caution as it is considered by some to be unlucky), Willow, moss, raffia, plastic or copper tubing can all add interest to a design. Make sure that stones and copper tubing are spotlessly clean before use.

Customer requests

It's important to take your clients' requests into account while at the same time providing flowers that will last in a business environment. For example, if a client asks for a selection of Roses and Iris, but you know that these flowers will not last very long in their office, then you should explain to the client why these flowers are unsuitable and suggest some alternatives.

Sometimes clients request that you use their corporate colours in your arrangements. If it's not possible to supply these colours throughout the year in a selection that will last, you should explain this to the client.

Remember, if the flowers you provide do not last though the week then you will most likely lose the account.

Mid-week visit

It's a good idea to make a mid-week visit to check what state the flowers are in and whether they need a water change or added preservative. Take a digital camera with you and photograph the flowers for proof of their appearance. If any flowers have drooped or wilted unexpectedly, replace the flowers and email the photographs to your supplier for a refund.

The mid-week check not only shows your client that you care, but also may save you losing your client if the flowers haven't lasted as long as you said they would.

Costing

Having business clients can be lucrative but you need to factor in certain costs to ensure that you're pricing your products and services appropriately. In your costings, remember to take the following into account:

- the time it takes to create the arrangements, including possible overtime you'll pay your staff or yourself for creating arrangements on Sundays or early Monday mornings

- delivery time and transport
- mid-week visits, including time and transport
- materials needed, including flowers, foliage, vases and props
- rental fees for elaborate props.

For business accounts you'll need to develop a costing to cover the entire year. Remember that flower prices will change through the months of the year yet the figure to be paid to you will not vary. Your customers need to be aware that during the colder months flowers are scarce and your suppliers' prices will vary, therefore the selection your clients will receive may be smaller in quantity. Explain this to your client before you accept the account.

The margin on perishable goods is recommended to be 300% (by the Australian Association of Floral Designers). Many florists don't work on this figure but they really should, so that the standards of floristry supply to businesses are kept at a high level and so florists can continue to service businesses at an acceptable profit.

Suitable cut flowers for corporate and business decorating

The following is a list of flowers that are suitable for corporate and business use. They are listed alphabetically by common name and where their botanical name is different, this is listed after the common name in brackets.

For more information about using these flowers for commercial decorating, see the sub-heading 'Corporate and business use' on the individual flower listings in chapter 6. See chapter 4 for instructions on wiring methods for basic floral arrangements.

Agapanthus
Agonis
Alstroemeria
Amaranthus
Andromeda
Anemone
Anthurium
Arab's Eye (Ornithogalum)
Arum and Calla Lily (Zantedeschia)
Aster and Easter Daisy (Callistephus)
Astilbe
Baby's Breath (Gypsophila)
Banksia
Belladonna (Amaryllis)
Berzelia
Bird of Paradise (Strelitzia)
Blushing Bride (Seruria)
Bottlebrush (Callistemon)
Bouvardia
Broom (Cytisus)
Broom (Genista)
Bush Rose (Dryandra)
Campanula/Canterbury Bells
Carnations (Dianthus)
Chincherinchee (Ornithogalum)
Chrysanthemum
Clivea
Cockscomb (Celosia)
Cornflower (Centaurea)

Dahlia
Delphinium
Dogwood (Cornus)
Freesia
Garrya
Geraldton Wax (Chamelaucium)
Gerbera
Gladiolus
Globe Thistle (Echinops)
Gloriosa Lily
Godetia (Clarkia)
Golden Rod (Solidago)
Heliconia
Hyacinth (Hyacinthus)
Hydrangea
Icopogon
Iris
Ixia
Kalmia
Kangaroo Paw (Anigozanthos)
Knautia
Lambs Tail (Lachnostachys)
Larkspur (Consolida)
Lathyrus (Sweet Pea)
Leucadendron
Leucospermum
Liatris
Lilium
Lily of the Valley Tree (Clethra)

Limonium (Statice)
Lisianthus (Eustoma)
Lotus Pods (Nelumbo)
Molucca Balm (Molucella)
Nerine
Oncidium
Orchid
Pampas Grass (Cortaderia)
Peony Rose (Paeonia)
Pineapple Lily (Eucomis)
Polianthes (Tuberose)
Protea
Red-hot Pokers and Torch Lily (Kniphofia)
Scabiosa
Shasta Daisy (Leucanthemum)
Shell Heath (Erica)
Smoke Bush (Conospermum)
Snap Dragon (Antirrhinum)
South Australian Daisy (Ixodia)
Stock (Matthiola)
Straw Flower (Bracteantha)
Sunflowers (Heliathus)
Teasels (Dipsacus)
Water Lily (Nymphaea)
Watsonia
Zephyr lilies (Zephyranthes)
Zingiber
Zinnia

A-Z DIRECTORY OF CUT FLOWERS

How to use this directory

What flowers are included?

This comprehensive A-Z directory lists all flowers that can last for five or more days as cut flowers.

Finding a flower

The flowers are listed alphabetically by their botanical names, with their common names shown underneath. To search for a flower by its common name, see the Common name index on page 336. The Botanical name index on page 340 can be used a quick reference for finding a flower by its botanical name.

Understanding the information

Common names

Most flowers have several different common names by which they are known. In this directory only the most popular common names have been included.

Botanical varieties

Most flowers have many different botanical varieties. In this directory only the varieties that are commercially grown and available to purchase have been listed. The information given for each flower refers only to these varieties.

Family

For each flower the name of its family (or genus) has been listed. Where a flower comes from more than one family, all major family names are included.

Natural season

This refers to the season in which the flower is in bloom. Note that with the increase in hothouse and glasshouse production of flowers, many flower varieties are now available to buy all year round.

Colour availability

Only the flower colours that are commercially grown and available to purchase have been listed. You may find that other colours (not listed here) are grown in home gardens or in the wild.

Cut flower life span

This refers to the average life span of the flower, assuming it is fresh stock and is cared for and handled correctly.

ACACIA

(a-kay-sha) Common names: Wattle; Mimosa

BOTANICAL VARIETIES Acacia acinacea, Acacia baileyana, Acacia longifolia, (many other varieties) FAMILY Mimosaceae SUB FAMILY Legumnosae NATURAL SEASON All year as foliage, flowers in late winter and spring COLOUR AVAILABILITY White, yellow, purple, cream, green, red (rarely found) CUT FLOWER LIFE SPAN 5–7 days

Note: *be aware that there is a superstition regarding Wattle in the home. It is perceived as bringing bad luck.*

GENERAL USE

Acacia flowers (more commonly known as Wattle) are sold on their branches in bunches. The cut bunches are usually 30–80 centimetres in height. The leaves are pointed and prickly in some species and each flower has long stamens that make the mature flowers look fluffy.

Acacia is a suitable base foliage or flower for vases or floral foam designs. It is not suitable for use in air-conditioned or heated environments as it will dry out quickly. Acacia must have a constant water source or it will droop, shrivel and not revive.

The legume pod in the Acacia plant splits open to reveal a row of seeds. These seeds can be dried and used in floral designs.

The flowers are edible and they can be sprinkled over desserts or cakes.

Many people believe that Acacia pollen causes hay fever. This is untrue; however, convincing a hay fever sufferer of this may be difficult, so use with some caution.

Acacia is generally not suitable for corporate or wedding use.

GROWING CONDITIONS

Acacia is very hardy in all soil conditions, as long as the soil is well drained. It prefers full sun and grows from seed in autumn or spring.

CARE AND HANDLING

- Cut or purchase when the flowers are starting to open.

- Remove leaves that will sit under the waterline.

- The stem ends can be cut on an angle or lightly crushed.

- Preservative is recommended.

- Do not expose to direct sunlight.

- Replace water and conditioning solution after three days.

COMMERCIAL HANDLING

- Avoid cool room storage – if Acacia is kept in a cool room it will dry out faster when exposed to room temperature. The temperature change will shorten the flower's life span.

- Avoid using Acacia in hospital arrangements where the average temperature is 27 degrees Celsius.

HISTORY

Acacia's country of origin is Australia. In Europe it is known as Mimosa. The generic term Acacia is derived from the Greek word 'akis', meaning 'a sharp point' (referring to the prickly leaves in some Acacia species).

The Acacia variety of Golden Wattle is Australia's national floral emblem, officially proclaimed on 1 September 1988 by the Governor General, Sir Ninian Stephen. Previous to this, Australians celebrated 'Wattle Day' on the first day of September each year, wearing sprigs of Wattle to demonstrate patriotism and celebrate Australia's unique natural environment. In wartime, sending a sprig of Wattle to Australian soldiers was a popular custom. The wearing of a Wattle sprig on official occasions has become an Australian tradition.

ACANTHUS (a-can-thas) Common names: Oyster Plant; Bear's Breech; Mountain Thistle

BOTANICAL NAMES Acanthus spinosus (Mountain Thistle), Acanthus mollis (Oyster Plant and Bear's Breech) (over 2500 species) FAMILY Acanthacea NATURAL SEASON Plant dies back through summer, flowers in late winter and spring COLOUR AVAILABILITY Mauve, pink-grey, purple (leaves are glossy green) CUT FLOWER LIFE SPAN Up to 3 weeks for the leaves, 3–5 days for the flowers (if conditioned correctly)

GENERAL USE

Contrary to popular belief, Acanthus leaves are particularly good for floral design, both modern and natural. The leaf sizes vary and the flower spikes can be up to two metres tall, which is ideal for adding height to the back of large arrangements. Acanthus flowers are ideal for church, synagogue or event decoration.

In modern floral design you can pierce wire through the leaves for support. (To cover the piercing, place a small amount of moss around the stem where the wire has been inserted. Use the hairpin wiring method to fasten.)

WEDDING USE

Acanthus flowers can be used when dried. Do not use fresh Acanthus flowers or foliage for weddings as they will not last out of water.

CORPORATE USE

The flowers can be used dried or the leaves can be used if they are fully conditioned 24 hours before use. Constant water supply is vital.

GROWING CONDITIONS

Acanthus grows freely in the shade. For optimum growing results, the soil should be well drained and free of acidity. Use snail bait to deter pests.

The plant dies back after flowering. Divide the plant in early autumn and deadhead after the blooms have died back. Acanthus likes plenty of water, except when dormant.

CARE AND HANDLING

- Recut at least five centimetres off the stems if they have been out of water.

- Acanthus does not like being picked and without the right treatment it will droop and die within hours. Carry a bucket of water with you and place the stems into the water immediately after picking.

- After picking or purchasing, soak the stems overnight in deep water with conditioning solution.

- Acanthus is best in cool conditions and if the water supply is maintained, the leaves will harden and last up to three weeks. If handled correctly, it is strong enough to be kept in air-conditioned and heated environments.

COMMERCIAL HANDLING

- Avoid storing in the cool room. If Acanthus is placed in the cool room without being conditioned it will harden and look firm and strong, but will then soften and wilt when removed.

HISTORY

Acanthus is native to Greece and Turkey and the Greeks and Romans use the Acanthus pattern for adornments in their furniture, clothing and architecture.

Legend has it that Callimachos, the famous Greek architect from the 5th century BC, placed a basket of flowers on his daughter's grave, with a tile on top to keep the flowers from blowing away. When he came back to the grave some time later, an Acanthus plant had grown underneath the basket, with the leaves bent around it, reaching to the light. Callimachos was so pleased with the aesthetic shape of this that he adapted this decorative shape into a motif. He was building a temple at Corinth and used the motif to decorate the pillars of the temple.

Helen of Troy is believed to have worn the Acanthus pattern on her clothing and it is suggested in legend that Acanthus was one of the possible spiked flowers to form the Crown of Thorns worn by Jesus Christ at his crucifixion.

Some forms of Acanthus have been used in cough medicine.

ACHILLEA *(a-ki-lee-a)* Common names: *Yarrow; Sneezewort; Milfoil*

BOTANICAL VARIETIES Achillea cypeolata (Coronation Gold), Achillea filpendulina, (Fernleaf Yarrow), Achillea millefolium (Milfoil), Achillea ptarmica (Sneezewart), Achillea tormentosa (Woolly Yarrow, Sneezeweed), (a genus of around 100 species) FAMILY Asteraceae NATURAL SEASON Late spring/summer COLOUR AVAILABILITY Gold, lemon, deep pink with white centres; greenish white CUT FLOWER LIFE SPAN 7 days under average conditions (from bud form)

GENERAL USE

Achillea is suitable for general use in floral arrangements, as long as it has a constant water source (it will wilt quickly otherwise). It is a good posy filler and can be used as a single stem in most designs.

Achillea flowers can also be dried. Hang the bunches upside down with good airflow around them for optimum drying results.

Interestingly, Achillea is edible and can be cooked like spinach.

It is not suitable for corporate use.

WEDDING USE

Achillea is suitable for wedding designs that have a constant water source. Do not use in corsages or hairpieces as it will wilt quickly, even if sealed with binding tape.

GROWING CONDITIONS

Achillea requires well drained, conditioned and moderately fertile soil. It is relatively drought resistant. It needs occasional water and full sun to produce a full massed border in the garden. It can be propagated by dividing the plant in winter or from seed. The seeds will germinate in days.

Several bloomings can be expected through summer if stems are continually cut back. Cut back to ground level in winter and fertilise in spring.

HISTORY

Achillea is native to the Mediterranean region, and was named after Achilles, the hero of the Greeks, who used the plant as medicine. Legend has it that Achilles' soldiers treated their wounds with it. It was also used to keep colds and flu at bay and this is possibly why the meaning, or language of the flower, is 'good health'.

It was also thought to stop nose bleeds and therefore one of its folk names is 'nosebleed'.

CARE AND HANDLING:

- Cut or purchase when colour is visible in the blooms.

- Do not buy if any pollen falls when the blooms are shaken.

- Any brown tips or filmy substance on the stem indicates age.

- Recut two centimetres off the stems on an angle. Remove the leaves as they will not last as long as the flowers.

- Achillea needs a water source at all times, otherwise the flowers will droop quickly.

- As a cut flower, Achillea does not like deep water or direct sun.

- Achillea is very sensitive to ethylene so keep it away from cigarette smoke and ripening fruit.

- Use a preservative and change the water and preservative every three days.

- If the flowers droop, wrap them in a cone of paper (making sure the heads are upright) and place in warm water for up to three hours.

COMMERCIAL HANDLING

- Achillea will mould if bunched and refrigerated.

ACONITUM

(ak-o-nai-tum) Common names: Monk's Hood; Wolfbane; Granny's Nightcap; Captain over the Garden; Auld Wife's Hood BOTANICAL VARIETIES Aconitum carmichaelii (Monkshood) Aconitum napellus (Wolf's Bane, Granny's Nightcap, Captain over the Garden, Auld Wife's Hood) (over 250 species) FAMILY Ranunculacea NATURAL SEASON Flowers in late spring/summer, dies back in winter COLOUR AVAILABILITY Deep purple, blue, pale violet, white, pink, yellow CUT FLOWER LIFE SPAN 3–5 days

CARE AND HANDLING

- Aconitum is highly poisonous so always cut, handle and arrange wearing gloves.

- Buy or cut when one lower flower is open. The stems should be crisp and green.

- Place the stems in water immediately. If the stems are exposed to the air then recut 2–3 centimetres (on an angle).

- Strip the stems of all leaves that will sit below the waterline.

- Use a preservative as this will definitely hold the flowers for longer.

- Aconitum is sensitive to ethylene so keep it away from cigarette smoke and ripening fruit.

- Keep cool at all times.

COMMERCIAL HANDLING

- Do not place in the cool room.

GENERAL USE

The Aconitum plant is extremely poisonous in every part, including the roots. The poison is readily absorbed into the skin. It contains Alkaloid Aconite, which has an anaesthetic effect and it can even cause heart failure.

Given the poisonous nature of this flower it is not commonly used in flower arrangements, however, it can be a pretty posy or vase flower (if handled correctly). The blue-coloured variety lasts the longest as a cut flower.

Aconitum is not suitable for wedding or corporate use.

GROWING CONDITIONS

Aconitum is a herbaceous perennial. The seeds can take up to three years to flower and the stems can grow up to 1.5 metres high. It is not suited to warmer climates; it needs cool, rich soil and mulch around the plant. Aconitum will die in drought conditions. Cut back to the ground when the plant dies back.

HISTORY

Aconitum is native to China and Central Europe. It was used in potions in bygone days. Aconitum is even mentioned in the Harry Potter series!

ACTINOTIS

(ak-tin-oh-tas) Common names: *Flannel Flower*

BOTANICAL VARIETIES Actinotus hellanthi (a distant relative of the carrot) FAMILY Apiaceae NATURAL SEASON Spring and summer COLOUR AVAILABILITY Cream CUT FLOWER LIFE SPAN 5–7 days

GENERAL USE

Actinotus flowers are gaining popularity and can be used in bouquets and most forms of floral design. They give a modern effect when the stems are featured in floral foam designs.

The flowers can be dried by hanging them upside down in a well-ventilated room.

Do not use Actinotus flowers or foliage for corporate use as they will dry out.

WEDDING USE

Actinotis flowers are not hardy flowers for weddings but can still be used in bouquets if they are handled with care. Do not use if the temperature on the wedding day will be above 30 degrees Celsius.

GROWING CONDITIONS

Actinotis likes full sun in sandy, acid soil with a little gravel and humus. It does not like being disturbed. Once it is established it is quite hardy.

HISTORY

Actinotis is native to Australia. Its generic name means 'furnished with rays' or 'sunbeam'.

CARE AND HANDLING

- Cut or purchase when the flowers are half open. They should have a fluffy appearance.

- Avoid any stems with seed pod tops and floppy tips.

- Tiny, fine hairs cover the soft foliage and these can cause an allergic reaction to some. Wear gloves when handling.

- Remove any leaves that will sit under the water line.

- Recut 2–3 centimetres from the stem ends. Cut on a sharp angle.

- Use preservative. This will also assist the buds to open. If you don't use preservative, put bleach into the water.

- Replace the water and preservative every three days.

- Never crowd these flowers.

- Keep them cool.

- Do not keep these flowers in an air-conditioned environment as they will dry out.

COMMERCIAL HANDLING

- Do not place in the cool room. The foliage will mould if the stems are confined and they will shock on removal.

AGAPANTHUS

(a-ga-pan-thas) Common names: Lily of the Nile; African Lily

BOTANICAL VARIETIES Agapanthus Agapanthus africanus, Agapanthus orietalis, Agapanthus campanulatus (10 species of the South African genus) FAMILY Alliaceae NATURAL SEASON Summer COLOUR AVAILABILITY Blue (many different shades), pink and white CUT FLOWER LIFE SPAN 2 weeks

CARE AND HANDLING

- Cut or purchase when 1-3 flowers are opening on each stem.

- Avoid stems that have splits at the base.

- Recut on a sharp angle and place in deep vase water.

- Preservative is optional. Replace the water every second day if preservative is used.

- Cut any spikes from the plant once all the buds have opened.

- The spikes can be used in arrangements when fresh and green or when dried.

- Agapanthus is sensitive to ethylene gas. When the older florets die off around the edges, remove them as they are a source of ethylene and will affect the remaining blooms.

- Do not keep in airconditioned environments (their heads will drop off).

COMMERCIAL HANDLING

- Do not refrigerate.

GENERAL USE

Agapanthus is especially suitable for modern floral designs. Dwarf varieties provide a smaller flower for more delicate work. Dried Agapanthus husks can be used for arrangement work and they can be dyed any colour.

WEDDING USE

Individual Agapanthus florets can be used in wedding bouquets and corsages but must be singularly wired using the pierce and mount wiring method. They can be used in hairpieces, particularly circlets and tiaras, or as a smaller flower in bouquets.

Small heads (miniature varieties) can be used on their stems in hand-held natural stemmed bouquets. They last well in wired work.

CORPORATE USE

Agapanthus flowers will drop in air conditioning. The husk can be used if all spent flowers are removed.

GROWING CONDITIONS

Agapanthus requires full sun and well-drained soil. Half-hardy varieties need protection from frost.

The plants form full bushes but can be divided after flowering. The divided plants are ideal for lining paths or driveways.

The flower spikes can grow up to 1.5 metres tall.

HISTORY

Originally from South Africa, Agapanthus africanus were introduced to Europe in the 17th century and the first flowers to be publically viewed were at Hampton Court, England.

There were no attempts at hybridisation until the end of the 19th century. By the mid-20th century the full range of species became known.

AGERATUM *(aj-er-ah-tum)* Common names: *Floss Flower, Pussy Foot*

BOTANICAL VARIETIES Ageratum houstonianum (blue/mauve) (many other species) FAMILY Asteraceae NATURAL SEASON Spring through to early autumn COLOUR AVAILABILITY Mauve, blue, pink, white CUT FLOWER LIFE SPAN 7 days

GENERAL USE

Ageratum flowers (more commonly known as Pussy Foot) form great borders in the garden. As a cut flower they can be used as a vase flower or made into posies. They can be used in oasis arrangements but will droop quickly if there is a lack of water.

Do not use in wired work as they will wilt. Do not use in corporate decorations as the flowers and foliage will dry out.

WEDDING USE

Ageratum can be used in hand-tied bouquets if well supported by other blooms. Keep in water until the time of the service and then towel dry.

GROWING CONDITIONS

Ageratum is both an annual and perennial plant. It enjoys full sun or part shade, provided it is watered regularly in the garden. It can be moved in the garden at any time, even during flowering. Cut perennials back after flowering and protect them from frost.

HISTORY

Ageratum is originally from Central America, the West Indies, Southern Mexico and Guatemala. It is a member of the Daisy family, in spite of its appearance.

CARE AND HANDLING

- Buy when the flowers are starting to show colour.
- Pick when a third of all flowers are open.
- Remove most of the foliage.
- Always avoid purchasing bunches that have yellow leaves. This is a sign of age.
- Recut 2–3 centimetres from the stem ends. Cut on an angle.
- Wash the stems to avoid dirt particles settling at the base of the vase.
- Ageratum will foul the water if it is not changed regularly.
- Use a preservative or put bleach in the water.
- Ageratum likes shallow water and does not like heat as a cut flower.
- It is sensitive to ethylene so keep it away from cigarette smoke and ripening fruit.

COMMERCIAL HANDLING

- If you need to place Ageratum in the cool room, 6–8 degrees Celsius is recommended.
- It will mould if tightly bunched.

AGONIS (a-goh-nis) Common names: Willow Myrtle; West Australian Peppermint; West Australian Tea Tree BOTANICAL VARIETIES Agonis flexuosa FAMILY Myrtaceae NATURAL SEASON Spring COLOUR AVAILABILITY White CUT FLOWER LIFE SPAN 5 days

CARE AND HANDLING

- Select open or half-open flowers as the buds will not open once picked.

- Preservative in the water is optional.

- Remove any leaves that will sit below the waterline.

- Recut 2–3 centimetres from the stems ends. Cut on an angle. You can then shave the stem with a knife and gently bash or split the stems ends.

- Agonis flowers will drink a lot so ensure the vase water is always topped up.

- Agonis is mildly sensitive to ethylene gas.

- Keep in cool conditions.

COMMERCIAL HANDLING

- Agonis is sensitive to airconditioning.

- Do not place in the cool room.

GENERAL USE

Agonis is cut in lengths of 30–80 centimetres and the leaves have a pleasant peppermint aroma. These attributes make it ideal for vase arrangements.

The plant weeps elegantly and can be used in leaf or flower form. Some floral designers remove leaves that do not flow with the stem.

WEDDING USE

Agonis looks particularly elegant in cascading wedding designs such as reception arrangements and large bouquets.

CORPORATE USE

Agonis will just survive five days in corporate conditions. They drink heavily, so a mid-week visit to top up the water is recommended.

GROWING CONDITIONS

The Agonis plant grows in any soil conditions and will grow up to 14 metres high. It must have a warm climate. Frost will severely retard the plant.

HISTORY

Agonis is native to the south-west coast of Western Australia. Agonis flexuosa is the only variety used in commercial floristry.

ALCEA (al-see-a) Common names: Hollyhock

BOTANICAL VARIETIES Alcea rosea (double flower) (many other species) FAMILY Malvaceae NATURAL SEASON Spring, summer and early autumn

COLOUR AVAILABILITY A wide variety of colours are available CUT FLOWER LIFE SPAN 5 days

GENERAL USE

Alcea (more commonly known as Hollyhock) is a lovely house vase flower, but airconditioning and heating will dry it out. Do not place near a duct.

CORPORATE USE

Alcea will droop and dry out in office arrangements. However, it is ideal for function decorations where colour and height are required.

GROWING CONDITIONS

Alcea enjoys full sun, sheltered from wind. It thrives in rich, heavy soil, and can grow up to two and a half metres in height. Give it plenty of water in the dryer weather.

As a garden flower, Alcea is biennial and will therefore flower every two years. It is grown from seed, raked into the ground. Plant it in autumn. It will need to be staked when grown against walls or in garden beds.

Hollyhock Rust is a fungal disease that affects Alcea, but can be prevented by spraying the plant with a fungicide. Caterpillars are attracted to Alcea and can be a problem in some gardens.

HISTORY

Alcea is native to the eastern Mediterranean region. It is an old garden flower with a history of cultivation that goes back over five hundred years. The English consider Hollyhock to be a traditional English cottage flower. It was a popular and well known flower in England in the early 16th century.

Variegated Alcea flowers were introduced from Asia in the 18th century. By the 19th century they were a popular florist's flower, but the arrival of Hollyhock Rust in the 1870s waned their popularity and they survived from then on mainly as a garden cottage flower.

Romantic flower meaning: ambition

CARE AND HANDLING

- Alcea must be conditioned when picked.

- It is subject to blockage in the stem when out of water, so make sure it is purchased with a water source and keep the stems in water at all times.

- Buy Alcea with strong, straight stems. Some lower flowers should be open with many buds showing strong colour. Foliage should be green and firm.

- Avoid purchasing bunches with many flowers already open.

- Remove any foliage that will sit below the waterline.

- Recut 2–3 centimetres from the stem ends. Cut on an angle and under water if possible.

- Use preservative to assist the flowers to open.

COMMERCIAL HANDLING

- Alcea can be placed in the cool room at temperatures of 6–8 degrees Celsius.

ALLIUM *(al-lee-yum) Common names: Onion Flower; Lily Leek; Turkish Leek; Drumsticks*

BOTANICAL VARIETIES Allium giganteum (Onion Flower), Allium aflatunense (Flowering Onion), Allium sphaerocephalon (Drumsticks), Allium moly (Lily Leek), Allium karataviense (Turkish Leek) (over 700 species) FAMILY Amaryllidacaea SUB FAMILY Alliaceae NATURAL SEASON Spring and summer (Allium sphaerocephalon flowers in summer) COLOUR AVAILABILITY Mauve, green, purple, burgundy, yellow and white (white and yellow are rare) CUT FLOWER LIFE SPAN 5–7 days

CARE AND HANDLING

- Pick when a third of all blooms of the flower cluster are open.

- Recut at least 2–3 centimetres from each stem and place in water immediately.

- Never bash the stems.

- Use a preservative and change every two days.

- Ensure vases are very clean as the stems will absorb small particles of dirt from the base of the vase, decreasing their life span.

- As Allium ages, the flowers and stems will droop and fade, and will also smell more of garlic.

COMMERCIAL HANDLING

- If placed in the cool room the temperature should be 6–8 degrees Celsius.

- Allium is sensitive to air-conditioning.

GENERAL USE

Allium looks fantastic in modern, dramatic floral design work. The smell of Alliums is not pleasant to some, so use with caution if the flowers are a gift. The hollow, tubular leaves smell like garlic when crushed.

WEDDING USE

Allium is visually effective in modern bouquets and the flower heads can be split and wired into clusters. However, the garlic smell can be overpowering so use sparingly.

CORPORATE USE

Allium can look striking in half bud; however it will drop if open and the smell can be overpowering in office environments.

GROWING CONDITIONS

Allium requires full sun and shelter from strong winds. It is easy to grow in any soil conditions. Plenty of water is needed during foliage growth and it can be propagated using offsets or bulbils. You can also raise Allium from seed.

Allium is closely related to edible onions and garlic. Many Allium plants have one ball shaped purple/blue flower head. The leaves are blue/green in colour.

HISTORY

Allium is native to Europe and the Mediterranean and was first cultivated in 1604. Several species feature in European folklore as Allium was considered to have mystical properties. It was cherished for centuries as an ingredient for charms and counter charms and a number of species have been used in herbal medicine.

ALSTROEMERIA

(al-stro-mee-ree-a) Common names: New Zealand Christmas Bell; Lily of the Incas; Chilean Lily; Peruvian Lily BOTANICAL VARIETIES Alstroemeria aurantiaca (orange, known as Flower/Lily of the Incas), Alstroemeria hybrid (Striped Bird, also known as the Chilean Lily), Alstroemeria pulchella (a genus of around 50 species and numerous hybrids) FAMILY Alstromeriaceae NATURAL SEASON Late spring and summer but can be purchased all year round COLOUR AVAILABILITY Orange or hybrids in shades of white, pink, mauve, yellow, brick red and variegated with many tints and shades CUT FLOWER LIFE SPAN 3 weeks (the flowers can outlast the foliage)

GENERAL USE

Alstromeria is available in various lengths (most commonly shorts and longs). It is ideal for general use in floral design and the seed pods are widely used in posy work and modern designs.

STS-treated Alstroemeria lasts well in all wired work. It can be used singularly on individual stems or singularly wired with the pierce and mount wiring method.

If using Alstromeria in airconditioned or heated areas, strip the leaves and substitute with a hardy foliage, as the Alstromeria leaves will yellow and not last as long as the flowers.

If the flower heads are large they can be split for single stem use in floral foam. This gives a more delicate look.

The anthers of Alstromeria flowers will pollinate with maturity.

WEDDING USE

Alstroemeria can be used in bouquet holders and hand-tied natural stemmed bouquets. In most bouquets only a small amount of extra foliage is needed as the leaves of Alstroemeria provide sufficient padding to the flowers. Single florets can be wired individually for corsages and features.

GROWING CONDITIONS

Alstroemeria is one of the most widely grown cut flowers in the world. It can produce spikes up to 90 centimetres (depending on the hybrid), has tuberous roots and is a herbaceous plant that hybrids easily. It grows in sandy soils and likes sloped, well-drained areas. It is a wide spreading perennial and grows in full sun or under bushes in partial shade. It is planted from root division in autumn. Try to plant it where it can be left for some years.

CARE AND HANDLING

- It is best to buy Alstroemeria flowers that have been treated with STS (ask your florist).

- Cut or purchase with buds fully expanded and coloured with at least one flower open.

- If purchased in plastic sleeves remove immediately to avoid moulding

- Alstroemeria is ethylene sensitive. Remove any damaged or aged leaves in the bunch as they will emit ethylene and shorten the life span of the surrounding leaves and flowers.

- Ensure that there is plenty of room and airflow around each flower.

- Avoid yellow foliage and flowers that are faded or show any sign of pollination.

- Strip the foliage that will sit below the waterline then recut the stems and place in preservative solution.

- Avoid direct sunlight and drafty areas.

- Ensure that the vase water you use does not contain high levels of fluoride – this is detrimental to the life span of Alstroemeria.

COMMERCIAL HANDLING

- Avoid placing Alstroemeria in the cool room. If you must, ensure the temperature is between 6–8 degrees Celsius.

CORPORATE USE

STS-treated Alstroemeria lasts well in office decorating. However, the leaves do not last as long as the flowers (in office
conditions the leaves last 5–7 days before they start to yellow
and curl) so if the arrangement is needed to last longer than a
week, use the flowers only.

HISTORY

Alstromera is originally from Chile, Peru and Brazil and it was developed as a cut flower in England and Holland. The flower was
named after Baron Claus von Alstroemer by his close friend Carolus Linnaeus. (The Linnaean classification is named after him
and the system is still in use today.) The plant's seeds were collected by Alstroemer on a trip to South America in 1753.

Alstromera ligtu var angustifolia was introduced from Chile
by Harold Comber in 1933 and later crossed with Alstromera
haemantha to produce the Ligtu hybrids. These flowers come
in a wide range of colours.

The edulis varieties are grown all over the Andes and their tu-
bors are edible. It is said that they taste like Jerusalem artichoke.

ALYSSUM

(al-lis-sum) Common names: Sweet Alice; Yellow Alice; Yellow Tuft; Madwort

BOTANICAL VARIETIES Alyssum maritima (Sweet Alice, white and lilac colours), Alyssum montanum (Madwort), Alyssum saxatale (Yellow Alice), Alyssum spinosum, Alyssum murale (Yellow Tuft) (there are many species) FAMILY Brassicaceae NATURAL SEASON Spring COLOUR AVAILABILITY Pink, white, mauve, yellow and purple CUT FLOWER LIFE SPAN 7 days

GENERAL USE

The Alyssum (Sweet Alice) flower fits the cottage garden posy very well. They are dense yet delicate, and are honey scented. They can be used in small table centres as a filling flower. Do not use in airconditioned environments. Alyssum is not suitable for corporate use.

WEDDING USE

Do not use Alyssum on a warm day. It is very pretty but it will not last beyond the service unless it is in a bouquet holder where there is a water source. Use stronger flowers around Alyssum for flower support. Do not feature these flowers; use them as an accessory flower only.

GROWING CONDITIONS

Alyssum is an annual plant that is suited to rock gardens or trailing over retaining walls in full sun. The soil should be well-drained and solid. Occasional watering will assist its growth. It is prone to downy mildew attack.

HISTORY

Alyssum is native to the Mediterranean area as well as Caucasus and Siberia. Linnaeus *named* the *Alyssum* genus in 1753.

CARE AND HANDLING

- If purchased in plastic sleeves, remove the flowers immediately as any humidity will cause fungus to grow.

- Remove any foliage that will sit below the waterline.

- Recut 2–3 centimetres from the stem ends. Cut on an angle.

- Place in water immediately after cutting.

- Use a preservative and a small amount of bleach in the water.

- Alyssum does not like deep water.

COMMERCIAL HANDLING

- No need to place in the cool room.

Romantic flower meaning: incomparable worth

AMARANTHUS *(am-a-ran-thus) Common names: Love Lies Bleeding; Joseph's Coat; Molten Fire; Prince's Feather* BOTANICAL VARIETIES Amaranthus caudatus (Love Lies Bleeding) Amaranthus cruetus (Prince's Feather) Amaranthus hypochondriacus (upright in growth), (Over sixty species) FAMILY Amaranthaceae NATURAL SEASON Summer and autumn COLOUR AVAILABILITY Crimson red and green CUT FLOWER LIFE SPAN 10 days

CARE AND HANDLING

- Cut or purchase when three quarters of the flowers are open.

- Avoid spikes where the tip has bent over.

- Strip all leaves before arranging as they will not last.

- Recut the stems and place in clean, tepid water.

- Use conditioning solution or bleach in the vase water.

- Amaranthus is sensitive to ethylene so keep it away from cigarette smoke and ripening fruit.

- Avoid placing Amaranthus flowers in full sun as this will cause the colours to fade.

- Amaranthus flowers are heavy drinkers so check the water level regularly.

COMMERCIAL HANDLING

- Amaranthus should be kept cool and if placed in the cool room the temperature should be 6–8 degrees Celsius.

GENERAL USE

Most varieties of Amaranthus are effective for cascading floral designs, and particularly effective in linear (line directional placement) bouquets and arrangements. Amaranthus hypochondriacus (the upright variety) is better used in vertical designs.

WEDDING USE

Cascading Amaranthus is very striking, especially in lime green. It can be used in hand-tied natural stemmed bouquets, bouquet holders and wired work. It can be cut into sections for use in corsages.

CORPORATE USE

Amaranthus will last five days in most office environments but will start to look dry and faded beyond this time period.

GROWING CONDITIONS

Amaranthus is grown for its striking foliage as well as its cascading flowers. It grows outdoors in full sun and enjoys well-drained soil. It should be watered well during prolonged dry periods. Prepare the soil for planting with plenty of packaged fertiliser as well as manure, and plant the seeds 14 centimetres apart. The stems grow from 30–60 centimetres and may need staking for wind protection. Snails are attracted to Amaranthus and can be a problem, so use a suitable deterrent.

HISTORY

Amaranthus is native to South America. The name comes from the Greek word Amaranth, meaning 'never fading flower'. The Amaranth grain was believed to have been a staple in the diet of pre-Columbian Aztecs, who thought that it gave them supernatural powers. Amaranth grains can be toasted to make popcorn, and when combined with honey makes 'alegria' (meaning 'joy' in Spanish). Amaranthus is also grown for its leaves which can be used in salads, steamed dishes and stir-fries.

AMARYLLIS

(am-a-ril-lis) Common names: Belladonna Lily; Naked Lady

BOTANICAL VARIETIES Amarillis belladonna FAMILY Amaryllidaceae NATURAL SEASON Summer and autumn COLOUR AVAILABILITY Pink, red, white

CUT FLOWER LIFE SPAN Up to 10 days during opening (a further week after opening)

GENERAL USE

Amaryllis (more commonly known as Belladonna Lily) is pleasantly scented and effective in modern designs. If you cut up the stem in a quarter pattern using a knife and then place into deep water, the ends will curl dramatically, giving a strong visual effect for use in a clear vase. Advise recipients to wear gloves when handling Amaryllis flowers.

WEDDING USE

Amaryllis can be used in wired work or bouquet holders. Do not use if the temperature on the wedding day will be above 30 degrees Celsius. Amaryllis flowers are best used as a central feature of wedding arrangements (surrounded and supported by other blooms) due to their tendency to cause skin irritation.

CORPORATE USE

Amaryllis flowers can be used in office areas, but advise clients not to touch them. The flowers should be in bud form for corporate decorations.

GROWING CONDITIONS

Amaryllis enjoy a sheltered area in full sun and well-drained soil. They are frost hardy. It will flower quickly if planted in early summer with the neck of the bulb at ground level. The plant dies back through late autumn to winter. The flowers appear from the ground without foliage, hence the common name 'Naked Lady'.

HISTORY

Amaryllis is native to South Africa. It is named after a shepherdess in one of Virgil's plays, with the name Amaryllis meaning 'young rustic maiden'. Its common name 'Belladonna' is known to mean 'beautiful lady'. Amaryllis was also a woman's name in ancient Greece.

CARE AND HANDLING

- Cut or purchase when flowers are half to fully open. The leaves should be a glossy green.

- Avoid any stems showing brown marks.

- The Amaryllis flower has a fleshy stem, which will bruise easily if not handled carefully.

- Use preservative solution and replace daily.

- Using a sharp knife, recut 2–3 centimetres off each stem and place into water immediately. Cut on a sharp angle.

- Wear gloves when handling Amaryllis as some people are highly allergic to the sap. Welts on the skin (caused by sap) can last up to one month.

COMMERCIAL HANDLING

- Keep cool but do not place in the cool room as it will fade quickly when exposed to normal temperatures.

Romantic flower meaning: pride and beauty

AMMI *(am-mee) Common names: False Queen Anne's Lace; Bullwort; Bishop's Weed*

BOTANICAL VARIETIES Ammi majus FAMILY Apiaceae NATURAL SEASON Late winter and spring COLOUR AVAILABILITY White

CUT FLOWER LIFE SPAN Up to 7 days

GENERAL USE

Ammi is a very pretty, light looking bouquet flower. It can last for seven days but after this the flower will begin to pollinate and drop.

Ammi can be used in floral foam, but the stems should be cut short first – the longer the stem the shorter the flower's life span, as they are prone to air blockages.

Use with caution for hospital arrangements as Ammi will dry out in heated or airconditioned environments. Ammi is not suitable for corporate use as it dries out and drops very quickly.

WEDDING USE

Ammi is ideal for use in large wedding bowls (table centrepieces). It can also be used in bouquets, but only with a constant water source. It is a nice filling flower.

GROWING CONDITIONS

Ammi is an annual plant that needs well-drained soil with partial to full sun. Staking can assist against wind fall. It can be propagated from seed.

HISTORY

Ammi is native to southern Europe and Turkey. Ammi majus has antispasmodic properties and is commonly used as a cardiac tonic for treatment of angina, palpitations or weakness, as well as being used as a diuretic. It is also used in treatment of wheezing or cough. The ancient Egyptians used it as a treatment for skin diseases.

Ammi majus is sometimes confused with roadside Queen Anne's lace (Daucus carota).

CARE AND HANDLING

- Cut or purchase when the small white flowers are half open.

- Shake the heads to check for any flower fall.

- The leaves should be green and the stems strong enough to support the flowers.

- The sap of this flower can cause irritation and a skin rash so it is best to handle it wearing gloves.

- Strip any foliage that will sit under the water line.

- Recut 2–3 centimetres from the stem ends. Cut on an angle.

- Add bleach to the water. Preservative is also recommended.

- Change the vase water regularly to prevent the flowers fouling the water.

Romantic flower meaning: delicate femininity

ANANAS *(an-na-nas) Common names: Miniature Pineapples*
BOTANICAL VARIETIES Ananas comosus, Ananas bracteatus (tricolour) FAMILY Bromeliaceae NATURAL SEASON Spring and summer
COLOUR AVAILABILITY Green and tricolour (red/orange) CUT FLOWER LIFE SPAN Up to 4 weeks

CARE AND HANDLING

- Use preservative in the water.

- Using a sharp knife, cut 2–3 centimetres from the stem ends. Cut on an angle.

- Ananas is resistant to ethylene gas, however it does emit it, so consider this when using with other flowers.

GENERAL USE

The stems of the Ananas (Miniature Pineapples) are about 30 centimetres as a cut flower. They are ideal for modern, dramatic work. The foliage at the tops lasts well. Despite their similarity in appearance to the pineapple fruit, Ananas comosus and bracteatus are not edible.

CORPORATE USE

Due to its long-lasting quality, Ananas is ideal for corporate work. It is best used in the lower areas of designs.

GROWING CONDITIONS

Ananas propagation is mainly by basal sucker offsets. It likes warm temperatures in sub-tropical or tropical areas. Humus will assist its growth.

HISTORY

Ananas originated in Brazil and is native to Central America and northern South America. In architecture the pineapple motif symbolises 'hospitality'.

ANEMONE

(an-em-o-nee) Common names: Japanese Anemone; Wind Flower; Wind Poppy; Lily of the Field BOTANICAL VARIETIES Anemone coronaria (St Brigit, Wild Poppy) Anemone hupehensis (Wind Flower) Anemone japonica (Japanese Anemone) (family genus of over 120 species) FAMILY Ranunculaceae NATURAL SEASON Autumn and spring COLOUR AVAILABILITY White (cream), pink (light and dark), red, mauve, burgundy red, purple CUT FLOWER LIFE SPAN 7 days

Note: *A grower could dry store Anemone flowers at a temperature of 2–4 degrees Celsius for up to 7 days.*

GENERAL USE

Anemone flowers are good for use in posies and other small cottage designs. Their cut flower length is generally 30–40 centimetres. They make a nice vase flower and mix well with other bright flowers. If used in flower foam they may need to be wire-supported.

Anemone does not react well to freshly cut Narcissus, so don't put the two flowers together, otherwise the Anemone stems will become limp.

WEDDING USE

Anemone flowers can be used in clustered hand-tied bouquets as long as they are supported by other flowers. In bouquet holders, it is best to wire-support the heads and stems. For wired bouquets they should be wired and bound with binding tape.

CORPORATE USE

Anemone flowers in bud form may last for five days in corporate designs, but there is a risk that they may start to dry out or droop.

GROWING CONDITIONS

Anemone likes well-drained, rich, sandy soil and full sun if well watered (partial shade otherwise). As a plant it does not like to be disturbed, but once settled will grow steadily.

Cool climates produce the best flowers. As a perennial it should be split every three years.

CARE AND HANDLING

- Cut or buy when the flowers are showing colour in bud form and when the petals have separated from the centre.

- Pollen should not be visible in the flowers. Avoid any bunches with yellow leaves.

- Separate bunches, then wash and recut 2–3 centimetres from the stems before placing in vase water.

- Remove foliage that will sit below the waterline.

- Preservative or bleach in the water is recommended. Make sure the vase is spotlessly clean.

- Change the water every 2–3 days.

- Anemone tends to curve towards the light, so avoid placing it in direct sunlight.

- Anemone dislikes very deep water, however, it will drink more if it is in direct sunlight.

- Anemone is sensitive to ethylene so keep it away from cigarette smoke and ripening fruit.

COMMERCIAL HANDLING

- If placed in the cool room, the temperature should be 6–8 degrees Celsius.

HISTORY

Anemone is related to Buttercup and Ranunculus. It is native to China and other parts of Asia as well as the eastern parts of the Mediterranean. It has been cultivated since ancient times.

Anemone is thought to be named after the Goddess Namesis (goddess of retribution). The word also comes from the Greek word 'anemos' meaning 'wind'. Anemones can be seen at the foot of the cross in some paintings of the Christ's crucifixion. Greek mythology also says that the goddess, Flora, was jealous of the nymph Anemone and so transformed her into a wind flower and left her to the mercy of the wind.

Anemones are known as Japanese Anemones due to a documentation of the plant near Nagasaki in 1695. They reached the West in 1844 when Robert Fortune introduced them to Britain.

Romantic flower meaning: forsaken

When you buy or sell Kangaroo Paw always make sure it has a water source or it will wilt due to air blockage. When placed in water it cannot drink if the stem is air-blocked.

ANIGOZANTHOS

*(an-i-go-zan-thos) Common names: Kangaroo Paw;
Cat's Paw* BOTANICAL VARIETIES Anigozanthos manglesii (green and black), Anigozanthos flavidus (yellowish green and the most hardy), Anigozanthos macropidia, Anigozanthos fuliginosa (black), Anigozanthos pulcherrima (golden) and Anigozanthos rufa (reddish crimson) (there are 12 species) FAMILY Haemodoraceae NATURAL SEASON Flowers in winter and spring COLOUR AVAILABILITY Green/black, pink/red, green, yellow, gold CUT FLOWER LIFE SPAN Up to 4 weeks

CARE AND HANDLING

- When picking or purchasing, the first one or two florets should be open. All florets should be strong and firm.

- Anigozanthos needs to be conditioned when cut, or when it is out of water at any time. It can wilt quickly without a water source.

- Add sugar directly to the water. The flowers need sugar and this will not foul the water.

- Each stem has flowers that have fine hairs covering them (these give the flowers their colour). Wear gloves as some people are allergic to them.

- Remove all leaves.

- Recut stems 2–3 centimetres from the stem ends. Cut on an angle.

- Use preservative.

- Anigozanthos will dry out in airconditioned environments.

- If the stems flag, recut them and stand in deep water with sugar added.

- Do no place in direct sunlight – this will cause the flowers to fade.

COMMERCIAL HANDLING

- Do not place in the cool room. They will droop on removal.

GENERAL USE

Anigozanthos flowers (more commonly known as Kangaroo Paw) are available to purchase with stem lengths of between 30–90 centimetres. They can be used in most floral designs. They are long-lasting flowers and should remain hard, but if they start to soften, recut and follow the care and handling instructions. If hung upside down they will dry well (their colour will remain but the stems will partly shrivel).

WEDDING USE

Use Anigozanthos only in bouquet holders. Make sure they are well conditioned. They will wilt in hand-tied natural stemmed bouquets or wired bouquets.

CORPORATE USE

Anigozanthos is popular in corporate arrangements. The stems should be well conditioned with a constant water supply. They must be carried in water as they are heavy drinkers. They will start to dry out in airconditioned environments but will still look reasonable to the untrained eye.

GROWING CONDITIONS

Anigozanthos is a Western Australian perennial plant. It does not like humid summers or the cold of winter. It needs strong drainage, plenty of sun and rest after flowering. It is prone to the fungus Ink disease, which blackens and withers the foliage. If this occurs cut away the leaves and cover with fungicide.

HISTORY

All Anigozanthos species are native to Australia. Some species are also native to South Africa and also found in Tropical America. The flowers are mainly pollinated by birds.

The Greek term 'anises' means oblique or unequal and the name Anigozanthos probably derived from this term. Anigozanthos is the floral emblem of Western Australia.

ANTHURIUM *(an-thoo-ree-yum) Common names: Flamingo Flower; Palette Flower; Obake; Little Boy Flower* BOTANICAL VARIETIES Anthurium scherzerianum (Corkscrew Spadix) Anthurium andreanum (Flamingo Flower) (over 700 species in the Arum/Araceae family) FAMILY Araceae NATURAL SEASON Spring, summer and autumn COLOUR AVAILABILITY Cream, lime, burgundy, brown, red, flame, orange, pink and variegations CUT FLOWER LIFE SPAN 4 weeks or more

GENERAL USE

Anthurium is available all year round, with most stock sourced from commercial growing in Mauritius, where the climate for natural growing is ideal. They are also grown in hothouses around the world. To identify the freshness of Anthurium, the spadix is the best indicator. At its freshest it will be glossy in appearance and strong lime or yellow/lime in colour. If the end of the spadix shows brown discoloration, the flower is at the end of its life span.

Anthurium's wide colour range and long lasting qualities make it ideal for all types of floral designs. It is available in different sizes, including miniatures. It is especially suited for use in modern designs with other tropical flowers, and is also popular in wedding designs. Anthurium flowers are generally available with stem lengths of 30–70 centimetres.

WEDDING USE

Anthurium flowers are ideal for all forms of wedding work. The miniature variety is especially suited to corsages, buttonholes and hairpieces as well as bouquet work.

CORPORATE USE

Anthurium flowers and leaves are well suited to office decorating.

GROWING CONDITIONS

Anthurium is easy to grow in tropical climates. It likes a rich, moist compost of peat and sphagnum and high humidity as well as excellent drainage. Potted Anthuriums do not like to be moved. During winter it must grow in a climate above 15 degrees Celsius to flower in season. You can propagate it by dividing older plants. Do this in early spring. In cooler climates it can grow in sunrooms with central heating, but a hot house is preferable.

CARE AND HANDLING

- Anthurium flowers should never be refrigerated. Any sign of purple at the edges of the flower indicates they have been. Do not purchase in this instance.

- The tip of the spadix should be green or green/yellow if it is fresh (most varieties). Do not purchase if the tip of the spadix is brown. This indicates age.

- The top third of the spadix should be smooth.

- Always remove the spadix from the plastic sleeve or it will rot quickly.

- Keep them above 12 degrees Celcius.

- Anthuriums like to be misted with water.

- If they start to wilt they can be re-hydrated by submerging them in lukewarm water.

COMMERCIAL HANDLING

- Anthuriums can be dipped in commercial fruit wax to extend their vase life.

- They should never be kept in the cool room.

HISTORY

Anthurium originated in the rainforests of Columbia and was discovered by the West in 1876 by Edwuard Andre, a French botanist and landscape artist. The plants were taken to Kew Gardens in Britain in the late 19th century by Jean Linden, a botanist for the Belgian government. They were seen by the Hawaiian minister for finance, Samuel Mills Damon, who was a keen grower as well. He imported them to Hawaii in 1889, to a climate that suited them perfectly. Fifty years ago Anthurium could be found as mass ground cover in Hawaii.

The Scherzerianum varieties are from Guatemala and Costa Rica. The leaves of these varieties are dark green and the leaves are oblong or lanceolate in shape.

ANTIRRHINUM

(an-ti-rhai-num) Common names: Snap Dragon

BOTANICAL VARIETIES Antirrhinum majus (the genus has around 40 species) FAMILY Scrophulariaceae NATURAL SEASON Summer and autumn COLOUR AVAILABILITY Yellow, white, orange, pink, red, maroon and magenta (sometime several colours on one stem) CUT FLOWER LIFE SPAN Up to 14 days with STS treatment, or up to 7 days without

Romantic Flower Meaning: Presumption

GENERAL USE

Antirrhinums (more commonly known as Snap Dragons) are solid forms that can be used to create an outline or as a good filler in arrangements. They can be placed in designs horizontally, with the stems laid flat, and the stem tips will turn upwards. This can look dramatic in modern work. Allow for this in your designs.

Antirrhinums, with their solid forms and tall stems, are also suited to gift bouquet work. These flowers are also a good base for funeral designs as they provide an excellent outline on a sheaf or wreath.

WEDDING USE

Use Antirrhinum flowers in clusters only as they need support. They are best used in bouquet holders. The florets can be used singularly in corsage work. Single florets can be wired but their life span will be reduced to only 3–4 hours.

CORPORATE USE

Antirrhinum can be used for corporate designs but only if it has been STS treated.

GROWING CONDITIONS

Antirrhinum is grown as an annual plant but is naturally a woody perennial. Once germination occurs (usually 4–7 days indoors), place them into a seed raising mix that is compost rich. After six weeks, spread some lime and plant into well-drained soil with plenty of fertiliser and manure. You can pinch out the buds if you want the flower to fork.

HISTORY

Antirrhinum is native to Europe. It was cultivated in Russia primarily for its seeds, as these were thought to ward off witchcraft and spells. Some say the seeds are as pure as Olive Oil. The botanical name 'Antirrhinum' means 'like' and 'nose' in Greek.

CARE AND HANDLING

- Cut or purchase when one third of the florets are open. Check for imperfections in the flowers.

- Shake bunches before buying to ensure there is no fall.

- Antirrhinum will mould and foliage will deteriorate quickly if tightly bunched, so ensure that the flowers have plenty of room in the vase.

- Remove any foliage that will sit below the water line.

- Recut 2–3 centimetres from the stem ends and place into clean, tepid water.

- Use bleach in the water and change every two days. Preservative is also recommended.

- Antirrhinum is sensitive to ethylene so keep it away from cigarette smoke and ripening fruit.

COMMERCIAL HANDLING

- Avoid keeping Antirrhinum in the cool room, but if it is necessary make sure the temperature is 6–8 degrees Celsius.

APHELANDRA

(Af-el-an-dra) Common names: Zebra Plant; Golden Spike

BOTANICAL VARIETIES Aphelandra squarrosa (Louisae) (a genus of some 170 species) FAMILY Acanthaceae NATURAL SEASON Summer COLOUR AVAILABILITY Yellow (other varieties in pink and red) CUT FLOWER LIFE SPAN 5 days

CARE AND HANDLING

- Use a preservative.
- Cut 2–3 centimetres from stem end, on an angle.
- Foliage and flowers must have a constant water source.

COMMERCIAL HANDLING

- Do not place in the cool room.

GENERAL USE

Aphelandra has bright yellow flowers that can be used in many floral designs. The flower spikes can grow up to 45 centimetres. Sometimes the flowers need an internal wire support (1.25 or .90 gauge). The stems are a burgundy red and these are very striking in modern design when the stems are featured as well as the flowers. The foliage is also well suited in modern work, particularly wedding design. The leaves need a strong wire support across the middle of the backbone.

GROWING CONDITIONS

Aphelandra needs a warm climate and rich, porous soil. As an indoor plant the minimum temperature is 10 degrees Celsius. It will self seed in tropical gardens and will grow from cuttings. Prune down hard in spring after flowering.

HISTORY

Aphelandra is native to Central and South America. It is a member of the Acanthus family. Primarily grown as display pot plants, the flowers are also cut and used in floral designs.

AQUILEGIA

(ak-wil-ee-jee-ya) Common names: Columbine; Granny's Bonnett

BOTANICAL VARIETIES McKana hybrids (Granny's Bonnet), Biedermeyer and Vulgaris hybrids (Columbine) (a genus of some 70 species) FAMILY Ranunculaceae NATURAL SEASON Late spring and summer COLOUR AVAILABILITY Blue, purple, white, red and yellow CUT FLOWER LIFE SPAN 5–7 days

GENERAL USE

The inner petals of Aquilegia flowers form a trumpet, which feature well in posy work. Aquilegia is generally available in stem lengths of 20–50 centimetres. It is not suited to corporate use as it will dry out quickly in airconditioned or heated environments.

WEDDING USE

Aquilegia flowers can be used in hand-tied clusters or bouquet holders. Do not use in wired bouquets. Do not use on hot days.

GROWING CONDITIONS

Aquilegia grows best in semi-shade and in alkaline soil, kept moist. Give the flowers plenty of liquid fertiliser during growth. The seeds should be sown in early spring.

HISTORY

Aquilegia originated in Europe and North America. Some species were used medicinally by the North American Native Indians. The curved spurs or nectarines resemble the closing talons of an eagle, and the name Aquilegia is derived from the Latin 'aquila' meaning 'eagle', and 'lego' meaning 'to gather'.

CARE AND HANDLING

- Cut or purchase when the flowers are starting to open.

- Shake bunches with any open flowers to check for flower fall.

- Yellow foliage indicates age.

- Recut 2–3 centimetres from the stem ends before placing in water.

- Remove any leaves that will sit below the waterline.

- Always use a preservative as it will encourage flower development.

- Replace water and preservative daily.

- Aquilegia is sensitive to ethylene so keep it away from cigarette smoke and ripening fruit.

ARGYRANTHEMUM *(ah-ger-ran-thee-mum)*

Common names: Marguerite Daisy; Paris Daisy

FAMILY Asteraceae NATURAL SEASON Nearly all year in frost-free climates COLOUR AVAILABILITY White, cream, yellow and pink

BOTANICAL VARIETIES Argyranthemum frutescens (the genus has 22 species)

CUT FLOWER LIFE SPAN up to 2 weeks

CARE AND HANDLING

- Cut or purchase when two or three flowers are open.

- Avoid bunches with yellow leaves – this is a sign of age.

- Look for round flowers with tightly packed petals and tight centres.

- Argyranthemum bruises easily so handle with care.

- Ensure that the flowers have plenty of space in the vase, with airflow around each bloom.

- Remove foliage that will sit under the water line.

- Recut 2–3 centimetres from the stem ends. Cut on an angle.

- Preservative or bleach will assist the flowers to open and hold.

- Change the vase water regularly.

Romantic flower

meaning:

innocence (Daisy);

sentiments shared

(Garden Daisy)

GENERAL USE

Argyranthemums (more commonly known as Marguerite daisies) can have single or multiple flowers on each stem. The stems are usually 30–60 centimetres in length. The flowers mostly have yellow centres, but the pink variety has dark, small centres.

Argyranthemums are a pretty vase flower and because they are so easy to grow they are often used as a cut flower for casual arrangements, more suited to the kitchen or casual living areas than formal rooms. They are also a pretty posy flower.

As Argyranthemum flowers age they will pollinate in the centre and develop a scent that some people find unpleasant.

WEDDING USE

Argyranthemums can be used in all bouquets, although some find their odour to be a problem. Do not use them around the edge of a bouquet as they can bruise easily when knocked.

CORPORATE USE

Argyranthemums are best used in half bud for corporate designs (as they will last longer). Because they bruise easily they should be placed in an area where they will not be disturbed.

GROWING CONDITIONS

Argyranthemum grows just about anywhere, from cuttings or from seed. It will grow in any type of soil, but good drainage is of benefit, and it does not like frost. Cut back after flowering.

HISTORY

Argyranthemum is native to the Canary Islands, Mediera and Southern Europe. It is believed to have been around for thousands of years. The ancient Egyptians often decorated their pottery with daisy designs, and 4000-year-old old hairpins that feature daisy-like ornaments were recently discovered on the island of Crete.

The English were renowned in medieval times for the use of `daisy chains´ as hair circlets.

ASCLEPIAS *(as-klee-pee-as) Common names: Butterfly Wood; Milkweed* BOTANICAL VARIETIES Asclepias incarnata (pink), Asclepias tuberosa (bright orange) Asclepias rubra (red/purple) FAMILY Asclepiadacaea NATURAL SEASON Summer COLOUR AVAILABILITY Pink, red/purple, cream and orange CUT FLOWER LIFE SPAN 5–7 days

GENERAL USE

Asclepias can be used in posies and bouquets, and is a pretty filler in table centres and delicate work.

GROWING CONDITIONS

Asclepias likes deep, rich, moist soil. Use leaves under peat moss and fertilise the soil well, especially in spring. Propagate from seed or semi-ripe cuttings.

HISTORY

Asclepias is native to North and South America. The seed pods and tender shoots were boiled and eaten with buffalo meat by the North American Indians.

The latex of some species has been used as a substitute for rubber. The seed sap is acrid and poisonous (unless boiled) and butterfly larvae that feed on this are a danger to birds.

CARE AND HANDLING

- Asclepias produces a milky latex sap that exudes from the leaves and stem when cut. Wear gloves to avoid any allergic reaction.

- Cut or purchase when the blooms are starting to open.

- Shake the bunch to check for flower fall.

- Cut 2–3 centimetres from stems ends. Cut on an angle.

- Preservative or bleach in the water is optional.

- Asclepias is sensitive to ethylene so keep it away from cigarette smoke and ripening fruit.

COMMERCIAL HANDLING

- If placed in the cool room, make sure the temperature is 6–8 degrees Celsius.

ASTILBE

(as-til-bee) Common names: Goat's Beard; Herbaceous Spiraea; False Spiraea; Prince of Wales Feathers BOTANICAL VARIETIES Astilbe X arendsii (includes twelve species and many hybrids) FAMILY Saxifragaceae NATURAL SEASON Summer COLOUR AVAILABILITY pink, white and red CUT FLOWER LIFE SPAN 7 days

CARE AND HANDLING

- Cut or purchase when the flowers are in bloom as they do not develop after harvest.

- Do not purchase or cut bunches with yellowish leaves – this is a sign of age.

- Purchase STS-treated Astilbe if available.

- Remove the leaves as these will die before the flower and emit ethylene gas.

- Recut 2–3 centimetres from the stem ends and place in water immediately. Astilbe will bleed when cut, so remove from the water after two hours and place the stems in fresh, conditioned water.

- If stems flag, wrap them tightly in paper to hold the heads up, recut up to six centimetres off the stems and place in deep, warm water for three hours.

GENERAL USE

Astilbe has wide-branching, feathering flowers in strong colours, with stems that can grow up to 60 centimetres. A single plume (or stem) may contain hundreds of florets. Astilbe flowers are very striking and have a wide variety of uses in floral work. They give a solid, yet delicate outline to most designs.

Astilbe can also be hung and dried. Spray with hair lacquer lightly to hold the fluffiness.

WEDDING USE

Use Astilbe in hand-tied, natural stemmed bouquets or bouquet holders. Natural stems need a water source up to the time of use. Do not use on a hot day. They are a very delicate flower so spray them with hairspray on the day of use as this will assist them to hold.

CORPORATE USE

Only use STS-treated Astilbe for corporate work. It will last five days in the office environment.

GROWING CONDITIONS

Astilbe loves moisture and cool climates with rich and moist soil. Grow it in a shady position.

HISTORY

Astilbe originated in China, Japan and Korea. Astible in Greek means 'not glittering'. The Arendsii varieties owe their origins to two European growers: Goerge Arends of Ronsdorf, Germany and Lemoine of France. They crossed Astilbes davidii with Astilbes arendsii to obtain a stunning result. The name 'Spiraea' was mistakenly associated with this genus when they were introduced to England in the 1820s.

ASTRANTIA (as-tran-tee-a) Common names: Masterwort

BOTANICAL VARIETIES Astrantia major FAMILY Apiaceae NATURAL SEASON Summer COLOUR AVAILABILITY Pink, white, deep purple/red and green

CUT FLOWER LIFE SPAN 5 days

CARE AND HANDLING

- Cut or purchase when the upper flowers are fully open. The buds will not open once the flower has been harvested.

- Recut 2–3 centimetres from the stem ends. Cut on an angle.

- Add preservative and change water regularly.

- Do not use in airconditioned environments as it will dry out.

COMMERCIAL HANDLING

- If placed in the cool room, the temperature should be 8 degrees Celsius.

GENERAL USE

Astrantia, which grows up to 60 centimetres in height can be used in floral foam arrangements or hand-tied work such as bouquets.

GROWING CONDITIONS

Astrania grows well in shade or full sun. The soil must be moist as Astrantia cannot tolerate dry conditions. It is primarily a perennial plant. The time to propagate is in late autumn to early spring. It is propagated from divisions.

HISTORY

Astrania is native to southern Europe and the near East. The name Astrantia possibly comes from the Greek 'astro', meaning star, and therefore alluding to Astrantia's star shaped flowers.

AZALEA

(a-zay-lee-ya) BOTANICAL VARIETIES There are numerous hybrids FAMILY Ericaceae (in botanical terms Azaleas are a section of the Rhododendron genus) NATURAL SEASON Late winter, spring and often in autumn but some varieties flower nearly all year round COLOUR AVAILABILITY All colours CUT FLOWER LIFE SPAN 3–5 days

GENERAL USE

Azaleas are not generally a commercial flower, but used in corsage and wedding work. They are also available in bunches in the Australian states of Victoria and Tasmania and they are used predominantly for posy and cottage work. It is possible to use them for wired work for funerals, particularly wreaths. They should be cross-wired using fine wire. Azaleas are not suitable for corporate work as the flowers drop off their stems very easily.

WEDDING USE

Use the cross-wiring method for wired designs. Azaleas should be used in wired work only and the flowers should be used singularly. There is a lovely colour range available, including white for the traditional bride.

GROWING CONDITIONS

Azalea needs full sun, temperate climates and must be shallow rooted and planted quite firmly to prevent wind damage. It likes soil that is light with acidity. It can be propagated from cuttings.

A problem for Azalea is petal blight – a fungus that causes the flowers to rot in humid weather. Use spray regularly with recommended fungicide and burn all affected flowers.

HISTORY

Azalea is originally from China. In 1753 Carolus Linneas created the botanical grouping called Genus Rhododendron. He created a separate genus for Azaleas, containing six species. In 1834 the genus known as Rhododendron was divided into eight sections by George Don. Azalea comprises two of these sections. Azalea today is grouped into the Pentanthera subgenus and Azaleastrum subgenus.

CARE AND HANDLING

- Azaleas have very solid, woody stems. Recut 2–3 centimetres from stem base and then lightly crush or bash the stem ends.

- Azalea flowers will separate from their calyx. You may need to float the base of flowers to ensure water supply before use.

- Use preservative.

COMMERCIAL HANDLING

- Azaleas can be placed in the cool room at a temperature of 6 degrees Celsius.

Romantic flower meaning: temperance

BANKSIA

(bank-see-ya) Common names: Honeysuckle; Bottlebrush; Hookers' Banksia; Golden Banksia; Scarlet Banksia; Rickrack Banksia; Ashby's Banksia; Red Banksia **BOTANICAL VARIETIES** The main varieties used as cut flowers include Banksia coccinea, Banksia baxteri, Banksia menziesii, Banksia speciosa, Banksia prionotes, Banksia occidentalis, Banksia ashbyi, Banksia collina, Banksia hookeriana, Banksia spinulosa, Banksia burdettii and Banksia ericafolia. **FAMILY** Proteaceae **NATURAL SEASON** Mid-autumn to late spring for most varieties **COLOUR AVAILABILITY** Orange, red, lime green, cream, yellow **CUT FLOWER LIFE SPAN** 4 weeks

GENERAL USE

Banksias are generally available with stem lengths of 30–80 centimetres. Due to their large size, they are best used at the base of floral designs. They can used in floral foam, and can be cut in half or into disks for more delicate wired work. Banksia bracts can be wired in small clusters for posy work. Banksias can also be dried, but the leaves become very brittle and will drop, and they will fade in colour.

WEDDING USE

Banksias can be used in all forms of wedding work and are a popular native flower choice for casual outdoor weddings. The miniature varieties are popular for bouquets or corsages, or the larger varieties can be cut into sections or plates to reduce their size. Use a small saw to cut and then wire to use.

CORPORATE USE

Both miniature and larger varieties of Banksia can be used in corporate designs. The flowers last well but they are heavy drinkers, so make sure they have a water source at all times.

GROWING CONDITIONS

Banksia prefers sandy soil, rich in leaf mould. It grows best in warm climates with full sun. It is relatively slow growing, but stays in bloom for a long time, and is bird attracting. Banksia can be propagated from seed or tip cuttings.

HISTORY

Sir Joseph Banks possibly chose this genus to be his name-sake. He discovered Banksia on landing day at Botany Bay in April 1770. The first variety he discovered was the tree species Banksia baueri, known as the Red Honeysuckle. Approximately 80 more species have been found across the southern part of Australia since then.

Banksia was the first Australian plant to attract attention in England.

CARE AND HANDLING

- When Banksia flowers are fresh, their colour is strong and vibrant. If the colours are faded then this is an indication of age.

- Purchase or pick when one third of the flowers are open.

- Recut 2–3 centimetres from the stems ends, using secateurs. Cut on an angle. Do not bash the stems.

- Strip any leaves that will sit below the waterline.

- Banksias will drink heavily, especially when they have just been cut. Ensure the water supply is always topped up.

- Do not mist with water as the moisture will cause black marks on the flowers.

- Preservative is optional.

COMMERCIAL HANDLING

- Banksias should be kept cool but not placed in the cool room.

BEAUFORTIA (boh-fort-ee-a) Common names: Gravel Bottlebrush; Swamp Bot-

tlebrush BOTANICAL VARIETIES Beaufortia sparsa (Swamp Bottlebrush) FAMILY Myrtaceaa NATURAL SEASON Spring and early summer

COLOUR AVAILABILITY Red/scarlet CUT FLOWER LIFE SPAN up to 30 days

CARE AND HANDLING

- Cut or purchase branches with flowers that are half open (where the red bracts are visible). Any buds that are still tight buds will not open once cut from the plant.

- Recut 2–3 centimetres from the stem ends. Cut on an angle. Use secateurs as these stems are woody.

- Remove any leaves that will sit below the waterline.

- Use preservative to help the flowers last longer and retain their colour.

- Beaufortia are heavy drinkers so place into deep water

COMMERCIAL HANDLING

- Do not keep Beaufortia in the cool room.

GENERAL USE

Beaufortia can be used in modern floral designs. The fine bracts are ideal for corsage work and the flowers will dry if hung upside down. They will however, become brittle.

Beaufortia should not be placed in airconditioned environments as this will cause the flowers to dry out. They should have a constant water source that is topped up regularly.

GROWING CONDITIONS

Beaufortia will grow in warm temperatures and tropical conditions. It is often found growing in swampy areas. It can be raised from the seeds of the previous years' capsules or from cuttings of half-ripe shoots. Keep the seeds stored in a warm place until they open and then scatter them on damp sand and peat mixture, making sure they are lightly covered. Prune lightly after the flowers have died off.

HISTORY

Beaufortia is native to Australia. It was named for Mary, The Duchess of Beaufort, who is recognised as an early patron of botany.

BERZELIA (ber-zae-lea)

BOTANICAL NAMES Berzelia lanuginosa or Berzelia galpinii (larger ball-shaped flowers) FAMILY Bruniaceae NATURAL SEASON Late winter, spring and early summer COLOUR AVAILABILITY Green, yellow, white/pink CUT FLOWER LIFE SPAN Up to 30 days

GENERAL USE

Berzelia is often used in modern floral designs. It is a very hardy flower and can be used in heated or airconditioned environments. It is generally available with stem lengths of up to 70 centimetres.

WEDDING USE

Berzelia flowers can be wired singularly or used in natural stemmed bouquets as well as bouquet holders. They are especially effective in modern wedding design, especially when the ball-shaped flowers are featured. The strap-like leaves can be used in corsages when small pieces are from the main stem.

CORPORATE USE

Berzelia flowers are particularly effective and last well in corporate designs. Remove foliage if the arrangement will be placed near an airconditioning system as this can dry it out.

GROWING CONDITIONS

Berzelia can be grown in temperate and tropical climates. It prefers well-drained soil and grows well in moist sand and peat mixture. It can be trimmed after flowering for shape. Propagate from seed or from half-hardened tip cuttings taken from non-flowering stems.

HISTORY

Berzelia originated in South Africa. It was named in honour of Count Jons Jakob Berzelius (1779–1845), a well-known Swedish chemist. He created a number of medicines using Berzelia flowers. He was also a professor of medicine. The name Lanuginosa, meaning wool, is derived from Latin.

CARE AND HANDLING

- Cut or purchase when buds have developed.

- Any yellowing on the flowers indicates age.

- Strip any leaves that will sit below the waterline.

- Recut 2–3 centimetres from the stem ends. Cut on an angle. Use secateurs as these stems are woody.

- Do not bash or split the stems.

- Use a preservative.

BLANDIFORDIA

(bland-for-dee-ya) Common names: *Christmas Bells*

BOTANICAL VARIETIES Blandfordia grandiflora FAMILY Originally of the Liliaceae family, now part of the Blandifordiaceae family NATURAL SEASON Summer COLOUR AVAILABILITY Red flowers with yellow/orange tips CUT FLOWER LIFE SPAN 5–7 days

CARE AND HANDLING

- Cut or purchase when one bell is open and there are undamaged petals.

- Handle with care as the bells are easily crushed and brown/black creases will appear if the flowers are mistreated.

- Recut 2–3 centimetres from the stem ends. Cut on an angle.

- Use preservative – this will assist the buds to open.

- Blandifordia is a heavy drinker so keep the vase water topped up.

GENERAL USE

Blandifordia is suitable for natural and modern floral designs or simply in a vase of cut flowers.

GROWING CONDITIONS

Blandifordia is a perennial plant. It has deeply buried corm-like rhizomes. It likes well-drained, acidic, sandy soil with plenty of humus. Plant it in full sun (in autumn) and keep moist.

HISTORY

Blandifordia is native to Australia.

Note: *Blandifordia is a protected species in the wild. Dealers must have a 'Greens Right' to pick them and all bunches are tagged with their rights number attached when they are sold.*

BORONIA

(bo-roh-nee-ya) Common names: Kalgam Boronia; Lipstick

BOTANICAL NAMES Boronia heterophylla, Boronia megastigma (brown and yellow/brown) (there are over 70 species) FAMILY Rutaceae NATURAL SEASON Spring for brown Boronia; late spring for pink and yellow Boronia COLOUR AVAILABILITY Pink, blue, white, red, brown (brown is perfumed), yellow and yellow/brown (a more delicate perfume) CUT FLOWER LIFE SPAN 5 days

GENERAL USE

Boronia heterophylla (strong pink) has a very strong citris-like perfume which some find unpleasant. It is not advisable to give this variety to hayfever sufferers.

Boronia flowers, with their four-petalled form look very pretty in bouquets, especially when used to surround other flowers. They can be used as filling flowers in arrangements, table centrepieces and funeral sprays, although they are not suitable for corporate use as they dry out quickly.

Boronias can also be used when dried. Make sure all the leaves are removed beforehand as any moisture dripping on the flowers will cause them to rot, and dry the stems before hanging them upside down.

WEDDING USE

Boronia flowers are best used in bouquet holders with a water source. Do not use on a hot day.

GROWING CONDITIONS

Boronia is best suited to sandy, acid soil that drains fast and has plenty of humus (to avoid the ground drying out in summer). It is not easy to grow away from its native environment, and in cooler climates it will survive only in glasshouses. The plant only lives for about 3–5 years but the seeds can be used to reproduce.

HISTORY

Boronia is native to southern Western Australia, The violet-scented 'Oil of Boronia' comes from the Boronia megastigma varieties. This essential oil is used in perfumes.

There are over 70 species of Boronia; however, as a cut flower, the varieties listed here are the most popular.

CARE AND HANDLING

- Cut or purchase when half the flowers are showing colour. In brown or yellow/brown varieties, a strong perfume should be evident as an indicator of freshness.
- Avoid bunches with any yellowing on the leaves and check for any flower drop. The foliage should be crisp.
- Keep cool at all times.
- Use a preservative in the water as this will help the flowers to open and to look fresher for longer.
- Replace preservative daily.
- Remove any foliage that will sit below the waterline.
- Recut 2–3 centimetres from the stem ends. Cut on an angle. Place into water immediately.
- Boronia drinks from its head as well as its stem, therefore it needs to be misted at regular intervals during the course of each day.
- If Boronia starts to flag it can be fully immersed in cold water for up to two hours. However, this will affect its perfume.
- Do not use in airconditioned or heated environments.
- As the flowers age, their colour and perfume fades.

COMMERCIAL HANDLING

- Boronia can be wrapped in damp paper at the end of the day to retain moisture overnight.
- Boronia should not be placed in the cool room as it will dry quickly when removed.

BOUVARDIA (boo-vah-dee-ya)

BOTANICA_ VARIETIES Bouvardia humboldtii, Bouvardia longiflora (this genus has over 30 species) FAMILY Rubiaceae NATURAL SEASON November and December (available most of the year from hot houses) COLOUR AVAILABILITY White, mauve, pink, orange and red CUT FLOWER LIFE SPAN 5–7 days

CARE AND HANDLING

- Cut or purchase when the flowers are open and in full colour.

- Recut 2–3 centimetres from the stem ends. Cut on an angle.

- Remove any foliage that will sit below the waterline.

- Bouvardia needs to be placed in deep water with preservative added.

- Ensure the blooms are not squashed together in the vase – having air flow around the blooms will help keep them alive for longer.

- Bouvardia is subject to fungal disease and the petals will bruise if not handled with care.

- Do not place Bouvardia on a bench. It will bruise easily if the petals are in any way crushed. Stand the flowers in a container and select from this container as you make your arrangement.

COMMERCIAL HANDLING

- Do not place into the cool room.

GENERAL USE

Hothouse Bouvardia is available all year round and is generally larger and brighter in colour than natural season Bouvardia. The long-stemmed variety is only grown in hothouses.

Natural season Bourvardia is ideal for use in posies, especially when the white variety is used as this has the strongest perfume. Bouvardia is generally not suitable for corporate designs.

WEDDING USE

Bouvardia is a delicate, perfumed flower and can be used singularly or in clusters for wedding designs. It is best used with strong foliage surrounding it to protect the flowers. As hothouse Bouvardia can have extended length in the flower head, you may need to wire down the throat of the flower to support the trumpet and prevent it from bending.

When used in bouquets, advise the bride to handle with care, and to pass the bouquet to her bridesmaids for safekeeping while the wedding guests congratulate the bride.

GROWING CONDITIONS

Bouvardia will grow fairly easily in sheltered, well-drained, fertilised soil. Cut it to the ground after flowering and pick out the growing tips or they will look untidy in the garden. Propagate from cuttings. Bouvardia will not withstand frost and is susceptible to White Fly and Mealybug.

HISTORY

Bouvardia is mostly native to Mexico and South Central America. It is named after Charles Bouvard, a French chemist and physician of the 16th century. He became known for creating a number of medicines from common ordinary flowers, using his extensive knowledge of plants.

BRACTEANTHA

(brak-tee-yan-tha) Common names: Everlasting Daisy; Straw Flower; Helichrysum BOTANICAL VARIETIES (Bracteantha was formally known as Helichrysum bracteatum), Bracteantha bracteata cultivars, Rhodanthe species (formally known as Schoenia filiffolia), Xerochrysum bracteatum FAMILY Asteraceae NATURAL SEASON Summer COLOUR AVAILABILITY Yellow (in the wild) red, orange, pink, burgundy, white and pale to dark yellow (all commercially grown colours) CUT FLOWER LIFE SPAN Up to 10 days

GENERAL USE

The petals of Bracteantha flowers are actually papery bracts (modified leaves), surrounding a yellow centre. The flowers and stems grow up to 50 centimetres in height, and are used in a range of floral designs as a fresh flower but may sometimes need a wire support.

As a dried flower they are popular in posies and can be mixed with other flowers in dried arrangements. Once dried they are very strong and their colours remain vibrant.
Hang the flowers upside down to dry, but remove the foliage as it will become very brittle when dried.

WEDDING USE

Bracteantha can be used in clustered, hand tied, natural stemmed bouquets, and the flowers can be wired singularly for wired bouquets. It is best to use wire support for the heads and stems.

CORPORATE USE

Bracteantha will foul the water if it is not changed regularly. They are better used as a dried flower as they keep their colour and will last indefinitely.

GROWING CONDITIONS

Drainage and full sunshine are essential for growing Bracteantha. This plant is a summer annual and should be planted by seed in winter. For perennial varieties, use tip cuttings to propagate.

HISTORY

Bracteantha is native to Western Australia. Its species name 'Rhodanthe' is derived from the Greek words 'rhodon', meaning rose, and 'anthos', meaning flower.

CARE AND HANDLING

- Cut or purchase when most flowers are fully open and the buds are showing strong colour.

- Avoid any damaged or imperfect formations and ensure the foliage is a strong green colour.

- Keep the flowers and foliage cool.

- Recut 2–3 centimetres from the stem ends. Cut on a sharp angle.

- Remove any leaves that will sit under the waterline.

- Wash the stems before use.

- Use preservative. This prevents the water being fouled and will also assist buds to open. Bleach may be used to assist water cleansing instead of preservative.

- The vase water should be changed every 3–4 days.

COMMERCIAL HANDLING

- Do not place in the cool room. Bracteantha are a summer flower and dislike cold temperatures as it causes their foliage to deteriorate and mould.

Romantic flower meaning: unceasing remembrance

CALENDULA *(kal-en-du-la) Common names: Marigold; English Marigold; Gold Daisy*

BOTANICAL VARIETIES Calendula officinalis FAMILY Asteraceae NATURAL SEASON Late winter, spring, summer and autumn COLOUR AVAILABILITY Orange, yellow, gold, apricot and white CUT FLOWER LIFE SPAN 5–7 days

CARE AND HANDLING

- Purchase or cut when flowers are half open and showing colour.
- The leaves should be bright green with no sign of any browning.
- Remove packaging and open the bunches as soon as you bring them home, as the flowers need airflow around them to prevent deterioration.
- Keep Calendulas away from direct sunlight and draughty areas.
- Remove any foliage that will sit below the waterline
- Recut 2–3 centimetres from the stem ends. Cut on an angle.
- Use a preservative or bleach in the water to maintain open flowers and help them to last longer.
- Calendula flowers are heavy drinkers so always keep the water topped up.
- They are very sensitive to ethylene so keep them away from cigarette smoke and ripening fruit.
- Do not place in heated or airconditioned environments.

COMMERCIAL HANDLING

- Do not place in the cool room as they mould easily.

GENERAL USE

Calendula flowers have very strong stems and are ideal for use in posies. They may need a wire support to angle the heads. They also make an excellent surface flower for use in wreaths. Some varieties are edible and can be used in salads. These varieties are sometimes sold in boxes of edible flowers. Calendula flowers are not suitable for corporate decorating as they dry out very quickly. They do have a scent but it is not to everyone's taste.

WEDDING USE

Calendula flowers can be used in hand-tied natural stemmed bouquets, posy clusters or bouquet holders. Use wire support for the heads and stems and support with a strong foliage surround, such as Camellia leaves. Calendula flowers will only last for 3-5 hours when used in fully-wired bouquets.

GROWING CONDITIONS

Calendula can be planted from seed. It enjoys full sun (provided it is well watered) and fertile soil. It will flower approximately 10–12 weeks after planting. Calendula is one of the easiest of the annuals to propagate and bloom. Plant the seeds in spring for a summer flowering, and in summer for an autumn and early winter flowering.

HISTORY

Calendula is native to Mexico, the Mediterranean and Central America. It is thought that an ointment of this herb is supposed to cure acne and other skin problems.

Calendula flowers are sought after in India for religious purposes. The Buddhists use them solely to keep insects at bay and at the temples they are planted for this reason through rose and vegetable gardens. The name is derived from the Latin 'Calandae', meaning 'the first day of each month, and is named in reference to the long flowering period of this plant.

CALLISTEMON

(kal-lis-tem-on) Common names: *Bottlebrush*

BOTANICAL VARIETIES Callistemon montanus, Callistemon citrinus, Callistemon pityoides. FAMILY Myrtaceae NATURAL SEASON Spring and summer COLOUR AVAILABILITY Red, white, green, pink, lemon and purple CUT FLOWER LIFE SPAN 5 days

CARE AND HANDLING

- Cut or purchase branches with flowers that are half open (so that you can see the red bracts). Tight buds, where the bracts are not visible, will not open once the branches are cut from the plant.
- Recut 2–3 centimetres from the stem ends. Cut on an angle using secateurs, as these stems are woody.
- Remove any fine leaves that will sit below the waterline.
- Add preservative to the water to help the flowers last longer and retain their colour.
- Place into deep water as these flowers are heavy drinkers.
- Do not place in heated or airconditioned environments.

COMMERCIAL HANDLING

- Do not place or store in the cool room as they will mould.

GENERAL USE

Callistemon are best kept with other native flowers. They have colourful, compact and upright heads and sometimes have pendulous flower heads. The flowers consist mainly of fluffy stamens. They can be used in many types of arrangements and bouquets. The lime green flowers are striking when used in modern designs.

WEDDING USE

Callistemon can be used in all types of wedding bouquets.

CORPORATE USE

Callistemon can be used in corporate designs as long as it has an adequate water source.

GROWING CONDITIONS

Callistemon grows in sandy, well-drained soil. This plant is highly drought resistant and can be found growing near swamps or river banks. It can be propagated from spring seed.

Callistemon montanus is the hardiest variety and will even withstand a frost. The main flush of flowering will be through spring with a secondary flush in autumn. Leaves will extend from the tips of the blooms.

HISTORY

Callistemon is native to Western Australia with some varieties from the east and southeast coast areas of Australia. The flowers are sometimes referred to as Bottlebrush because of their brush-like, cylindrical blooms, which resemble a traditional brush used for cleaning bottles.

CALLISTEPHUS / ASTER (kal-lis-tef-as) (ass-ter) Common names: China Aster; Michaelmas Daisy; Easter Daisy BOTANICAL VARIETIES Callistephus chinensis, Aster novi-belgii and Aster eroides (Easter Daisy) FAMILY Asteraceae NATURAL SEASON Summer for annuals, autumn for perennials COLOUR AVAILABILITY Purple, mauve, pink, burgundy and white CUT FLOWER LIFE SPAN 7–10 days (the flower may last longer but the foliage will not)

GENERAL USE

Callistephus are ideal for use in posies and cottage designs mixed with other flowers. Sometimes their stems may need a wire support. They are a more traditional looking flower and can be used in many traditional designs.

The Easter Daisy variety is an excellent filling flower, especially in large wedding arrangements. They are available on stems up to one metre in length. Their foliage dislikes cool rooms and will brown quickly. These flowers, as named, are available at Easter and often feature in church arrangements as an outline flower or a filling flower.

WEDDING USE

The China Aster and Michaelmas Daisy varieties can be used in all types of bouquets, except when the bouquet is required on a hot day. For hand-held bouquets or bouquet holders, support the heads and stems with wire.

The Easter Daisy variety can be used in natural stemmed bouquets or bouquet holders, although they do not last well in wired bouquets.

CORPORATE USE

Callistephus can be used in corporate designs, provided the flowers are in bud form. The foliage should be removed if it is late in the season as it will yellow and start to dry out.

GROWING CONDITIONS

Callistephus should be planted in fertile, moist, retentive soil, in full sun or part shade. Add lime to the soil. Cut the plant back to the ground after the flowering season. It should not be planted where Callistephus has grown in the previous year. Perennial varieties should be cut back each year and divided every second year. Annuals should be pulled up and grown from seedlings.

CARE AND HANDLING

- These flowers are susceptible to fungus, so if they are purchased in a plastic sleeve it be removed immediately.

- Cut or purchase when some blooms are opening.

- Separate the bunches to circulate air around the stems.

- Recut 2–3 centimetres from the stem ends. Cut on an angle.

- Remove any foliage that will sit below the waterline.

- Use a preservative or bleach in the water.

- Keep Callistephus away from direct sunlight, draught areas and heat to avoid wilting.

COMMERCIAL HANDLING

- Do not place in the cool room as they may not acclimatise on removal.

- The foliage will blacken and mould if left tightly bunched in the cool room.

- They like to be kept as individuals in single stems, not bunched together. If they are squashed together the flowers will pollinate in the centres.

HISTORY

Callistiphus is originally from China. The name in Latin means 'star', and in Greek means 'small star'. In the language of flowers, Callistephus symbolises 'love' or 'daintiness'.

Aster ericoides is known in the Northern Hemisphere as Michaelmas Daisy. In the southern part of the world they are known as Easter Daisies. In the Middle Ages they were known by the British as Asters or Starworts. It was also thought at this time that the burning of Aster leaves drove serpents away.

CAMELLIA

(kah-meel-lee-ya) Common names: Japonica; Chinese Rose; Sazankwa

BOTANICAL VARIETIES Camellia japonica (there are thousands of cultivars) FAMILY Theaceae NATURAL SEASON Winter/spring flowering COLOUR AVAILABILITY White, pink, red, lemon, yellow, apricot, peach and striking variegations CUT FLOWER LIFE SPAN 5–7 days

GENERAL USE

Camellia flowers are available in a fabulous range of colours and varieties. Some varieties are peony-like in appearance. They can be used for corsages, wedding bouquets and various other arrangements. They are most attractive when displayed in a float bowl, which is the traditional method of display for Camellias in floral art. The mature leaves are also used widely in floral work. They are usually deep green in colour but there are variegated leaves as well.

Camellia flowers are not used very much commercially; however, the heads of the flowers can be used for funeral work. The flowers will cover a funeral wreath quickly. They need to be cross-wired and the wire support should be then be fastened to wooden pegs (also known as picks).

WEDDING USE

Camellia flowers and foliage can both be used in wedding designs. Camellia flowers need support with cross wires as the sepals are likely to separate from the flower. Camellia flowers used in bouquets that are not fully-wired will still need to be wired before use. For bouquets made with a bouquet holder, insert the wired stem into the holder with a double fork-wired end.

CORPORATE USE

Camellia foliage may be used for corporate designs, but the flowers should not be as they will drop from the stem.

GROWING CONDITIONS

Camellia is a woody plant that grows well in deep, well-drained soil that is neutral, to slightly acidic. It grows well in mountainous and subtropical areas in partial shade. The Sasanqua variety can take more sun than the Japonica variety.

CARE AND HANDLING

- The flower will separate from its calyx and fall.

- Preservative is optional.

- Camellia leaves will not deteriorate under water.

COMMERCIAL HANDLING

- Flowers and foliage can be placed in the cool room at a temperature of 6–8 degrees Celsius.

Romantic flower meaning:

exquisite loveliness (white); unpretentious excellence (red)

HISTORY

Most Camellia varieties are native to China although a small percentage are native to Japan. They were named for Georg Kamel, a Jesuit priest who lived from 1661 to 1706 and collected plants from China and the Philippines. It is widely believed that he brought the seeds back to Europe. He also wrote a book on the plants of Luzon.

The first Camellia plants grown in England were grown in greenhouses and subsequently died as it was too hot. These were in the garden of Lord Petre in 1739 in Essex. In 1792 John Slater (of the East India Company) re-introduced Camellias. Alfred Chandler began raising new varieties from seed around 1830. Camellia breeding peaked in the 1840s.

Financially, the most important species is Camellia sinensis, known as the Tea Plant. It is the national beverage of China and greatly associated with the English.

Romantic flower meaning: gratitude

CAMPANULA *(kam-pan-yoo-la)* Common names: *Canterbury Bells; Bellflower; Bluebell* BOTANICAL VARIETIES Campanula medium (Canterbury Bell) (Campanulas are a large genus of some 300 species) FAMILY Campanulaceae NATURAL SEASON Spring and early summer COLOUR AVAILABILITY Purple, mauve, pink, white and lemon CUT FLOWER LIFE SPAN 3 weeks (if conditioned correctly)

GENERAL USE

Campanula flowers, generally available with stem lengths of up to 60 centimetres, can be used for numerous purposes but are most attractive in glass vases.

These flowers do not like change. Always give the flowers time to settle in water. If any stems droop, recut and allow them to settle again. Campanulas can shrivel up within hours if they stop drinking but in most cases they can still be revived if recut and placed in deep water with preservative added. If the leaves begin to turn yellow it is a sign that there are drinking problems and if this is ignored, the flowers will die.

If using Campanula in floral foam, allow the flowers to condition, i.e. make the arrangement, then leave it overnight to see if all flowers are in peak condition. Remove and re-condition any blooms that are in doubt.

Remember that Campanula flowers will outlast their foliage so consider this when putting the arrangement together.

CORPORATE USE

Campanula flowers must be STS-treated for corporate use. If treated correctly they will last up to three weeks. Never transport them without a water source as they air block very easily. It is best to arrange them the day before to make sure they have adjusted, especially if used in floral foam.

GROWING CONDITIONS

Campanula is a herbaceous perennial. It thrives in rich, moist, well-drained soil and in full sun. It can be propagated from seed sown outdoors from spring and summer. The roots can be divided in spring and autumn or by striking them from soft cuttings under glass in early spring.

HISTORY

Campanula originated from southern Europe. Its common name may have derived from the horse bells used by pilgrims visiting the shrine of Saint Thomas Beckett at Canterbury Cathedral.

CARE AND HANDLING

- Commercially grown Campanula flowers should be STS-treated – ask your florist when purchasing.

- Check the flowers for purple edging – this is an indication of refrigeration damage.

- If cutting from the garden, make sure the lower blooms are opening and the upper buds are showing colour.

- Keep cool at all times.

- Remove any foliage that will sit below the waterline.

- Recut 2–3 centimetres from stem ends, on an angle, then stand in the stems in deep water containing preservative.

- If the flowers are removed from the vase for arranging or water change, the stems must be recut again before placing back into the vase.

- Use a tall vase with deep water.

- Campanula flowers are extremely long lasting and resilient to airconditioning, but if they're not treated correctly they can die within 24 hours.

- Campanula is sensitive to ethylene so keep it away from cigarette smoke and ripening fruit.

COMMERCIAL HANDLING

- Campanulas can be placed in the cool room at temperatures of 6–8 degrees.

CARTHAMUS

(kar-tha-mas) Common names: Matches; Safflower

BOTANICAL VARIETIES Carthamus tinctorius FAMILY Asteraceae NATURAL SEASON Summer COLOUR AVAILABILITY Mainly orange/gold (most popular as a cut flower), yellow, orange/red and (rarely) white CUT FLOWER LIFE SPAN 7 days

CARE AND HANDLING

- Cut or purchase when the thistle-like flowers are about to open and the orange colour is showing. Any buds that are still tightly closed will not open once the stems have been cut from the plant.

- Recut 2–3 centimetres from the stem ends, on an angle, using a knife or secateurs.

- Remove any leaves that will sit below the waterline.

- Foliage of a different variety can be added to the vase, but before doing so strip all the leaves from the Carthamus stems as they will not last as long as the flower.

- Use a preservative and change the vase water daily.

- Carthamus is sensitive to ethylene so keep it away from cigarette smoke and ripening fruit.

COMMERCIAL HANDLING

- Do not place in the cool room.

GENERAL USE

Dried Carthemus flowers are popular for dried arrangements. They are not a popular arranging flower, however, their colour is bright and strong and blends well with Australian natives. They are heavy drinkers.

GROWING CONDITIONS

Carthamus grows in most soil conditions, provided there is good drainage. It is considered by some to be a weed as it spreads easily by seed.

HISTORY

Carthamus is native to the Mediterranean region. Folk history records that seeds of Carathamus were used for treating tumours, particularly inflammatory tumours of the liver. The flowers were considered a diaphoretic, emmenagogue, laxative (in large doses), sedative, and stimulant. They were once used as a substitute or adulterant for saffron in treating measles, scarlatina, and other diseases.

Charred safflower oil was used for rheumatism and sores and the seeds were used as a diuretic and tonic. It was prescribed in China as a uterine astringent in dysmenorrhea. It is also recorded that the oil was used as a salve for sprains and rheumatism in Iran.

Carthamus was also used as a pigment source for yellow and red dyes.

CELOSIA (sel-oh-see-ya) Common names: Cockscomb; Prince of Wales Feathers;
Wheat Celosia BOTANICAL VARIETIES Celosia argentia pyramidalis (Prince of Wales Feathers), Celosia argentea, Celosia cristata (Cockscomb) and Celosia spicata (Wheat Celosia) FAMILY Amaranthaceae NATURAL SEASON Late spring and summer COLOUR AVAILABILITY Yellow, orange, red/pink, coral, green (green also with veins of colour) CUT FLOWER LIFE SPAN up to 30 days for the flower and 5–7 days for the foliage

GENERAL USE

The different varieties of Celosia (generally available with stems of up to 60 centimetres) vary dramatically in appearance. The Cockscomb variety has rippled flower heads that resemble coral (or to some, brains). The flowers are fan shaped. With its strong colours, Cockscomb is commonly used in modern arrangements, posies and bouquets. It should be wire supported if the heads are heavy.

The Prince of Wales Feathers variety has tall sprays of plumes that look like coloured feathers. They have a fluffy appearance, similar to the look of brightly coloured Pampas Grass. The flowers can be dried. Remove all foliage before drying and hang it upside down.

Wheat celosia has short, wheat-like spikes about 20–30 centimetres long.

Celosia has a dramatic texture. It needs to be conditioned prior to use in floral foam.

WEDDING USE

Celosia can be used in hand-tied, natural stemmed bouquets if supported by other flowers. Use wire support for use in bouquet holders. The flowers can be split into smaller sections if required.

Celosia does not last in wired bouquets in temperatures over 30 degrees Celsius. Always make sure the Cockscomb variety is fully conditioned before use in wired work.

CORPORATE USE

Celosia can be used in vase arrangements rather than foam. It lasts well when only the flowers (not foliage) are used.

CARE AND HANDLING

- Cut or purchase when the flowers are fully developed and in full colour. Any flowers still in bud form will not open once the stems have been cut from the plant. The leaves should be perfect with no discolouration.

- Recut 2–3 centimetres from the stem ends, on an angle, using secateurs.

- Remove any leaves that will sit below the waterline.

- Use preservative and change the vase water daily as Celosia is a big drinker.

- Do not place in airconditioned environments or it will dry out.

- As a cut flower Celosia does not like direct sunlight.

COMMERCIAL HANDLING

- Celosia can be placed in the cool room with a temperature of 6 degrees Celsius.

GROWING CONDITIONS

Celosia is a fast-growing annual plant. It likes hot summers and rich, sandy soil that is well-drained. Soil rich in humus and manure is desirable.

HISTORY

Celosia is native to Africa and Asia. The name Celosia is derived from the Greek word 'kelos' which means burn. This aptly describes the flame colours of this flower.

In India the leaves of Celosia argentea are eaten as a vegetable and other species are used medicinally.

CENTAUREA

(sen-tor-ee-ya) Common names: *Cornflower; Bachelor's Button; Bluebottle; Knapweed; Sweet Sultan; Century* BOTANICAL VARIETIES Centuria cyanus (Blue Cornflower); Centuria macrocephala, Centuria montana (Knapweed), Centaurea cyanus (over 55 varieties and around 450 species) FAMILY Asteraceae NATURAL SEASON Late winter and early spring and in colder climates they will flower in summer COLOUR AVAILABILITY Pink, blue, white, lemon, red/crimson and purple CUT FLOWER LIFE SPAN 7 days

Coloured Cornflowers fade to white with age

GENERAL USE

Centaurea (the Cornflower variety) is a good single stem flower to use in most arrangements. However, the flowers will not last if any pollen is visible. Centaurea flowers are generally available with stem lengths of 30–60 centimetres.

WEDDING USE

Centaurea can be used in all types of bouquets. Wire support the head and stem for use in bouquet holders. If the petals are removed, the base of the flower can be used for fine-wired designs.

CORPORATE USE

Centaurea flowers can be used in corporate designs but their colour will fade after six or seven days and their foliage may start to dry out. The water should be changed every couple of days.

GROWING CONDITIONS

Centaurea can be grown in most climates but prefers a sunny position in well-drained, light soil. It should be watered regularly while the buds are forming. It is easy to grow from seed and can flower continuously for months in ideal conditions.

Perennial varieties can be propagated from division as well as from soft wood cuttings from non-flowering stems. These plants are straggly and are best planted in clumps.

CARE AND HANDLING

- Cut or purchase when the flowers are half open. The flowers should be strong in colour and leaves should be a vibrant green.

- Centaurea is sensitive to fungal disease. This can be prevented by ensuring that the bunches are separated so that the foliage does not mould.

- Recut 2–3 centimetres from the stem ends. Cut on an angle.

- Do not stand in deep water.

- Preservative is essential.

- Centaurea is sensitive to ethylene so keep it away from cigarette smoke and ripening fruit, and remove the foliage before arranging the flowers (the foliage does not last as long as the flowers and will emit ethylene when it starts to die)

- Do not keep Centaurea in airconditioned environments.

COMMERCIAL HANDLING

- Do not place Centaurea in the cool room. The temperature will cause the flowers to fade and the stems will mould if there is insufficient airflow around the flowers.

Romantic flower meaning: celibacy (Bachelor's Button)

HISTORY

Centaurea is native to Europe and the Middle East and has been grown since ancient times. It may have been used medicinally, as it is said to have healed a wound in the foot of Chiron, the wisest of all senators and mentor of Hercules. It was once a common weed in the cornfields and it was known, perhaps appropriately, as Hurt-Sickle. Artists used to prepare a blue coloured paint from its petals. It was a very popular posy flower in Victorian and Colonial times.

From 1968 the blue Cornflower has been the national flower of Estonia. In the language of flowers the Cornflower symbolises refinement and delicacy. Centaurea is often used as a buttonhole flower on Derby Day (Melbourne Cup).

CENTRANTHUS

(ken-trathas) Common names: *Fox's Bush; Red Valerian; Jupiter's Beard* BOTANICAL VARIETIES Centranthus ruber FAMILY Valerianaceae NATURAL SEASON Spring and early summer COLOUR AVAILABILITY pink, red and white CUT FLOWER LIFE SPAN 5–7 days

GENERAL USE

Centranthus is a pretty vase flower and a nice bouquet flower. Do not attempt to wire these flowers as they must have a constant water source as a cut flower.

GROWING CONDITIONS

Centranthus likes well-drained soil with full sun. It is drought resistant. The seeds can be sown into the garden soil.

HISTORY

Centranthus flowers are native to Europe, Asia Minor and Northern Africa. Centranthus has been cultivated for many centuries.

In southern Italy the leaves are used in salads. The seeds were once used by Egyptians in the embalming process of the dead.

CARE AND HANDLING

- Cut or purchase when the base flowers are showing colour.

- Do not crush the leaves as an unpleasant odour will be emitted.

- Recut stems 2–3 centimetres from the stem ends. Cut on an angle.

- Use preservative and bleach in the water.

- Do not place in airconditioned environments.

COMMERCIAL HANDLING

- Do not place in the cool room.

CEPHALARIA (kef-a-lear-ee-a) Common names: The Tartar Pincushion

BOTANICAL VARIETIES Cephalaria gigantea FAMILY Dipsacaceae NATURAL SEASON Summer COLOUR AVAILABILITY Yellow

CUT FLOWER LIFE SPAN 5–7 days

CARE AND HANDLING

- Cut or purchase when the flowers are showing colour.

- Remove any foliage that will sit below the waterline.

- Recut stems 2–3 centimetres. Cut on an angle.

- Use preservative.

- Cephalaria is sensitive to ethylene so keep it away from cigarette smoke and ripening fruit.

- Do not place in airconditioned environments.

COMMERCIAL HANDLING

- Cephalaria can be kept in the cool room at temperatures of 6–8 degrees Celsius.

GENERAL USE

Cephalaria flowers are suited to vases and floral foam as well as natural designs.

GROWING CONDITIONS

Cephalaria will grow in any soil conditions and is frost hardy. It does favour clay-based soils so long as they are moist. It is a herbaceous perennial. It should be dead- headed after flowering and cut back to the ground in late autumn. It can be grown from seed, and can grow up to 1.5 metres in height.

HISTORY

Cephalaria is native to the Caucasus mountains of Siberia (home of the Tatars)

CERATOPETALUM (ke-ra-toh-pet-a-lam)

Common names: *Christmas Bush; Festival Bush* BOTANICAL VARIETIES Ceratopetalum gummiferum FAMILY Cunoniaceae

NATURAL SEASON Summer COLOUR AVAILABILITY White, yellow/red, cherry/red to purple CUT FLOWER LIFE SPAN 14 days

GENERAL USE

Ceratopetalum flowers are generally best used in native bouquets and arrangements. Make sure they always have a good water source. The white flowers and the coloured sepals are both widely used as cut flowers.

GROWING CONDITIONS

Ceratopetalum grows into small, slender trees that can grow up to ten metres tall. They enjoy deep, rich, sandy, well-drained soil. The first flowering is tiny white flowers that drop from the tree, leaving behind the sepals, which enlarge and darken in colour to a yellow/red or cherry/red colour and sometimes, purple.

HISTORY

Ceratopetalum is native to Australia and in particular, coastal New South Wales. The name Ceratopetalum comes from two Greek words that translate to mean 'horned petal' (one of the Ceratopetalum species has petals resembling horns).

CARE AND HANDLING

- Cut or purchase when the yellow/red colour is visible.
- Dark purple sepals are older and should be avoided.
- Recut 2–3 centimetres from the stem ends. Cut on an angle, using secateurs.
- Do not bash the stems.
- Remove any leaves that will sit below the waterline.
- Use preservative.
- Ceratopetalum flowers are very heavy drinkers so keep the vase water topped up.
- Mist regularly as they drink through the surface area of the flower and foliage as well as the stem.
- Do not place in airconditioned environments.

COMMERCIAL HANDLING

- Do not keep Ceratopetalum in the cool room.

CHAMAEMELUM *(ka-mee-meel-am)*

Commcn names: *Chamomile; Roman Camomile* BOTANICAL VARIETIES Chamaemelum nobile FAMILY Asteraceae NATURAL SEASON Spring and autumn COLOUR AVAILABILITY White with yellow centres, yellow CUT FLOWER LIFE SPAN 5 days

CARE AND HANDLING

- Cut or purchase when flowers are showing colour.
- The yellow centres should be tight with no visible sign of pollen.
- Remove any foliage that will sit below the waterline.
- Recut 2–3 centimetres from the stem ends. Cut on an angle.
- Use preservative.

COMMERCIAL HANDLING

- Do not place in the cool room.

GENERAL USE

Chamaemelum flowers are more likely to be cut from a garden than purchased commercially. They have aromatic leaves, and look very pretty when used in small table centrepieces and posies. These flowers should be used singularly or in small numbers rather than in larger clusters. They are not suitable for use in wired designs as they don't last when out of water. They are not suitable for wedding or corporate designs.

GROWING CONDITIONS

Chamaemelum should be cut back after flowering. If the bush is divided it will keep flowering each year. It likes rich soil and enjoys plenty of sun. Chamaemelum can be grown from cuttings.

HISTORY

Chamaemelum is native to Europe. One purpose for its growth is to make Chamomile tea. The flowers are also used for flavouring fine liqueurs as well as for their excellent oil, used in the making of perfume. The dried flowers are used medicinally in the treatment of sleeping and nervous disorders.

Chamaemelum also makes a solid, drought-resistant lawn (Cultivar treneague). There is a Chamomile lawn at Buckingham Palace.

CHAMELAUCIUM

(kam-e-lor-kee-am) Common names: Geraldton Wax; Wax Flower; Bud Wax; Wax Plant BOTANICAL VARIETIES Chamelaucium megalopetalum, Chamelaucium uncinatum (Geraldton Wax), Chamelaucium ciliatum FAMILY Myrtaceae NATURAL SEASON Late winter and spring COLOUR AVAILABILITY White, pink/red, cream/yellow CUT FLOWER LIFE SPAN Up to 12 days

GENERAL USE

Chamelaucium flowers are popular for use in many types of floral designs. They are best used with other Australian natives, but remember they are heavy drinkers, so use a vase that holds a large amount of water.

WEDDING USE

Chamelaucium is a delicate filling flower that can be used in all types of bouquets.

CORPORATE USE

Chamelaucium can be used for most corporate designs, but will partly dry out by the end of the week. The foliage will drop as it dries.

GROWING CONDITIONS

Chamelaucium has brittle roots and prefers gravelly, alkaline soil. It does not like too much water or acidic soil. Prune lightly after flowering and the plant will grow quickly into a shrub.

HISTORY

Chamelaucium is native to Western Australia. The name possibly comes from the Latin term 'uncinatum' used to describe the headwear of medieval popes. This word originally came from 'uncinatus', meaning 'hooked', referring to the apices of the leaves.

CARE AND HANDLING

- Cut or purchase when several of the flowers are open. Check for any flower fall as this can indicate age. The leaves should be green and flowers perfect (damaged blooms may be due to fungal infection).

- Remove any leaves that will sit below the waterline.

- Recut 2–3 centimetres from the stem ends. Cut on an angle, using secateurs.

- Add chlorine or bleach to the clean vase water. Do not use a preservative.

- Do not mist this flower as they are subject to Botrytis and fungal disease.

- Chamelaucium is a heavy drinker so top up the vase water daily.

- If the flowers have been STS-treated they will not be sensitive to ethylene. Check with your florist.

- Do not place in airconditioned environments or the flowers will drop and the foliage will dry out.

COMMERCIAL HANDLING

- Do not place in the cool room.

CHRYSANTHEMUM / DENDRANTHEMA

(kris-an-tha-mum) Common names: Painted Daisy; Pockets (Disbuds); Mums; Buttons; Paris Daisy; Spider BOTANICAL VARIETIES Dendranthema morifolium, Chrysanthemum grandiflorum (known under Dendranthema as well as Chrysanthemum species) FAMILY Asteraceae NATURAL SEASON Autumn and early winter COLOUR AVAILABILITY All colours CUT FLOWER LIFE SPAN Up to 4 weeks

GENERAL USE

There are numerous varieties of Chrysanthemum with many different sizes and shapes and different uses.

Most Chrysanthemum varieties are clustered and feature thin petals. They have long stems and appear very large due to multiple heads or one large head. Clustered flowers are more difficult to arrange and are best used in larger designs such as arrangements for weddings and corporate functions. Single flowers can be separated or cut from the cluster and used in wreath construction, but sometimes they will need a wire support so that the head is facing in the right direction. Use the pierce and mount wiring method and fork the wire so that there are equal wire lengths to insert in the base.

Pocket Chrysanthemums have one large head and can also be used in the arrangements described above.

Field Chrysanthemums are very hardy and can be used in arrangements as well as bases with no water source, such as wreaths made with dry foam.

Glasshouse or hothouse Chrysanthemums will develop air embolisms very easily and must not be removed from water. If there are embolisms in the stems, the lower leaves will start to droop. Do not ignore this because if one leaf droops then they will all start to droop, and eventually the flower will die. The stems must be recut to save the flowers. Single flowers can be wired for delicate work such as hairpieces and corsages.

Disbud Chrysanthemums (such as Pocket and Mum varieties), are disbudded by the grower to create single stemmed flowers. This is done by hand picking all buds on a stem except for one, so that all the nourishment goes to the remaining single bud. There are, however, some side effects to this process. Sometimes the remaining single head is too heavy for the stem, or if too much nourishment goes to the one bloom, treat with care as they can disintegrate or shatter very easily.

CARE AND HANDLING

- When cutting or purchasing Disbud Chrysanthemums (Pocket or Mum varieties), check that the centres are tight.

- When cutting or purchasing spray Chrysanthemums, make sure at least one flower is in full bloom.

- The Spider varieties should be firm. Some petals do grow downwards and this should not be considered a sign of age, as long as the flowers 'spring' when you lightly press on them.

- The leaves of the Chrysanthemum will age and yellow before the flowers. Consider this when creating arrangements.

- Recut 2–3 centimetres from the woody stem ends. Cut on an angle. If drooping occurs cut the stems again.

- Remove any leaves that will sit below the waterline.

- Do not bash the stem ends.

- Use preservative.

- Chrysanthemums are resilient to heating and airconditioning.

COMMERCIAL HANDLING

- Chrysanthemum can be placed in the cool room at temperatures of 6–8 degrees Celsius.

If the petals are peeling back on the large 'pockets', spray with floral wax or drip candle wax on the calyx. This will hold the base of the petals more firmly.

WEDDING USE

Chrysanthemums are available in a range of colours and can be used in wedding work of all kinds. The single flowers give a more casual look to bouquets and can also be used for hairpieces. They should be wired using the pierce and mount method, but make sure that hothouse or glasshouse Chrysanthemums are conditioned and are therefore strong before wiring.

Chrysanthemums can be used in a bouquet holder where they have a water source. They will last in hand-tied natural stemmed bouquets if pre-treated with preservative.

CORPORATE USE

For corporate use, hothouse or glasshouse Chrysanthemums must have a constant water source and be pre-conditioned. The flowers will outlast the leaves. Field Chrysanthemums will last well even if they are not conditioned.

GROWING CONDITIONS

Chrysanthemum thrives in rich, well-drained soil. Blooming begins about three months after seeds are sown, and peak bloom is in late autumn, triggered by the lengthening night hours. Deadhead the blooms to prolong flowering.

HISTORY

Chrysanthemum is native to China. The Chinese cultivated it in 500 BC. It first appeared as a small yellow flower and was cultivated as a herb. It was believed to have the power of life. It is thought that the boiled roots were used as headache medicine and the leaves were brewed as a festive drink. The petals were used in salads.

Chrysanthemum was widely cultivated in both China and Japan before the 18th century. The Mikado took the flower to be his personal emblem in 797 AD and at one time, the flowers could only be viewed by the Emperor and his nobles.

Japan celebrates National Chrysanthemum Day on the 9th of September and this day is called the Festival of Happiness. The Chrysanthemum flower is the national flower of Japan and is represented in the Japanese Imperial Crest.

Chrysanthemums were introduced to Europe in the late 18th century. The name is derived from the Greek Khrusanthemon flower.

CLARKIA

(klah-kee-a) **Common names:** Godetia; Farewell to Spring; Satin Flower; Summers Darling **BOTANICAL VARIETIES** Clarkia amoena **FAMILY** Onagraceae **NATURAL SEASON** Late spring and summer **COLOUR AVAILABILITY** Red, burgundy, white, pink, lilac and orange **CUT FLOWER LIFE SPAN** 14 days

GENERAL USE

Clarkia is a very good posy and bouquet flower. It can be used in all floral designs.

WEDDING USE

Clarkia flowers can be used in bouquet holders if the heads and stems are wire-supported. They can also be used in natural stemmed bouquets. Use the pierce and mount wiring method for single florets. Clarkia flowers mix well with roses.

CORPORATE USE

Clarkia flowers can be used in corporate designs if in half bud form. Keep an eye on the foliage as it can start to dry out after 3-5 days.

GROWING CONDITIONS

Clarkia likes well-drained soil that is between neutral and acidic. It should be kept moist. The plant has simple, minutely toothed leaves, with terminal racemes of flowers. The petals flow from a tubular calyx. Many double flowers are produced. Most Clarkia varieties are annuals. They grow from seed and can be planted in autumn.

HISTORY

Clarkia is native to North America and was originally a desert flower. The flower was named after Captain William Clark, an American explorer who, along with Captain Meriwether Lewis, crossed America in 1806.

CARE AND HANDLING

- Cut or purchase when the coloured buds are half open. All buds will open if they are showing colour when picked, but green buds will often not open.

- There should be no sign of yellowing on the leaves.

- Remove any foliage that will sit below the waterline.

- Preservative is essential.

- Clarkia is sensitive to ethylene so keep it away from cigarette smoke and ripening fruit.

- Separate purchased bunches to prevent mould growth.

- As the flower ages, any visible veins or purple edges on the petals is a sign that the refrigeration was too cold.

COMMERCIAL HANDLING

- Clarkia can be kept in the cool room with temperatures of 6–8 degrees Celsius.

CLETHRA

(kleth-rah) Common names: Lily-of-the-Valley Tree; Sweet Pepperbush; Summersweet; White Alder BOTANICAL VARIETIES Clethra alnifolia (White Alder) FAMILY Cyrillaceae NATURAL SEASON Summer flowering COLOUR AVAILABILITY White CUT FLOWER LIFE SPAN 7–10 days

CARE AND HANDLING

- Cut or purchase when the base florets are in bloom (the florets open from the base upwards).
- Recut 2–3 centimetres from the stem ends. Cut on a sharp angle using secateurs.
- Do not bash the woody stems.
- Use preservative.
- These flowers are heavy drinkers so keep the vase water topped up.
- Clethra is sensitive to ethylene so keep it away from cigarette smoke and ripening fruit.
- Keep the flowers at room temperature.

COMMERCIAL HANDLING

- Do not place in the cool room.

GENERAL USE

Clethra has strong, green, long lasting foliage as well as variegated foliage and strong spiked white flowers. Clethra flowers can be used for a wide range of designs including corsages and posies, and are particularly suited to cascading designs. The florets can be wired individually for delicate work. These flowers look great in glass vases as the water will remain clear with the use of a preservative.

WEDDING USE

Clethra flowers have a sweet, spicy fragrance and are suitable for use in all types of bouquets, hairpieces and cake tops. They can be used with their stems, cut into sections or wired individually using the pierce and mount or hairpin method. They are especially suitable for bouquets with a cascading trail.

CORPORATE USE

Clethra flowers can be used for corporate designs. Clethra foliage is quite hardy and suitable for long lasting designs.

GROWING CONDITIONS

Clethra grows well in wet, sandy soil in swamps and woods. It must be planted in well-drained soil in gardens and should be watered regularly. Clethra grows into a tree up to two and a half metres tall.

HISTORY

Clethra is native to North America. The name Clethra translates from the Greek word 'alder' meaning 'tree'. 'Alder' is a translation from the term 'alnifolia'. There is a resemblance to the slightly obovate-shaped leaves to those of the genus, alnus.

CLIVIA *(klai-vee-a) Common names: Fire Lily; Cape Clivia; Kaffir Lily*

BOTANICAL VARIETIES Clivia miniata, Clivia nobilis (Cape Clivea) FAMILY NAME Amaryllidaceae (also known as Imantophyllums) NATURAL SEASON Late spring and summer COLOUR AVAILABILITY Yellow/orange, red and some tipped with green (other varieties have different colours) CUT FLOWER LIFE SPAN 7 days

GENERAL USE

Clivia miniata has yellow/orange trumpet flowers and Clivia nobilis has more tubular flowers that are orange tipped with green. Clivia stems are quite thick and are therefore not suited to use in floral foam, however they do look effective in bouquets and vases. If you cut the stem ends, running vertically upwards with a knife with several cuts around the stem, the ends will curl up in water. This can look effective in a glass vase. The flowers on the bush are followed by red berries. These are clusters and take almost a year to ripen. They can be used in modern designs.

WEDDING USE

Clivia can be used in hand-tied, natural stemmed bouquets or wired as single florets. Use the pierce and mount wiring method.

CORPORATE USE

Clivia flowers in half bud form can be used for corporate designs.

GROWING CONDITIONS

Clivia is a bulbous plant. It likes well-drained soil with plenty of humus and prefers a shady position. It is severely affected by frost. Clivia requires little water through winter and is a dependable plant. It can be separated to grow in other parts of the garden.

CARE AND HANDLING

- Cut or purchase when the first flowers of the cluster are showing colour.
- Using secateurs, cut 2–3 centimetres from the stem ends. Cut on an angle.
- Do not bash the stems.
- Use preservative.
- Clivia foliage can be cut and used with the flower in vases.

COMMERCIAL HANDLING

- Do not place in the cool room.

HISTORY

Clivia is native to South Africa. William Burchell, an English naturalist, first recorded the Clivia nobilis in the wild at the mouth of the Great Fish River in the Eastern Cape. James Bowie, a Kew (England) gardener and botanical collector, sent Clivia to England in the 1820s.

In 1828 the Kew botanist and horticulturalist John Lindley named Clivia in honour of Lady Charlotte Florentine Clive, the Duchess of Northumberland and the governess of Queen Victoria. Clivias were very popular in Victorian times.

The first yellow form of Clivia was discovered around 1888 in Zululand, by Mr W Watson.

CONOSPERMUM

(koh-no-spur-mum) Common names: Smoke Bush; Smoke Grass BOTANICAL VARIETIES Conospermum amoenum, Conospermum incurvum, Conospermum stoechadis, Conospermum crassinervium FAMILY Proteaceae NATURAL SEASON Spring and early summer COLOUR AVAILABILITY Grey/white CUT FLOWER LIFE SPAN 30 days

GENERAL USE

Conospermum is a very pretty native flower and it can be used in all types of floral designs.

WEDDING USE

Conospermum is delicate and can be used in all forms of bouquets.

CORPORATE USE

Conospermum can be used in corporate designs, although it will only last five days in an office environment.

GROWING CONDITIONS

Conospermum is a shrub-like plant that grows up to a metre in height. It is a member of the Protea family. It can be grown from summer cuttings and will grow in poor, gravel type soil. It is drought resistant and only needs water in extremely hot weather.

HISTORY

Conospermum is native to Australia.

CARE AND HANDLING

- Purchase bunches with flowers that appear fluffy. The fluffiness is an indication of freshness.
- Remove any leaves that will sit below the waterline.
- Recut 2–3 centimetres from the stem ends. Cut on an angle.
- Use preservative.
- Do not place in airconditioned environments.

COMMERCIAL HANDLING

- Do not place Conospermum in the cool room as it will mould easily.

CONSOLIDA

(kon-sol-i-da) Common names: Larkspur; Sweet Rocket

BOTANICAL VARIETIES Consolida ajacis, Consolida ambigua FAMILY Ranunculaceae NATURAL SEASON Spring and summer COLOUR AVAILABILITY Pink, blue, white, carmine, mauve and lilac CUT FLOWER LIFE SPAN 10 days (treated)

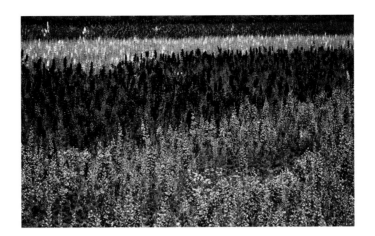

CARE AND HANDLING

- Look for strong stems with green foliage. One third of the flowers should be starting to open from the base.

- Purchase Consolida that has been STS-treated by the grower. It is very sensitive to ethylene and STS treatment prevents flower fall.

- Remove any foliage that will sit below the waterline.

- Recut 3–5 centimetres from the stem ends. Cut on an angle.

- Consolida must be placed in water immediately. If it dries the flowers will die.

- Use preservative.

- Always keep indoors and cool.

COMMERCIAL HANDLING

- Consolida can be kept in the cool room at temperatures of 6–8 degrees Celsius.

GENERAL USE

STS-treated Consolida can be used in all types of floral designs. If untreated, the flowers will fall within three days. This flower should not be placed in areas with central heating as it dries out easily. It will tolerate airconditioning but its life span will be shortened. Consolida flowers can give a traditional outline to an arrangement or a modern look to designs when used in clusters.

WEDDING USE

Use STS-treated Consolida in bouquet holders. If the flower spikes are too large then they can be cut into sections. The florets can be singularly wired, using the pierce and mount method and then wrapped with binding tape.

CORPORATE USE

Only STS-treated Consolida can be used for corporate designs. It will last up to three weeks.

GROWING CONDITIONS

Consolida likes well-fertilised alkaline soil and full sun. It should be planted in clumps. Use stakes to support the stems as these flowers are on spikes and will break in the wind. Give the plants extra feed when buds appear and deadhead them to prevent self seeding.

HISTORY

Consolida is native to southern Europe. The name comes from the Latin 'consilidare', which means 'to make whole'. It also refers to the medicinal qualities of the plant to heal wounds. The seeds are poisonous and the juice of the leaves was once used in herbal tonics. Consolida is a cousin of Dephinium.

CONVALLARIA

Common names: *Lily-of-the-Valley; European Lily-of-the-Valley*

BOTANICAL VARIETIES Convallaria majalis FAMILY Convallariaceae NATURAL SEASON Late spring COLOUR AVAILABILITY White and pink

CUT FLOWER LIFE SPAN 3–5 days

GENERAL USE

Convallaria is a delicate perfumed flower and it can be used in wired work. The stems should be wire supported through the florets (using very fine wire) or they can flop. These flowers can be used in bouquets with miniature roses. They also look pretty as vase flowers.

WEDDING USE

Convallaria was very popular in weddings for many decades up to the 1980s. It must be well-conditioned before use. Each stem must be wire-supported or the flower can droop. Use a fine wire. Hook the end and wind the wire down through the bell flowers. You can use a stronger wire to support the stem to use in a bouquet.

Convallarias are pleasantly perfumed. Traditionally this flower is used on its own or with Gardenias.

CORPORATE USE

For corporate designs Convallaria is best used in a bud vase at the front desk of an office. It will need to be removed by the third day. Its perfume is pleasant and it looks lovely, but is more of a treat than a reliable office flower.

GROWING CONDITIONS

Convallaria has running rootstock and pendulous flowers approximately 15 centimetres in length. It likes humus soil in indirect sunlight. It should be kept moist in a dim, warm spot until flower spikes appear, then moved to a brighter place. Cut back after flowering.

HISTORY

Native to all continents of the Northern Hemisphere, Convallaria is the very symbol of spring in many places. For the French, May Day would not be complete without the Convallaria fragrance.

CARE AND HANDLING

- Cut or purchase when the first terminal bell has lost its deep green colour.

- Recut 1 centimetre from the stem ends and place in water immediately after cutting.

- Use conditioning solution or preservative.

- Avoid placing it in heat, sunlight or draughty areas.

- If the heads droop, place the stems into ice water for one minute. They should revive. Alternatively, lay stems over ice.

COMMERCIAL HANDLING

- Convallaria can be kept in the cool room at temperatures of 6–8 degrees Celsius. It should not remain in the cool room for longer than 24 hours or else it will droop quickly on removal.

Romantic flower meaning: increased happiness

COREOPSIS *(ko-re-yop-sis) Common names: Tickseed; Sea Dahlia; Callopsis*

BOTANICAL VARIETIES Coreopsis lanceolata (there are more than 80 annuals and perennials in this genus) FAMILY Asteraceae NATURAL SEASON Spring and early summer COLOUR AVAILABILITY Yellow CUT FLOWER LIFE SPAN 5 days

CARE AND HANDLING

- Cut or purchase when all the flowers are fully open.
- Check the foliage. Any curled or discoloured leaves indicate age or damage.
- Remove any leaves that will sit below the waterline.
- Recut 2–3 centimetres from the stem ends. Cut on an angle.
- Use preservative or bleach in the vase water.
- Keep it cool.

COMMERCIAL HANDLING

- Coreopsis usually does not need to be kept in the cool room. However, if absolutely necessary, the temperature should be set at 8 degrees Celsius.

GENERAL USE

Coreopsis is a pretty posy flower with stem lengths of up to 60 centimetres. It is single stemmed and suited to lower designs such as table centrepieces. Coreopsis is not suitable for corporate designs as the flowers will dry out in heating or airconditioning.

GROWING CONDITIONS

Coreopsis is an annual and perennial plant. It self-sows and grows from a rosette of slender dark green leaves. It will grow in any soil condition.

HISTORY

Coreopsis is native to America. The genus Coreopsis is the state flower of Florida. It is a pest in the garden, but when controlled it provides a beautiful show of yellow flowers. This flower can be seen growing along the roadside in New South Wales.

CORNUS

(kor-nas) Common names: Dogwood; The Dogwood of America; Cornel

BOTANICAL VARIETIES Cornus sanguinea, Cornus florida (The Dogwood of America) FAMILY Cornaceae NATURAL SEASON Spring

COLOUR AVAILABILITY White, pink and reddish/green CUT FLOWER LIFE SPAN 5 days

GENERAL USE

Cornus flowers can be used in both traditional and modern designs. They add height and can help to achieve an informal look in most designs. Watch for correct proportion in the choice of vase or container – the height and width of the container should balance with the height of the flowers. Cornus features greyish stems that look very effective when displayed on their own. The flowers can also be used in dried form.

The branches can be used for decorating functions. Their life span is limited in floral foam so use on occasions where their life span beyond the function is not a consideration.

WEDDING USE

The single florets of Cornus can be used for fully-wired bouquets using the pierce and mount wiring method.

CORPORATE USE

Cornus stems and branches can be used in corporate designs. The flowers should not be used as they will dry out.

GROWING CONDITIONS

Cornus flowers are not common in Australia but do feature in some Australian gardens. They enjoy cool conditions and grow in well-drained, humus soil. They lose their leaves in autumn. Cornus florida bears purple tinged, white petals which gives the flower an overall pinkish appearance. The bracts are the distinctive feature of this flower. Cornus sanguinea has creamy white, four-petalled flowers that are succeeded by black berries after flowering. The berries are bitter tasting.

HISTORY

Cornus is native to Japan, China and North America. The Dogwood variety was introduced into Britain in 1783.

The wood of the Cornus is very hard and previously arrows were made from it. In France it was also used to make skewers.

Cornus florida is the state flower of Virginia.

CARE AND HANDLING

- Cut or purchase branches when approximately half of the flowers are open. The buds should be firm and plump. Yellow leaves are a sign of age.

- Recut stems on a sharp angle using secateurs.

- The stems can be mildly crushed but do not bash them.

- Keep cool at all times.

- Always use a preservative. This will assist in maintaining the flowers.

- Replace the vase water daily and add new preservative to increase the flowers' life span.

COMMERCIAL HANDLING

- Do not place in the cool room.

CORTADERIA

(kor-ta-deer-ee-ya) Common names: *Pampas Grass*
BOTANICAL VARIETIES Cordaderia selloana FAMILY Poaceae NATURAL SEASON Autumn and winter COLOUR AVAILABILITY White/cream, pink, cream
CUT FLOWER LIFE SPAN Up to 4 weeks

Note: although Pampas is a grass, it has been included in the directory as it is popular in floral designs.

CARE AND HANDLING

- Cut or purchase when the flowers are tight and not fluffy in appearance.
- Cortaderia foliage has a razor edge so handle with care.
- Do not place near heating or air-conditioning ducts as the flower can seed and separate. It will filter across a room with seeds flying everywhere.

COMMERCIAL HANDLING

- Cortaderia flowers can be sprayed with hairspray to avoid flower shatter.

GENERAL USE

Cortaderia looks great when displayed in tall vases. It is ideal for adding height to designs. It can also be dried.

WEDDING USE

Cortaderia may seem an unlikely choice for wedding use but if fine sections are 'feathered' or split from the pampas, it can be used in all types of wedding work. It can look very delicate and can be coloured with floral spray colours.

CORPORATE USE

Cortaderia can be used in corporate work. The flowers can be sprayed with floral spray colours to change or blush the colour of the blooms. The flowers can also be misted with hairspray to prevent them from bursting.

GROWING CONDITIONS

Cortaderia will grow just about anywhere, although it grows best in well-drained soil. The plant grows into large clumps that can be separated in spring. If garden size allows it, this plant can be burnt to the ground to control its size.

HISTORY

Cortaderia is native to North America. It was traditionally popular in Victorian parlours. In Australia it is listed as a noxious weed as its seeds spread quite rapidly.

COSMOS *(kos-mos) Common names: Mexican Aster; Bidens*

BOTANICAL VARIETIES Cosmos bipennatus, Cosmos sulphureus, Cosmos Sstrosanguineus FAMILY Asteraceae NATURAL SEASON Summer and early autumn COLOUR AVAILABILITY Yellow and orange, chocolate brown, pink, white, crimson CUT FLOWER LIFE SPAN 5–7 days

GENERAL USE

Cosmos is used mainly as a posy flower or a filler flower in arrangements. The colours are vibrant and eye-catching and the leaves are very fine and fern-like. Cosmos is not suitable for use for corporate designs as it will dry out.

WEDDING USE

Cosmos flowers can be used in bouquet holders with a water source. Do not use around the perimeter as they can bruise easily.

GROWING CONDITIONS

Cosmos grows best in full sun. It grows quickly in any soil, but especially in soil that is slightly dry. Apply heavy mulch in winter. Taller varieties may need staking. Annual varieties of Cosmos can be propagated from seed and perennial varieties from basal cuttings. Do not overfeed as they can become top heavy.

HISTORY

Cosmos is native to Mexico. Cosmos is the Greek word for harmony, or 'ordered universe'. Spanish priests planted Cosmos in their mission gardens in Mexico.

CARE AND HANDLING

- Cut or purchase when the flowers are showing colour. The flowers' centres should be tight and not showing pollen.

- Remove the flowers from their packaging immediately and separate the stems.

- Remove all foliage.

- Recut 2–3 centimetres from the stem ends. Cut on an angle.

- Use preservative.

- Keep the flowers cool but not in airconditioned environments.

COMMERCIAL HANDLING

- Cosmos can be kept in the cool room at temperatures of 6–8 degrees Celsius.

COTONEASTER (ko-toh-nee-yas-ta) Common names: Rock Spray; Berries

BOTANICAL VARIETIES Cotoneaster salicifolius FAMILY Rosaceae NATURAL SEASON Spring to summer (followed with ornamental fruit and berries in autumn) COLOUR AVAILABILITY Shades of pink and white with red berries CUT FLOWER LIFE SPAN 3 days for flowers and up to 2 weeks for berries

CARE AND HANDLING

- Cut or purchase when the flowers are showing colour and if using the berries make sure they are tight on the stem.

- Remove any yellow leaves.

- Recut 2–3 centimetres from the woody stems. Cut on an angle.

- Use preservative.

- Do not use in airconditioned environments.

- The foliage lasts well and if the berries are fresh they will last for up to a week before falling.

COMMERCIAL HANDLING

- Do not place in the cool room.

GENERAL USE

The small white flowers of Cotoneaster are of very limited use in floral work as their life span is short and they will fall; however, the berries that follow have a range of uses. The flowers can be used for decorating a function the day of picking.

The foliage is very hardy and it can be used in corsages, bridal work and in general arrangements. The berries can be wired singularly or arranged on stems. They will drop, but this can be prevented by gluing wire into the berry with floral glue.

GROWING CONDITIONS

Cotoneaster is suited to a wide range of soil types and situations. Well-drained soil is preferable. Cotoneaster is extremely hardy.

HISTORY

Cotoneaster is native to China and the Himalayas.

CROCOSMIA *(krok-oz-mee-a) Common names: Montbretia; Falling Stars* BOTANICAL VARIETIES Crocosmia crocosmiiflora (Falling Stars), Crocosmia masoniorum FAMILY Iridaceae NATURAL SEASON Spring and summer COLOUR AVAILABILITY Red, yellow and orange CUT FLOWER LIFE SPAN Up to 7 days

GENERAL USE

Crocosmia is available with stem lengths of up to 80 centimetres. The flowers and foliage can be used to create natural floral designs. Remove spent flowers as they age.

Crocosmias develop seed pods in early autumn and these can also be used in floral work. The foliage can be split as well as curled.

GROWING CONDITIONS

The foliage of this flower is similar to Agapanthus and Gladiolus. They grow wild in unkept gardens and can be seen growing by the roadside in some parts of Australia. Set the corms out in winter in rich, well-drained soil, in a spot that gets the morning sun. Water reguarlly in summer to achieve the best flowering result.

HISTORY

Crocosmia is native to South Africa.

CARE AND HANDLING

- Cut or purchase when the lower buds are showing colour.

- Shake the stems and avoid those where flowers drop off.

- Recut 2–3 centimetres from the stem ends. Cut on an angle.

- Use a preservative in the water.

- Crocosmia is very sensitive to ethylene so keep it away from cigarette smoke and ripening fruit.

- To prevent flower fall keep it out of airconditioned environments.

COMMERCIAL HANDLING

- Crocosmia can be kept in the cool room at temperatures of 6–8 degrees Celsius.

CROCUS (kroh-kuss) Common names: Meadow Saffron; Saffron Crocus; Dutch Crocus

BOTANICAL VARIETIES Crocus tommasinianus, Crocus vernus FAMILY Iridaceae NATURAL SEASON Early spring COLOUR AVAILABILITY Mauve, white, cream, wine purple (Crocus vernus is available in blue, beige and mauve with striped bi-colours) CUT FLOWER LIFE SPAN 4–5 days

CARE AND HANDLING

- Cut or purchase when blooms are showing colour.
- Recut 2 centimetres from the stem ends. Cut on an angle.
- Use preservative.
- Keep it cool, away from heating and airconditioning.

COMMERCIAL HANDLING

- Crocus can be kept in the cool room at temperatures of 4–6 degrees Celsius.

GENERAL USE

Crocus flowers are usually not purchased commercially. They can be used as a cut flower in small designs. The colour is strong yet delicate and the form of the flower is very attractive.

GROWING CONDITIONS

These delicate, pretty flowers pop out of the ground and their leaves follow after the flowers starts to die back. The flowers will even appear through melting snow. They enjoy well-drained, leaf-rich soil. If spring is hot, the corms will not form for the ensuing year of flowering.

HISTORY

Crocus is native to the Mediterranean region. Saffron Crocus (Crocus sativus) was a source for dye and medicine in the Middle Ages. The dye is sourced from the dried stigmas of the flowers. Italian women would dye their hair with saffron to give blonde locks, like those of Northern Europe and Scandinavia. In 1591 Christopher Colton discovered that Saffron benefited health and happiness.

Romantic flower meaning: spring; youthful gladness

CROWEA (kroh-wee-ya)

BOTANICAL VARIETIES Crowea exalata, Crowea saligna FAMILY Rutaceae NATURAL SEASON Summer and autumn COLOUR AVAILABILITY Pink and white CUT FLOWER LIFE SPAN Up to 7 days

GENERAL USE

Crowea can be used in many styles of floral design. Its life span is limited so use it in floral work for special occasions where longevity is not a consideration.

GROWING CONDITIONS

Crowea will grow from hardwood cuttings struck in peat and sand mixture. Plant in late summer or early autumn. Crowea is related to Boronia but does not flower at the same time and its flowers are not perfumed.

HISTORY

Crowea is native to Australia. Homesick settlers in Australia's early colonial days referred to this flower as the 'Native Rose'. It is not related to the Rose, but its leaves are aromatic.

CARE AND HANDLING

- Cut or purchase when flowers are in coloured bud or half open. The flowers will drop if they are older.

- Recut 2–3 centimetres from the stem ends. Cut on an angle.

- Remove any leaves that will sit below the waterline.

- Use preservative to assist the buds to open and help maintain open flowers.

COMMERCIAL HANDLING

- Do not place in the cool room.

CYCLAMEN

(si-kla-men) Common names: Alpine Violet; Sowbread BOTANICAL VARIETIES Cyclamen persicum (there are 19 species belonging to the Cyclamen family) FAMILY Primulaceae NATURAL SEASON Winter and spring COLOUR AVAILABILITY all colours and variegations CUT FLOWER LIFE SPAN Up to 5 days

Romantic flower meaning: diffidence

CARE AND HANDLING

- Cut when flowers are showing colour.
- Use preservative.
- Mist occasionally.
- Keep it away from direct sunlight, heating and airconditioning.

COMMERCIAL HANDLING

- There is no need to place Cyclamen in the cool room.

GENERAL USE

Cylamen is generally thought of as a potted plant. It can be used in potted arrangements where a bowl is placed into a ceramic dish or a basket base and a selection of potted plants are arranged with cut flowers in foam in the central dish.

As a cut flower, Cyclamen can be used in bud vases. The leaves can be used in floral designs. They need a vein wire support.

WEDDING USE

Cyclamen can be used in all types of bouquets as long as their stems are wire supported. Bouquet holders with a water source are an ideal base. Use with caution in fully wired bouquets if it is a warm day as the flower may collapse. Cyclamen flowers can also be used in other forms of wedding work if they are wired internally. The leaves look very elegant when teamed with Phalaenopsis Orchids.

Unlike some other white wedding flowers, white Cyclamens look white, not cream, against a white gown.

CORPORATE USE

For corporate designs Cyclamen is best placed in pots rather than arranged in a vase.

GROWING CONDITIONS

Cyclamen is best grown in pots with gritty compost and chalk or limestone for drainage. It is grown from fleshy circular tubers. In the garden it can be planted under trees. Do not water potted cyclamen from the top as this will rot the corms. It is best to place the pot in a saucer or pot base with water added so that it can drink from the roots. Cyclamen usually dies back after flowering.

HISTORY

Cyclamen persicum is native to Asia minor, Israel and the Greek Islands.

CYTISUS *(sit-iss-as) Common names: Broom; White Spanish Broom; Bridal Veil Broom*

BOTANICAL VARIETIES Cytisus multiflorus (White Spanish Broom) FAMILY Fabaceae NATURAL SEASON Spring and early summer COLOUR AVAILABILITY White, pink, yellow and deep red CUT FLOWER LIFE SPAN 5–7 days

GENERAL USE

Cytisus is a delicate looking flower that is best used in modern designs.

WEDDING USE

Cytisus is lovely in all types of wedding bouquets, although it is best suited to bouquet holders that have a constant water source. The Bridal Veil Broom variety has beautiful weeping branches.

Cytisus is ideal for creating cascades in table centrepieces, and service and reception arrangements. Do not use it when the florets are fully open as they can collapse.

CORPORATE USE

Cytisus can be used in corporate designs but will dry quickly in airconditioned environments.

GROWING CONDITIONS

Cytisus will grow in slightly acidic soil, even if the soil is of poor quality. The plant grows upright and develops into an arching habit. Most varieties of Cytisus are evergreen shrubs. Keep the plant moist during flowering. A sunny position will provide the best display of flowers. Spent flowers and shoots should be removed after flowering.

HISTORY

Cytisus is native to the Mediterranean and the Atlantic Islands.

CARE AND HANDLING

- Cut or purchase when the lower buds are showing colour.
- Recut 2–3 centimetres from the stem ends. Cut on an angle.
- Remove any foliage that will sit below the waterline.
- Use preservative.

COMMERCIAL HANDLING

- Do not place in the cool room.

DACTYLORHIZA

(dat-til-oh-rai-za) Common names: Marsh Orchid; Hyacinth Orchid; Spotted Orchid BOTANICAL VARIETIES Dactylorhiza elata (Marsh Orchid) Dactylorhiza foliosa, Dactylorhiza fuchsii (Spotted Orchid) FAMILY Orchidaceae NATURAL SEASON Spring to summer COLOUR AVAILABILITY Dark pink, red/violet. CUT FLOWER LIFE SPAN 7–14 days

CARE AND HANDLING

- Cut or purchase when the lower flowers are showing colour.
- Remove all leaves that will be below the water line.
- Recut 2–3 centimetres from the stem ends. Cut on an angle.
- Preservative is optional.
- Remove lower blooms as they will emit ethylene as they die.
- Do not place in heated or airconditioned environments.

COMMERCIAL HANDLING

- Do not place in the cool room.

GENERAL USE

Dactylorhiza flowers are strong in colour and form. They are best used in home decorations but can also be used in gift floral items and bouquets. Remove the lower flowers as they die off to prevent ethylene emissions, affecting the other blooms.

GROWING CONDITIONS

These Hyacinth-looking orchids grow best in cool conditions. They like shaded positions in rich, moist, slightly limey soil. They do not like to be moved, but if necessary they can be replanted in autumn. Their spikes can grow up to 60 centimetres. Propagation is by division.

HISTORY

Dactylorhiza is native to south-western Europe and Algeria.

DAHLIA *(dah-eel-a)*

BOTANICAL VARIETIES Dahlia pinnata, Dahlia hybrid cultivars FAMILY Asteraceae NATURAL SEASON Summer COLOUR AVAILABILITY Wide range CUT FLOWER LIFE SPAN 5–7 days

GENERAL USE

Commercially-grown Dahlia stems are sometimes scalded or burned by the grower to force out air blockages (embolisms) in the stem. When recutting the flowers, at home, look for a scald line on the stem and cut below it. If the flowers flag then this means the embolism has travelled further up the stem, and you may need to recut the stems again, above the scald line. If this is necessary, you will need to re-scald or sear the stem ends with a naked flame. Always follow occupational health and safety guidelines while doing this.

Dahlias are very attractive vase flowers for the home. They are related to the Chrysanthemum family. Florists use Dahlia flowers for wreath and funeral designs as they have a solid surface area and are available in an array of strong colours. They are not suited to hospital floral displays as they dislike heating and airconditioning.

The Cactus varieties last well as a cut flower for arrangements. In large floral displays such as church, synagogue or reception venue arrangements, Dahlias are an excellent filling flower due to their lovely colours and size.

Dahlias are available in many shapes; anemone flowered, ball, cactus, collarette, decorative, miscellaneous, pompon, semi-cactus, single-flowered and waterlily.

WEDDING USE

The smaller sized Pompom Dahlia varieties are suited to hand-held bouquets and bouquet holders. Their heads will need wire support. Some white Pompom Dahlias are lightly perfumed and delicate in appearance. Some varieties are blushed with another colour.

CARE AND HANDLING

- Cut or purchase when the flowers are showing colour. The outer petals should be open but the centres should be very tight. Tight buds may not open at all.

- Recut 2–3 centimetres from the stem ends. Cut on an angle.

- Remove any foliage that will sit under the waterline.

- Use preservative.

- Do not place in direct sunlight.

- Make sure the stems have plenty of room in the vase. Dahlia leaves will die before the flowers and if the stems don't have enough air circulating around them, the dead leaves will rot and infect the stems.

- If Dahlias flag, they may be revived by placing the stems in boiling water for 1–2 minutes and then transferring them into cool water. Their life span will have already diminished at this stage, but this process may help to revive them for a few more days.

COMMERCIAL HANDLING

- Dahlia can be kept in the cool room at temperatures of 6–8 degrees Celsius.

Romantic flower meaning: changeable

CORPORATE USE

The Pompom varieties are suited to office designs, as long as the heads are wire-supported. They may start to dry around the edges by the end of the week. The vase water should be changed mid-week. Use bleach in the water as well as preservative.

GROWING CONDITIONS

Dahlia should be planted in soil that is conditioned deeply with fertiliser or sand (if the soil is heavy). The flowers will need support as they grow so place stakes near where Dahlias are planted. The tubers are normally lifted after flowering and stored for winter in cool, dry water. A miniature Dahlia, called Hi Dolly, is a popular border or it can be grown in baskets.

HISTORY

Dahlia is native to Mexico and it is the country's national flower. It is named after the Swedish botanist, Dr Andreas Dahl. Dahlias were known and used by the Aztecs as a treatment for epilepsy. In later years, specialists turned to the Dahlia for other medicinal reasons. Before insulin was discovered, diabetics were given a substance called Atlantic Starch or diabetic sugar, which was made from Dahlia tubers.

The Dahlia flower first reached Europe in 1789 through Vincent Cervantes, superintendent of the Botanical Gardens of Mexico.

DAPHNE

(daf-nee) Common names: Garland Flower

BOTANICAL VARIETIES Daphne odora (pink), Daphne blagayayana (cream/white), Daphne laureola (lime), Daphne cneorum (bright pink) FAMILY Thymelaeaceae NATURAL SEASON Winter and spring COLOUR AVAILABILITY white flower tinged pink, white, bright pink and lime CUT FLOWER LIFE SPAN 5 days

CARE AND HANDLING

- Cut or purchase when the small wax-like flowers are at least three-quarters open. The flowers should be perfumed.

- Cut 1–2 centimetres from the stem ends. Cut on an angle using secateurs.

- Once cut, the stem ends can be gently split, but do not bash them.

- Remove any leaves that will sit below the waterline.

- Place the stems in cool water.

- Preservative is essential.

- Keep it cool.

- The sap is poisonous if consumed.

COMMERCIAL HANDLING

- Daphne can be refrigerated at temperatures of 4–6 degrees Celsius.

GENERAL USE

Daphne is very attractive as a specimen vase flower. Its perfume is delightful. It can be purchased in short-stemmed bunches, although some florists do not stock it as it is not used widely in floristry. It will not last out of water and therefore its commercial use is limited. Spent flowers will fall.

Daphne cannot be used in wired work, although it can be used in floral foam and as a feature on wreaths. There is a variety of Daphne with variegated leaves and this foliage can be used as a posy base. All varieties of Daphne are suitable in unwired floral work with an adequate water source.

WEDDING USE

Daphne is highly perfumed, so use with caution for hayfever or asthma sufferers. The flowers can be used in bouquet holders but cannot be wired.

CORPORATE USE

Daphne flowers look lovely when placed at a reception desk, but their life span is limited to three or four days.

GROWING CONDITIONS

Daphne is a hardy plant. It needs well-drained, humus rich soil that does not dry out. It grows best in neutral to alkaline soil. Mulch the plant to keep the roots cool in summer and use a small amount of fertiliser after flowering. It grows best in a semi-shaded position. Propagate by seed or by cuttings or layers. Daphne is often planted near house entry points for the scent to waft into the home.

HISTORY

Daphne is said to originate from western China. It is native to Europe, North Africa and parts of Asia. It is documented that Daphne grew in Chinese gardens over a thousand years ago.

DELPHINIUM

(del-fin-ee-yum) Common names: Candle Larkspur

BOTANICAL VARIETIES Delphinium grandiflorum, Delphinium hybrid cultivars FAMILY Ranunculaceae NATURAL SEASON Late winter, spring and early summer (it is also now widely grown out of season) COLOUR AVAILABILITY Purple, mauve, blue, pink, white, red, lemon CUT FLOWER LIFE SPAN up to 3 weeks with STS treatment, 3 days without treatment

GENERAL USE

Delphinium is a very adaptable flower and it is used in all areas of floristry. It has hollow stems and you may need to make a hole in floral foam to avoid putting pressure on the stems when you insert them into the foam.

These flowers are popular as backing flowers to give height and visual strength to a design. They can also be cut into sections and used as a filling medium in arrangements. The smaller Butterfly varieties are popular in commercial floristry. The single florets can be used in wired work (corsage, hairpiece, bridal) in early spring, in cooler climates.

Delphinium can be dried if hung upside down. Do this when all flowers are just open. Untreated Delphinium can be turned upside down and sprayed with hairspray. This will help the flowers to last longer before dropping petals.

WEDDING USE

The single florets of Delphinium can be used in wired work including hairpieces and corsages. Use the pierce and wiring method. Do not use these flowers on a hot day as they may not last.

CORPORATE USE

STS-treated Delphinium will last up to three weeks if right water levels are maintained.

GROWING CONDITIONS

Delphinium enjoys full sun, out of the reach of strong winds. Staking will prevent breakage. The plant must have good drainage. It revels in lime and requires deep soil that is rich in manure. Do not let it dry out in summer. Using chemical fertilisers in natural seasons will prolong flowering.

Many varieties have poisonous leaves, but this won't deter slugs – the plants are prone to slug attacks, especially in spring.

CARE AND HANDLING

- Cut or purchase when the stems are strong and fully supportive of the flower weight. Make sure at least one third of the lower flowers are open.

- Delphinium that is STS-treated by the grower will last longer as a cut flower.

- Avoid spikes with hooked tips.

- Untreated Delphiniums can be lightly misted to prevent them from drying out.

- Recut 2–3 centimetres from the stem ends. Cut on a sharp angle. Do not bash the stem ends.

- Place into cold water with preservative.

- Make sure the there is plenty of airflow around the flowers.

- Untreated Delphinium flowers are ethylene sensitive and will not last long in airconditioned environments, their petals will drop.

- Do not place Delphinium in direct sunlight or draughty areas.

COMMERCIAL HANDLING

- Try to avoid placing Delphinium in the cool room, but if needed the temperature should be 6–8 degrees Celcius.

- The foliage will rot quickly and mould if left bunched tightly.

- When removed from the cool room allow time for the flowers to acclimatise.

The Delphinium elatum varieties need frequent renewal as old plants tend to deteriorate. Delphinium can be grown from seed or cuttings.

HISTORY

Delphinium has been cultivated in the countries around the Mediterranean since ancient times. Ancestors of these flowers came mainly from China. It is named from the Latin 'delphus' or the Greek word 'delphinion', meaning 'dolphin'.

The Egyptians believed Delphinium seeds had the ability to fight off body vermin. Greeks and Romans were first interested in this flower as its medicinal properties were said to be an antidote for scorpion bites. The juice of the flowers, mixed with alum was also used to make blue ink. Delphinium contains an alkaloid called Delphinidin. This is very toxic and can cause vomiting when eaten.

It was not until the 16th century that Delphiniums were grown for their beauty. In the language of flowers, Delphinium means 'fun and enjoyment' whilst the Larkspur variety means 'lightness' or 'an open heart'.

DIANTHUS

Common names: Carnation; Pinks; Gillyflower; Sweet William; Sim; Spray; Chinensini; Egan; Micro; Indian Pink BOTANICAL VARIETIES Dianthus caryophyllus (Sim and Spray) Dianthus chinensis (Chinensini), Dianthus barbatus (Sweet William) (300 or so species in this genus) FAMILY Caryophyllaceae NATURAL SEASON Grown all year round (although volume decreases in winter) COLOUR AVAILABILITY Wide range of colours and variegations CUT FLOWER LIFE SPAN 2–3 weeks

GENERAL USE

Dianthus are one of the world's most popular flowers. They were unfashionable through the 1990s, but are now making a comeback. They are available in fantastic colours and are perfumed. Dianthus is suited to all aspects of flower design. When there are several blooms to one stem, they are known as 'sprays'. They last very well as a cut flower.

WEDDING USE

Dianthus flowers are suitable for all wedding uses. They can be split or 'feathered' into tiny flowers for delicate wedding designs such as hairpieces and tiaras. Spray Carnations are smaller in form than standard Carnations. They will last on the hottest of days. Micro-carnations are very small and delicate for bridal work.

CORPORATE USE

Dianthus is suited to corporate designs and is very resilient, although the Sweet William variety will have some dead heads by the end of the week. A wide range of colours and varieties are available. These flowers are very hardy if conditioned correctly.

GROWING CONDITIONS

Dianthus thrives in neutral, sandy to alkaline soil with a little lime. It enjoys full sun. Feed regularly to promote excellent flowering. Pinching the buds will produce bushier growth. Dianthus can be grown from cuttings in winter, from healthy side shoots and can be potted when the roots form and then planted out in late spring.

The most popular of the annuals is the Dianthus chinensis (Indian Pink). The Sim Carnation variety features a larger flower. This is obtained by pinching the buds so that the nourishment and strength goes to one bloom only rather than several.

Dianthus is prone to rust as well as thrips, aphids and caterpillars.

CARE AND HANDLING:

- Cut or purchase when the flowers are in half-bud form with petals that are not curling inwards.

- Check for grey-looking film or slime on the stems – this indicates age.

- The sap is poisonous so wear gloves when handling.

- Recut 2–3 centimetres from the stem ends. Cut on an angle, above the node (the nobbly joint in the stem). The flowers will drink better if the cut is above the node.

- Stem length for sims (large heads) is up to 80 centimetres.

- Remove any foliage that will sit below the waterline.

- Field carnation stems should be washed so that any loose particles of dirt are removed.

- Watch for rust damage in the node area. It can make stems brittle.

- Change water with preservative every 3–4 days.

- Dianthus are ethylene sensitive and are usually STS-treated by the grower.

COMMERCIAL HANDLING

- Dianthus can be placed in the cool room at 6 degrees Celcius but this is usually not necessary. Cool room placement can increase the risk of fungal diseases.

Romantic flower meaning; bravery (Sweet William); my poor heart (Carnation Deep Red); refusal (Striped); disdain (Yellow)

HISTORY

Dianthus flowers are native to southern Europe and the Mediterranean region. The first record of cultivated Dianthus dates from 1460 in Spain.

Dianthus is the flower of Zeus, the Greek god of the sun. The ancient Greeks held the flower as sacred and many called it the 'heavenly flower'. They used this name to describe the annual and perennial Carnations and Pinks.

Dianthus caryophyllus is the forerunner of the modern Carnation. It was brought to England at the time of the Norman conquests and Carnations have been sold in England since the 16th century. The name Carnation refers to the use for them as coronary garlands. The English names of 'Sops in Wine' and 'Gillyflower' refer to the practise of using petals in wine and ale for the purpose of adding perfume and flavour.

Pink coloured carnations were in fact not bred commercially until the 19th century.

In the Language of Flowers a pink carnation stands for 'woman's love', yellow means 'disdain' and a red carnation means 'divine love'.

DIGITALIS *(di-ji-tah-lis) Common names: Foxglove; Thimble Flower*

BOTANICAL VARIETIES Digitalis purpurea (around 20 species in this genus) FAMILY Scrophulariaceae NATURAL SEASON Spring and early summer COLOUR AVAILABILITY White, cream, yellow, magenta, purple, lavender, yellow and pink (also spotted yellow or white throats) CUT FLOWER LIFE SPAN 5–7 days

GENERAL USE

Digitalis is a nice vase flower with an excellent colour range. It is suited to decorating functions where their life span beyond the function is not a consideration. It is a limited flower for commercial usage as the lower florets need to be removed. Do not use in corporate designs.

GROWING CONDITIONS

Digitalis prefers temperate and cool climates, but will grow in warm areas if given light shade. It likes well-drained soil that has been enriched with compost before planting.

Seeds should be sown in late summer or early autumn. Keep the seedlings frost free. Water regularly and remove spent flowers to prolong blooming. If the main stem is cut it will develop secondary spikes. Digitalis will self seed.

HISTORY

Digitalis is native to western Europe and is a common wildflower in the woods of northern Europe. It was first cultivated in Switzerland in 1830. In Latin, 'digitus' means 'a finger'. The flower name originated in Greek mythology when the goddess Flora slipped the bell-shaped flowers over her fingers.

The dried leaves contain medicinal properties called cardiac glycosides and they are used in conjunction with heart complaints especially regulating the heart rate. Herbalists use Digitalis for fever and liver complaints.

In New Zealand Digitalis is classed as a noxious weed.

CARE AND HANDLING

- Cut or purchase when at least one-third of the florets are open.

- Wear gloves when handling. All parts of Digitalis are toxic.

- Recut at least 2–3 centimetres from the stem ends. Cut on an angle.

- Remove all leaves that will sit below the waterline.

- Use preservative to assist the remaining florets to open.

- Digitalis need conditioning time (let them sit in water and preservative) to test their strength before us in floral foam.

- Remove spent florets as they emit ethylene and will affect the life span of the stems if left on.

- Do not place in airconditioned environments as this will dry the leaves quickly.

COMMERCIAL HANDLING

- Separate bunches to create airflow around the stems.

- Refrigerate at 6–8 degrees Celsius if needed.

Romantic flower meaning: insincerity

DIPSACUS

(dip-sa-kas) Common names: Teasel; Fuller's Teasel

BOTANICAL VARIETIES Dipsacus fullonum, Dipsacus sativus (Fuller's Teasel) FAMILY Dipsacaceae NATURAL SEASON Spring COLOUR AVAILABILITY Tiny, massed white or mauve pink flowers CUT FLOWER LIFE SPAN 4 weeks (for heads with flowers removed)

GENERAL USE

Dipsacus heads can be used in fresh or dried arrangements. Mauve Dipsacus is popular in fresh arrangements. Dipsacus is also purchased in dried, beige coloured, clustered heads on 60 centimetre stems. Remove the thorns on the stem with a rose stripper or a knife.

The flowers can be purchased already coloured or you can use floral spray colours to add any colour to the surface. Dried Teasels can be used with fresh flowers in water. The stems will not deteriorate easily.

WEDDING USE

Dipsacus flowers suit native arrangements with Banksias, Smoke Bush and Leucandendrons. They can be used on stems or wired and coloured with floral spray paints.

CORPORATE USE

Dried Dipsacus is ideal for use in corporate designs.

GROWING CONDITIONS

Dipsacus is a biennial plant and is raised from seed. It is easily cultivated in temperate climates. It prefers moist humus soil and should be watered regularly.

HISTORY

Dipsacus is native to Europe. Teasels were once used in the textile industry to remove raised pile from finished woollen cloth (because the bracts are hooked they are ideal for this process). Teasels are still used in this manner today on the very best fabrics. This process is better than any machine.

CARE AND HANDLING

- Remove from plastic sleeves.
- Remove the thorns from the stems for easier handling.
- Recut 2–3 centimetres from the stem ends.

COMMERCIAL HANDLING

- Dipsacus can be kept in the cool room at temperatures of 6–8 degrees Celsius.

DORYANTHES (dor-ree-yan-thas) Common names: Gymea Lily; Spear Lily; Giant Lily

BOTANICAL VARIETIES Doryanthes excelsa FAMILY Doryanthaceae SEASONAL AVAILABILITY Spring and summer COLOUR AVAILABILITY Red CUT FLOWER LIFE SPAN Up to 10 days

CARE AND HANDLING

- Cut or purchase when the red buds are beginning to open and extend out from the top of the stem.

- Avoid any bunches with dry heads or very tight flowers.

- Recut 5–6 centimetres from the stem ends using a knife or a saw. Cut on a sharp angle.

- Use preservative and change the water every 2–3 days.

- Keep them out of direct sunlight.

- Break off each flower as it dies.

- Doryanthes flowers are very thirsty drinkers so keep the water level topped up.

COMMERCIAL HANDLING

- Do not place in the cool room.

GENERAL USE

Doryanthes spikes grow up to three metres in height. They are mainly used in decorating, as they have fabulous height and a strong look.

GROWING CONDITIONS

Doryanthes is slow growing and often does not flower for up to ten years. It likes moist soil and a semi-shaded position. It can be propagated by seed or by separation or division of the suckers.

HISTORY

Doryanthes is native to Australia, in particular to the sandstone country of the Sydney Basin and northern New South Wales. In the Lake Macquarie district of New South Wales in 1836, Aborigines were observed roasting the stems, which were of arm thickness. They were also seen roasting the roots and these were used to make a cake-like substance. 'Gymea', meaning 'giant lily', was the name given to Doryanthes by the Aborigines.

In 1800 John William Lewin (1770–1819) was the first free artist to visit the colony of New South Wales. In 1801 he visited the Hunter Valley on two separate expeditions and painted the Gymea Lily. This painting, titled 'The Gigantic Lyllie of New South Wales', hangs in the Art Gallery of New South Wales. Two other studies hang in the Mitchell Library.

DRYANDRA

(drai-yan-dra) Common names: *Bush Rose*

BOTANICAL VARIETIES Dryandra formosa, also known as Showy Dryandra (from 2007 it is known as Banksia Formosa), Dryandra polycephala, Dryandra quercifolia (most popular variety as a cut flower), Dryandra praemorsa FAMILY Proteaceae NATURAL SEASON Late winter and spring COLOUR AVAILABILITY Yellow, yellow/green, yellow/orange CUT FLOWER LIFE SPAN up to 4 weeks

GENERAL USE

Dryandra flowers are adaptable to most designs. They are related to the Banksia family and arrange well with Banksia flowers.

Dryandra flowers can be dried. The foliage will become faded and brittle but the colour remains on the flowers.

WEDDING USE

Dryandra flowers can be used with native flowers for strong, textured bouquets, or with softer flowers where Dryandras will contrast. They can be wired using the pierce and mount method, or used in bouquet holders or other wired designs, including corsages.

CORPORATE USE

Dryandra holds well in corporate designs. It si a heavy drinker so use a sensible container that can hold lots of water.

GROWING CONDITIONS

Most Dryandra varieties will only grow in dry heat and sandy soil and dislike lime in the soil. They are evergreen. Dryandras need their own space in the garden. They are propagated from seed and they must be sheltered.

Dryandra polycephala can be grown in all soil conditions. The seeds of this plant are only released when the plant dies, or in the event of a bushfire. The leaves are saw-toothed with golden flower heads.

HISTORY

Dryandra is native to Australia. The genus Dryandra (family Proteacea) was named by the explorer/botanist Robert Brown in honour of the Swedish botanist Jonas Dryander, the first librarian of the Linnean society in London and curator of Joseph Banks' collections. The first European collector of Dryandra was Archibald Menzies in 1791. By 1827 English nurseries were propagating plants of this genus from seed.

CARE AND HANDLING

- Cut or purchase when the flowers have swelled, but the stamens have not yet popped out.

- Dryandras are prickly, so wear gloves.

- Remove any leaves that will sit below the waterline (their deterioration is slow, but it is best to remove).

- Recut 2–3 centimetres from the stem ends using sharp secateurs. Cut on an angle.

- Use preservative to keep the flowers looking fresh and assist the buds to open.

- Keep cool at all times.

- Replace the vase water and preservative every 3–4 days and top up the vase water daily.

COMMERCIAL HANDLING

- Do not place Dryandra in the cool room.

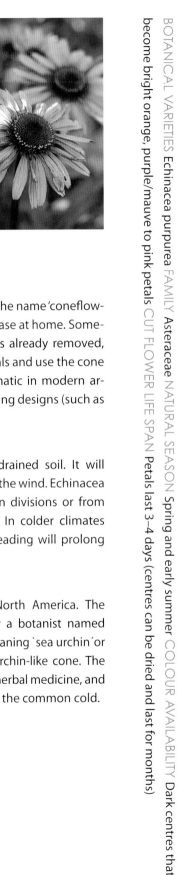

ECHINACEA

(ek-in-a-see-ya) Common names: Purple Coneflower; Coneflower

BOTANICAL VARIETIES Echinacea purpurea FAMILY Asteraceae NATURAL SEASON Spring and early summer COLOUR AVAILABILITY Dark centres that become bright orange, purple/mauve to pink petals CUT FLOWER LIFE SPAN Petals last 3–4 days (centres can be dried and last for months)

CARE AND HANDLING

- Cut or purchase when the flowers are open and the petals are relaxing downwards. The leaves should show no sign of aging.

- Remove any leaves that will sit below the waterline.

- Recut 2–3 centimetres from the stem ends, using secateurs. Cut on an angle.

- Always use a preservative and change every three days.

- Remove petals as they start to fade.

- Keep cool.

COMMERCIAL HANDLING

- Do not place in the cool room

GENERAL USE

Echinacea petals reflex backwards, hence the name 'coneflower'. The flowers are pretty when used in a vase at home. Sometimes the flowers are sold with the petals already removed, and floral designers often remove the petals and use the cone centre only. These cones look quite dramatic in modern arrangements and can also be used in wedding designs (such as corsages) for something different.

GROWING CONDITIONS

Echinacea thrives in full sun with well-drained soil. It will survive in dry conditions with exposure to the wind. Echinacea purpurea can be multiplied from autumn divisions or from winter root cuttings grown under glass. In colder climates they can be cut back in autumn. Deadheading will prolong the flowering season.

HISTORY

Echinacea is native to the prairies of North America. The genus Echinacea was named in 1794 by a botanist named Moench, after the Greek word 'echinos' (meaning `sea urchin´or `hedgehog´), in reference to the plants' urchin-like cone. The dried and powdered rhizomes are used in herbal medicine, and Echinacea extracts are used for alleviating the common cold.

ECHINOPS (e-kin-ops) Common names: Globe Thistle

BOTANICAL VARIETIES Echinops bannaticus (around 120 species) FAMILY Asteraceae NATURAL SEASON Spring and summer

COLOUR AVAILABILITY Mauve/Blue, pink CUT FLOWER LIFE SPAN Up to 2 weeks

GENERAL USE

Echinops can be used in a range of flower arrangements including posies and table centrepieces. The heads can be dried and used in long-lasting designs.

WEDDING USE

Echinops flowers can be used as filling flowers. They need to be wire-supported for use in bouquet holders or hand-tied natural stemmed bouquets.

CORPORATE USE

Echinops can be used for corporate work. Make sure all foliage is removed and the stems are wire-supported.

GROWING CONDITIONS

Echinops can be grown from seed or from root divisions taken in colder weather. During the flowering period it likes plenty of water. It can be deadheaded to prolong the flowering season.

HISTORY

Echinops is native to south-east Europe, central Asia and Africa. The generic name refers to the prickles with which the heads of inflorescence are thickly beset. The name is derived from the Greek 'echinos', meaning sea urchin or hedgehog. It refers to the shape of the flower.

CARE AND HANDLING

- Cut or purchase when half of the flowers are open. They should be clear blue in colour. Avoid yellow leaves.

- Remove all leaves as they will not last as long as the flower.

- Change the water and preservative every 3–4 days.

- These flowers are not ethylene sensitive but preservative is essential.

- Keep cool at all times.

COMMERCIAL HANDLING

- Do not place in the cool room.

- The foliage will mould if confined. Ensure there is sufficient airflow around the stems.

ECHIUM (ek-ee-um) Common names: Pride of Madeira; Tower of Jewels

BOTANICAL VARIETIES Echium candicans, Echium wildpretii FAMILY Boraginaceae NATURAL SEASON Spring and summer COLOUR AVAILABILITY Mauve blue to purple and pink CUT FLOWER LIFE SPAN 5 days

CARE AND HANDLING

- These flowers are not often sold commercially.
- Cut when the lower third of the flowers are showing colour.
- Remove all leaves that will be below the waterline.
- Recut 2–3 centimetres from the stem ends, using secateurs. Cut on a sharp angle.
- Use preservative.

COMMERCIAL HANDLING

- Do not place in the cool room.

GENERAL USE

Echiums feature long, pointed, parallel-veined leaves that are covered in silver silky hairs. The flowers are a long panicle of purple/blue-shaped flowers. They can give height and structure to most designs. The lower flowers may need to be removed. Echium flowers are best used in decorating where they are required for a specific function and not for longevity. Do not use in corporate work as they will dry out and drop.

GROWING CONDITIONS

Echium is a varied genus including annuals, perennials and shrubs. It will grow in any garden soil and will withstand beach conditions. All Echium varieties are frost tender. The plants can be propagated very easily from seed. Faded flower heads should be removed or they will self-seed. The flowers attract bees.

HISTORY

Echium is native to the Mediterranean, west Asia and some islands of the Eastern Atlantic. Echiums wildpretti is native to the Canary Islands.

EMILIA *(em-i-l-ee-ya) Common names: Tassel Flower; Flora's Paintbrush; Cacalia*

BOTANICAL VARIETIES Emilia sonchifolia (Flora's Paintbrush) (About 24 species in this genus) FAMILY NAME Asteraceae SUB FAMILY Compositae NATURAL SEASON Late spring and summer COLOUR AVAILABILITY Orange, scarlet, yellow CUT FLOWER LIFE SPAN 5–7 days

GENERAL USE

Emilia flowers are ideal for use in posies and bouquets. The flowers do not completely open. The flowers will last longer than their foliage so consider this when creating arrangements. Emilia flowers can be dried and used in cottage-style designs.

GROWING CONDITIONS

Emilia requires sandy soil in full sun. It needs to be kept well fed and watered. Deadhead spent flowers to promote blooming.

HISTORY

Emilia is native to the tropics in both hemispheres (eastern and southern Asia and the western Pacific). The Tassel flower variety, from the Far East, was introduced into England in 1799.

Leaf extracts from Emilia have been used medicinally to treat convulsions.

CARE AND HANDLING

- Cut or purchase when flowers are half open (they will not open completely).
- Recut stems 2–3 centimetres from the stem ends. Cut on a sharp angle.
- Remove all foliage that will sit below the waterline.
- Add preservative to the water.
- Emilia is sensitive to ethylene so keep it away from cigarette smoke and ripening fruit.

COMMERCIAL HANDLING

- Do not place in the cool room.

EPACRIS *(ep-a-kris) Common names: Australian Heath; Native Fuchsia*

BOTANICAL VARIETIES Epacris impressa, Epacris longiflora (about 40 species in this genus) FAMILY Epacridaceae NATURAL SEASON All year COLOUR AVAILABILITY Red, white, pink CUT FLOWER LIFE SPAN 2 weeks

CARE AND HANDLING

- Cut or purchase when one third of the lower flowers are opening.

- Recut at least 2–3 centimetres from the stem ends using sharp secateurs. Cut on a sharp angle.

- Remove any foliage that will sit below the waterline

- Use preservative to assist all flowers to open.

- Epacris flowers are heavy drinkers, so keep the vase water topped up.

COMMERCIAL HANDLING

- Do not place in the cool room.

GENERAL USE

Epacris flowers are suitable to use with all Australian natives in designs. They can also be mixed with other flowers. Do not use in hospital gift arrangements as they will dry out in heating or airconditioning.

GROWING CONDITIONS

Epacris needs acidic, well-drained, sandy soil. It is best kept moist. Cutting the spent flowers encourages bushy, dense growth and this ensures more blooms in the next season.

The seeds are difficult to germinate. In summer, take semi-hardwood cuttings and strike in moist sandy soil.

HISTORY

Epacris is native to Australia. In 1951 Epacris impressa was named as the state emblem of Victoria (the first flower to be proclaimed a state emblem in Australia). The generic name Epicris comes from the Greek 'epi' (meaning 'upon') and 'akris' (meaning 'hill') and this alludes to the elevated habitat of some of the species.

EREMURUS

(er-em-yoo-ras) Common names: Foxtail Lily; Desert Candle

BOTANICAL VARIETIES Eremurus robustus (about 50 species in this genus) FAMILY Asphodelaceae NATURAL SEASON Spring and early summer COLOUR AVAILABILITY Pink, white, yellow CUT FLOWER LIFE SPAN 7–10 days

GENERAL USE

These lovely spiked flowers mix well with Irises and Delphiniums. If you use these in flower foam you may need to make an insertion first. Do not use these flowers in corporate designs as the spent florets must be removed or the flower loses its visual appeal.

GROWING CONDITIONS

Eremurus is a clump-forming herbaceous perennial suitable for free draining, sandy soil in full sun. Do not disturb by digging around it as the roots are fleshy and break easily. Their tubers are octopus shaped and are best laid on a bed of sand. Use mulch for ground protection in the winter months.

HISTORY

Eremurus is native to western and central Asia. The leaves of some varieties are eaten in Afghanistan as a vegetable.

CARE AND HANDLING

- Cut or purchase when two or three flowers are open on the spike. The Foxtail Lily variety is purchased without foliage and dies back from the base.

- Avoid bent spikes – these will not straighten again.

- Remove any leaves that will sit below the waterline.

- Recut 2–3 centimetres from the stem ends. Cut on a sharp angle.

- Use preservative.

- Remove any wilted flowers as they are a source of ethylene gas and will affect the other flowers in the bunch.

COMMERCIAL HANDLING

- Do not place in the cool room.

ERICA

(eh-ri-kah) Common names: Shell Heath; Cape Heath; Scrub Heath; Heather

BOTANICAL VARIETIES Erica sessifolia, Erica hybrida (Cape Heath), Erica baccans, Erica patersonia, Erica lusitanica and Erica cerinthoides (numerous varieties) FAMILY Ericaceae NATURAL SEASON Flowers most of the year with the main profusion in late winter and spring COLOUR AVAILABILITY White, pink, lime, red, orange-red CUT FLOWER LIFE SPAN Up to 2 weeks

CARE AND HANDLING

- Cut or purchase when approximately half the flowers are open.
- Make sure there are no deteriorated flowers on the spike.
- Recut 2–3 centimetres from the stem ends. Cut on a sharp angle.
- Remove any leaves that will sit below the waterline.
- Ensure there is sufficient airflow around the stems.
- Keep cool and do not place in direct sunlight.
- Use preservative and change the water and preservative every 2–3 days.
- Keep the water levels topped up. When lacking in water, the tops of the flower spikes will begin to drop down.

COMMERCIAL HANDLING

- Do not place in the cool room.

GENERAL USE

Erica is used for the base of wreaths and is also a good base for all forms of bowl work. It has no fragrance. The foliage dries quickly in airconditioning. The Scrub Heath variety is excellent for a wreath or funeral sheaf base.

WEDDING USE

Erica flowers can be used as a filling flower in bouquet holders. Make sure they are not fully matured as they will drop. They are hardy and if well conditioned they can make a nice edge around the bouquet as well. Cut off the tops as they can fall.

CORPORATE USE

Erica flowers can be used for corporate designs but will dry out by the end of the week. They still look reasonable, but in the latter part of their season they will drop.

GROWING CONDITIONS

Erica is best grown in slightly acid, porous yet water-retentive soil. Plant in raised beds for perfect drainage. Most species can be raised from seed. They dislike animal manure and lime.

HISTORY

The varieties of Erica that are used as cut flowers are native to South Africa. They are related to Australian Heath but are not from the same genus. William Rollisson, an English nurseryman in Tooting, hybridised Cape Heaths in the 1790s. By 1826 there were 285 varieties.

ERIOSTEMON

(eh-ree-yos-tem-on) Common names: Waxflower; Pink Waxflower; Eastern Waxflower; Native Daphne BOTANICAL VARIETIES Eriostemon australasius, Eriostemon myoporoides (Native Daphne) (over 30 species) FAMILY Rutaceae NATURAL SEASON Late winter and spring COLOUR AVAILABILITY Pink, white CUT FLOWER LIFE SPAN 7–10 days

GENERAL USE

Despite its similarity in common names, Eriostemon is not related to Geraldton Wax. It is a nice vase flower and can be used commercially in bouquets and a range of flower designs. It is an excellent filling flower in all designs. Eriostemon dislikes heating and airconditioning.

The flowers of Eriostemon australasius (Pink Waxflower) are profuse and perfumed. Their fragrance is unappealing to some. Eriostomen myoporoides (Native Daphne) has foliage that has a sharp citrus smell. Some also find this fragrance unappealing.

WEDDING USE

Eriostemon can be used as a filler flower in all types of wedding bouquets.

CORPORATE USE

Eriostemon will last five days in airconditioned environments if the water supply is constant. It is best used in bud form.

GROWING CONDITIONS

Eriostemon require perfect drainage otherwise it is susceptible to root rot. Soak the seeds for 24 hours before sewing or strike from semi-hardwood cuttings taken in autumn.

HISTORY

Eriostemon is native to Australia, specifically the east coast region. One species is native to New Caledonia.

CARE AND HANDLING

- Cut or purchase when the buds are just opening.

- Shake the stems or bunches and avoid any with flower drop. Flower drop is common at the end of the season (late spring).

- Avoid bunches with any shrivelled flowers and yellowing leaves. The leaves should be glossy green.

- Remove any foliage that will sit below the waterline.

- Recut 2–3 centimetres from the stem ends, using sharp secateurs. Cut on a sharp angle.

- Lightly crush the stem ends after recutting.

- Use preservative to assist the buds to open.

- Keep it away from direct sunlight.

- Eriostemon is very sensitive to ethylene so keep it away from cigarette smoke and ripening fruit.

ERYNGIUM

(eh-ring-gee-yum) Common names: Sea Holly; Eryngo; Miss Willmott's Ghost BOTANICAL VARIETIES Eryngium planum, Eryngium bourgatii (over 200 species in this genus) FAMILY Apiaceae NATURAL SEASON Summer COLOUR AVAILABILITY Grey and green (almost metallic in appearance) CUT FLOWER LIFE SPAN 5–7 days

CARE AND HANDLING

- Cut or purchase bunches with straight stems and check that the leaves are clear blue in colour. Avoid any yellow leaves.

- Eryngium is extremely prickly. Use gloves when handling.

- Recut 2–3 centimetres from the stem ends. Cut on an angle.

- Remove any foliage that will sit under the waterline.

- Place the stems in conditioning solution for up to four hours. Once they have acclimatised, place them in water with preservative.

- If the flowers start to wilt it can be due to extreme change in conditions and air blockage of the stems. Recut the stems and place into deep water with preservative. After three hours they can be transferred to the vase.

COMMERCIAL HANDLING

- Do not place in the cool room as they will shock on removal.

GENERAL USE

The head of Eryngium is elongated and domed in shape. The spiky collar can be removed for floral work. It can be used in modern designs, bouquets and a range of floral items. Eryngium can also be dried. Do not use in office decorations as they will droop and dry out.

GROWING CONDITIONS

Ergyngium is a member of the carrot family. The blooms are spiny-collared. The plant prefers sandy, well-drained soil and with light but regular watering it may reach up to 60 centimetres in height. It can be grown from winter root cuttings planted under glass, then removed when foliage appears and planted in the garden in the following autumn.

HISTORY

Eryngium is native to Europe and South America. Legend has it that the shoots of Eryngium can be boiled and consumed like Asparagus. The roots are said to add youth to the elderly if preserved with sugar. The leaves have a slight aromatic smell.

The common name 'Sea Holly' comes from the mixture of two references; one being Spiky Holly and the other being Eryngium maritimum, a variety that grows naturally on the sandy sea shores of Britain and Europe.

ERYSIMUM

(e-riss-i-mum) Common names: Wallflower; Treacle Mustard; Blister Cress

BOTANICAL VARIETIES Erysimum cheiri (Wallflower), Erysimum perofskianum (Treacle Mustard) FAMILY Brassicaceae NATURAL SEASON Late winter, spring and early summer COLOUR AVAILABILITY Pink, mauve, golden yellow, brown CUT FLOWER LIFE SPAN 4–5 days

GENERAL USE

Erysimum flowers are commonly used for colour in posies. They are ideal for use in pretty, cottage-style posies. Their use for other types of floral arrangement is limited. They can be used in vases for show but they won't last very long. Do not use for corporate designs as they will not last in airconditioned environments.

GROWING CONDITIONS

Erysimum likes well-drained soil with average loam (a mixture of sand, silt and clay) and regular watering. It can be raised from seed. Once established it self-seeds easily. It needs full sun in winter and part sun in summer. It is fragrant in perfume. In the garden it is compatible with Violas and Forget-Me-Nots.

HISTORY

Erysimum is native to the Northern Hemisphere. In Elizabethan times, Wallflowers were known as 'Gilliflowers' or 'Yellow Flowers'. They were known for their medicinal uses such as counter-irritants.

CARE AND HANDLING

- These flowers are rarely sold commercially.
- Pick when the flowers are half open.
- Recut 2–3 centimetres from the woody stem ends. Cut on a sharp angle using secateurs.
- Remove any foliage that will sit below the waterline.
- Use preservative.
- Do not place in airconditioned environments.
- Erysimum is sensitive to ethylene so keep it away from cigarette smoke and ripening fruit.

ETLINGERA *(et-lin-ger-a) Common names: Torch Lily; Rose de Porcelaine; Philippine Wax Flower* BOTANICAL VARIETIES Etlingera elatior (About 60 species in this genus) FAMILY Zingiberaceae NATURAL SEASON Autumn, summer and late spring COLOUR AVAILABILITY Scarlet/red with a gold edge CUT FLOWER LIFE SPAN Up to 4 weeks

Note: *Torch Lilies look similar to the Australian Waratah (Telopea)*

CARE AND HANDLING

- Cut or purchase when the outer bracts are unblemished (these will die first).

- Recut 2–4 centimetres from the stem end. Cut on a sharp angle.

- Add preservative to the water.

- Do not place in airconditioned environments. The outer bracts will turn dark in colour and start to shrivel and the life span of the flowers will be severely shortened.

COMMERCIAL HANDLING

- Do not place in the cool room.

GENERAL USE

Etlingera flowers are dramatic and dominant when used in modern designs. If using in floral foam, make sure the foam is deep, and cut or shave the stem on a sharp angle before use. Etlingera flowers are best featured lower on the axis of the design. They will dry quickly in airconditioning so avoid using them in corporate work.

GROWING CONDITIONS

Etlingera only grows in warmth environments, although it is very hardy and will thrive in any well-drained soil. Feed regularly during the growth cycle.

HISTORY

Etlingera is native to New Guinea, Indonesia and the Malay Peninsula. The young buds are traditionally eaten as a vegetable. This species was named to honour botanist Edred John Henry Corner (1906–1996)

EUCALYPTUS (yoo-ka-lip-tas) Common names: Flowering Gum

BOTANICAL VARIETIES Eucalyptus caesia (red with gold tips), Eucalyptus ficifolia (pale pink to red), Eucalyptus erythrocorys (lime flowers) (over 800 species in this genus) FAMILY Myrtaceae NATURAL SEASON Late spring and summer COLOUR AVAILABILITY Lime, crimson, scarlet to pale pink, yellow to orange Cream to white is the most prolific CUT FLOWER LIFE SPAN 5 days in ideal conditions

GENERAL USE

Flowering Eucalypts will just last five days in ideal conditions. The flowing branches look effective when cascading down from the base of arrangements and the strong colours of the flowers can complement any design. Their silvery leaves may need some trimming for directional flow.

CORPORATE USE

Eucalyptus foliage can be used in corporate work but do not use the flowers as they will not last in heating or air-conditioning. When the flowers are removed they leave a striking calyx base (known as gumnuts when dried). These are effective in corporate work when used on the branch.

GROWING CONDITIONS

Eucalyptus will grow in dry conditions and just about anywhere in warmer climates.

HISTORY

Eucalyptus is native to Australia. The first Eucalypts known to Europeans were collected and transported to England by Joseph Banks in 1770. On Captain Cook's third expedition in 1777 the botanist, David Nelson, collected a Eucalypt on Bruny Island in southern Tasmania. This specimen was taken to the British museum in London where it was named Eucalyptus obliqua by the French botanist Charles-Louis L 'Heritier. The English botanist James Edward Smith named a number of species of Eucalypt from 1788 to 1800.

CARE AND HANDLING

- Cut or purchase when the flowers look fluffy and are half to three-quarters open.
- Recut 2–3 centimetres from the stem ends, using sharp secateurs.
- Lightly crush the stem ends after recutting.
- Remove any leaves that will sit below the waterline.
- Use preservative.

COMMERCIAL HANDLING

- Do not place in the cool room.

EUCOMIS *(yoo-ko-mis) Common names: Pineapple Lily*

BOTANICAL VARIETIES Eucomis comosa (other varieties available but this one is the most commercial) FAMILY Hyacinthaceae

NATURAL SEASON Summer and autumn COLOUR AVAILABILITY White to pale pink to light purple, buds are a lime colour, stems are green/red to purple

CUT FLOWER LIFE SPAN Up to 4 weeks

CARE AND HANDLING

- Cut or purchase when about a third of the lower flowers are open. The stems should be straight.

- Recut 2–3 centimetres from the stem ends. Cut on an angle.

- Use preservative.

- Remove any flowers from the base of the stem as they die off.

- Keep cool at all times.

- Eucomis is sensitive to ethylene so keep it away from cigarette smoke and ripening fruit.

COMMERCIAL HANDLING

- Eucomis can be kept in the cool room at temperatures of 6–8 degrees Celsius.

GENERAL USE

Eucomis flower spikes are usually around 30 centimetres in height. It makes an interesting vase flower and its colour mixes well with many other varieties of flowers. If the flower spike is used in floral foam a strong wire can be inserted into the centre of the fleshy stem for extra support. If necessary the stem can be cut and used in sections in floral foam.

WEDDING USE

The green colour of Eucomis mixes well with other flowers. The small florets can be wired using the pierce and mount method and look very delicate in hairpieces or corsages. It can also be used from the top of the stem in wired bouquets or bouquet holders. The stem can be cut into sections.

CORPORATE USE

Eucomis flowers are suited to corporate work, but make sure the flowers are only partly open (about one third from the base). These flowers are hardy but may need wire support as they can bend over. A constant water source is vital.

GROWING CONDITIONS

Eucomis is best planted in groups, in full sun and well-drained soil. Plant out the bulbs in early spring for autumn flowering.

HISTORY

Eucomis is native to South Africa. The name Eucomis is derived from the Greek word 'eukomos', meaning 'lovely haired'. This relates to the crown of leaves that appear at the top of each spike. The flower is commonly named Pineapple Lily due to the topknot of leaves above the flower head that resemble a pineapple.

EUPHORBIA

(yoo-for-bee-a) Common names: Cushion; Snow on the Mountain; Ghostweed; Fire in the Mountain; Poinsettia; Crown of Thorns; Poison Spurge

BOTANICAL VARIETIES Euphorbia marginata, (white and green) Euphorbia polychroma, (yellow and green), Euphorbia schillingii, Euphorbia wulfenii and Euphorbia molii (pale green) (over 2000 species in this genus) FAMILY Euphorbiaceae NATURAL SEASON Spring and early summer COLOUR AVAILABILITY Yellow, orange, red, pink, purple, flush purple, lime green CUT FLOWER LIFE SPAN 7–10 days

GENERAL USE

The Poison Spurge variety has large pale green heads and is suited to larger decorating designs. The flowers can be cut back in size if desired. The Snow on the Mountain variety can be used in vase work and bouquets. It should not be used in floral foam as it will die within hours if watering is missed and the stem dries. Do not use Euphorbia in corporate designs.

GROWING CONDITIONS

Euphorbia requires well-drained soil and plenty of water. Prune heavily after bloom, shortening the flowered stems by at least half. All perennial Euphorbias can be propagated from division between autumn and spring. They can also be grown from seed. They are intolerant to frost.

HISTORY

Euphorbia is native to Madagascar, Eurasia and North America. The name Euphorbia comes from the Greek surgeon Euphorbus, who was the physician to King Jubis II of Numidia. Euphorbus believed that the milky latex of the stems yielded powerful emetic and cathartic products. He used it for medicinal purposes. It was also believed to have been used for arrow poison and stupefying fish for capture.

In 1753 Linnaeus assigned the name to the entire genus. The common name of Spurge came from the middle English/old French 'espurge', meaning 'to purge', due to the use of the plant's sap as a purgative.

CARE AND HANDLING

- Cut or purchase Euphorbia polychroma (Cushion) when the yellow-green flowers are open.

- Cut or purchase Euphorbia marginata (Snow on the Mountain and Ghostweed) when the white bracts are fully open.

- Use gloves when handling. Euphorbia contains a milky, poisonous sap that may cause skin irritation.

- Recut the stems under water if possible, as this prevents the milky latex seeping from the stems.

- After recutting, place the stems into deep water as soon as possible. If they are left out of water the sap will dry, forming a crust over the stem ends – this will prevent the flowers from drinking and they will deteriorate quickly.

- Remove any foliage that will sit below the waterline.

- Never bash or split the stems.

- Use preservative to assist the flowers to open.

- Do not place in airconditioned environments.

COMMERCIAL HANDLING

- Do not place in the cool room as the flowers will wilt quickly on removal.

Note: *Poinsettias belong to the Euphorbia family. A white Poinsettia is Euphorbia leucocephala. A double red Poinsettia is Euphorbia pulcherrima. Euphorbia milii is known as the Crown of Thorns.*

Common names: Lisianthus; Prairie Gentian; Tulip Gentian; Lissie

BOTANICAL VARIETIES Eustoma grandiflorum (Lisianthus, Prairie Gentian) (3 species in this genus) FAMILY Gentianaceae NATURAL SEASON Late spring and summer

COLOUR AVAILABILITY Deep purple, mauve, pink, white, cream, lemon and variegations CUT FLOWER LIFE SPAN 3 weeks

GENERAL USE

Eustoma blooms in late spring and summer, but due to it's popularity is available all year round. It is an extremely popular flower in all forms of floral design. It is suited to bouquets and many other arrangements, including both traditional and modern designs. Never crowd these flowers, as their beauty should be featured.

WEDDING USE

Eustoma flowers are very popular in wedding work. They look like roses and mix well in bouquets with roses. The florets and buds can be wired singularly. They can be used in hand-tied, natural stemmed bouquets, bouquet holders or wired bouquets.

CORPORATE USE

Eustoma flowers will last well in corporate designs if they are STS-treated and have not been kept in a cool room.

GROWING CONDITIONS

Eustoma can be raised as an annual from summer cuttings or from seed in spring. It likes full sun and good drainage and flowers well in summer. In warmer climates it will grow up to one metre. It is frost intolerant.

HISTORY

Eustoma is native to North America. It originated from an American wild flower, the Prairie Gentian, also known as the Prairie Rose. Eustoma nigrescens is known as the Funeral Flower of Mexico. These flowers are pendulous and nearly black in appearance, hence the funeral connotation. Eustoma is named after the Greek words 'eu', meaning 'good, beautiful, well' and 'stoma', meaning 'mouth'. The meaning of Eustoma is 'good tasting' or 'well spoken'.

CARE AND HANDLING

- Look for straight stems and strong green foliage. Any yellowing is a sign of age.

- Choose stems that have at least one bloom open. The tips should not be hooked.

- Check that there is no visible pollen in the centres of the blooms.

- Eustoma is a very sensitive to ethylene, but if STS-treated their life span will be greatly increased.

- Recut 2–3 centimetres from the stem ends. Cut on a sharp angle.

- Remove any foliage that will sit below the waterline.

- Preservative will assist longevity and also help the buds to open, however preservative is not essential.

- Eustoma is a thirsty drinker so keep the vase water topped up.

COMMERCIAL HANDLING

- If placed in the cool room make sure the bunches are not in sleeves and are separated for good airflow (otherwise they will mould).

- The cool room temperature should be 8 degrees Celsius.

- Allow conditioning time on removal from the cool room, especially in warm weather.

- If the cool room is too cold, a dark edge will appear on the flowers and the buds will collapse.

FATSIA

(fat-see-a) Common names: *Aralia*

BOTANICAL VARIETIES Fatsia japonica (only 3 species in this genus) FAMILY Araliaceae NATURAL SEASON Spring COLOUR AVAILABILITY White/cream

CUT FLOWER LIFE SPAN 5–7 days

CARE AND HANDLING

- Cut or purchase when the flowers are open. Check for any imperfections or brown tips in the flowers.

- Recut 2–3 centimetres from the stem ends. Cut on a sharp angle.

- Use preservative.

- The sap is toxic so avoid any contact with skin.

COMMERCIAL HANDLING

- Do not place into the cool room.

GENERAL USE

Fatsia flowers can be used singularly in wired work such as corsages, cake tops and hairpieces. They are also very effective in modern or Ikebana style designs. The leaves will last up to one month and are practical in modern designs, particularly as a base to linear designs made either in the hand or in floral foam. They are used in Europe instead of paper or cellophane to circle bouquets. Do not use the light green foliage in arrangements as it is too young and will droop.

GROWING CONDITIONS

Fatsia is an evergreen shrub that grows in most soil conditions and enjoys well-drained soil. It grows best in the shade. In late spring it sends up showy panicles of milky white flowers.

HISTORY

Fatsia is native to Japan. Fatsia japonica was introduced from Nagasaki, Japan, to Europe by a German employee of the East India Company, Dr Siebold. According to Japanese mythology, Sojobo, the King of Tengu, possessed mystical powers. He carried a fan made of Fatsia leaf and used it to create a storm.

FORSYTHIA

(for-sai-thee-ya) Common names: Golden Bells

BOTANICAL VARIETIES Forsythia intermedia (7 species in this genus) FAMILY Oleaceae NATURAL SEASON Late winter and early spring COLOUR AVAILABILITY Yellow/gold CUT FLOWER LIFE SPAN 7 days (if conditioned correctly)

GENERAL USE

Forsythia is bright in colour and makes an excellent backing flower in arrangements for a function. Do not use in corporate designs as the flowers will fall in airconditioned environments.

GROWING CONDITIONS

Forsythia does not like sub-tropical conditions. It grows well in rich, well-drained soil. Propagate from soft tip cuttings taken in summer or take hardwood cuttings in winter.

HISTORY

Forsythia is native to China. This plant was named in honour of one of the founders of The Royal Horticultural Society in London. His name was William Forsythe and he was a director of the Chelsea Physic garden in the latter part of the 1700s.

CARE AND HANDLING

- Cut or purchase when some of the flowers are open on the stem.
- Recut 2–3 centimetres from the woody stem ends, using secateurs. Cut on a sharp angle.
- The stem ends can be crushed or bashed after recutting.
- After recutting, submerge the stems in a bath of warm water for 3–4 hours to soften. This will help the water to flow up the stems and the flowers to open. If 3–4 hours is not possible then one hour in warm water will suffice.
- Use preservative to assist the buds to open.
- Replace the preservative every two days.

COMMERCIAL HANDLING

- Do not place into the cool room.

FREESIA

(free-zha)

BOTANICAL VARIETIES Freesia hybrida FAMILY Iridaceae NATURAL SEASON Late winter and spring (availability increased through hothouse growth) COLOUR AVAILABILITY Cream and lemon centre, pink, deep pink, mauve, deep purple, white, red/burgundy CUT FLOWER LIFE SPAN Up to 10 days

GENERAL USE

Freesia flowers can be used in a wide range of floral items, including table centrepieces, tributes and wedding bouquets. If used in wired work, use fine wire to support them, as their sap makes it difficult to air-lock with binding tape. Superior, commercially grown Freesias with long stems (30–50 centimetres) are available from some florists. These are strong and of excellent quality. They are grown in hothouses.

WEDDING USE

Freesia flowers have a pleasant perfume and are delicate in appearance. They can be used in hand-tied, natural stemmed bouquets, bouquet holders or wired bouquets. They combine well with Roses and Lisiathus.

CORPORATE USE

Freesia flowers can be used in corporate designs, but be prepared for a mid-week visit, as spent florets need to be removed to keep the flowers looking fresh.

GROWING CONDITIONS

Most Freesia varieties have a fragrant perfume. They like well-drained, light soil with full sun. Freesia will grow from seed or from autumn planted corms. Cease watering once the leaves turn yellow in late spring. Water frequently the rest of the time.

HISTORY

Freesia is native to South Africa. Its history in South Africa goes back over 200 years when all species were discovered. It was named after the German botanist Freidrich HT Freese, by his friend the Danish botanist Dr Christain P Ecklon, who researched Freesia at the Cape of Good Hope. Freesia was relatively unknown outside of South Africa until the mid 1950s. It is grown and sold across the world today. In the language of flowers, the Freesia signifies 'innocence and trust.'

CARE AND HANDLING

- Cut or purchase when the first flower is opening. There should be 5–7 flowers per spike, with no brown tips.

- Separate the bunch to allow airflow around the flowers.

- Remove any foliage that will sit below the waterline.

- Recut 2–3 centimetres from the stem ends. Cut on an angle.

- Use preservative to assist all the flowers to open.

- Replace the vase water and preservative every two days for maximum life span.

- Freesia is sensitive to ethylene so keep it away from cigarette smoke and ripening fruit.

- Do not place Freesias in the same vase as freshly picked Daffodils or Jonquils as the sap from these flowers will kill the Freesias. If the Daffodils or Jonquils have been purchased commercially the likelihood of this problem is diminished as their sap will have already dissipated.

COMMERCIAL HANDLING

- Freesia can be kept in normal cool room temperatures of 4–6 degrees Celsius.

- Freesia can be stored in the cool room for future use at 0–2 degrees Celsius at a high humidity. It can be stored for up to 3 weeks in water. Avoid prolonged refrigeration as this will diminish its fragrance.

GALTONIA

Common names: *Summer Hyacinth; Berg Lily; Giant Snowdrop*

BOTANICAL VARIETIES Galtonia candicans (Summer Hyacinth) – now known as Ornithogalum candigans FAMILY Hyacinthaceae SUB FAMILY Liliaceae

NATURAL SEASON Mid-summer COLOUR AVAILABILITY White/cream CUT FLOWER LIFE SPAN 5 days

CARE AND HANDLING

- Cut or purchase when about half of the bell-shaped flowers are open. The flowers should be lime to white in colour with no sign of any visible marks.

- Recut 2–3 centimetres from the stem ends. Cut on an angle.

- Make sure the stems are clean before placing them in the vase.

- Preservative in the vase water is essential.

- Do not place in airconditioned environments.

COMMERCIAL HANDLING

- Galtonia can be kept in the cool room at temperatures of 6–8 degrees Celsius.

GENERAL USE

Galtonia flowers are tall, waxy and fragrant. Despite their common name Summer Hyacinth, their scent is quite unlike that of Hyacinths. They can be used in modern designs, but do not use them in corporate designs as the flowers die from the base upwards and florets need to be removed as they die.

GROWING CONDITIONS

Galtonia is often planted with Kniphofia for borders in the garden. The large bulbs should be planted in autumn, in warm spots in the garden. Plant the bulbs about 15 centimetres deep into compost-rich, well-drained soil. Allow them to dry out in winter. They are subject to slugs and they should be divided every three years.

HISTORY

Galtonia is native to South Africa and was named after Sir Francis Galton. In South Africa it is also known as the Cape Hyacinth.

GARDENIA (gah-dee-nee-ya) Common names: Cape Jasmine

BOTANICAL VARIETIES Gardenia augusta, Gardenia jasminoides (Over 250 species in this genus) FAMILY Rubiaceae NATURAL SEASON Late spring and summer COLOUR AVAILABILITY White CUT FLOWER LIFE SPAN 2–4 days

GENERAL USE

Gardenia flowers are perfumed and are ideal for use at home in a float bowl. They are not suited to corporate designs.

WEDDING USE

Gardenia was once one of the most popular wedding flowers. Gardenia flowers are costly to buy commercially; however, they are a magnificent bouquet flower and also well suited to corsages and buttonholes, and when mixed with Stephanotis give a delicate look for wedding designs.

The flowers are best kept in an airtight plastic box until ready to use. When the time comes, remove the flowers from the box and sit them on the edge of a shallow dish to allow them to drink for up to an hour. Then remove the sepal and wire using the pierce and mount method.

Gardenia leaves can be wired and placed around the flower to lift the outer petals up, giving the flower maximum surface area. To do this, some floral designers use white cardboard or plastic circles with holes in the centre (known as 'Gardenia backs'). The stem is placed through the hole and then a pin or a short piece of wire is inserted through the stem to stop the back sliding down. Do this with caution as Gardenia flowers will bruise if the fibres are crushed.

GROWING CONDITIONS

Gardenia likes neutral to acidic soil that is moist but well-drained. It likes plenty of water and feeding once a month. Some sunlight is preferable but avoid positions of full sun. When grown commercially, Gardenia is picked by the head and usually sealed with six flowers and some leaves in an airtight container.

HISTORY

Gardenia is native to China and some varieties are also native to South Africa. It was named after Dr Alexander Garden (1730–1731).

Note: *The Gardenia thunbergia (Star Gardenia) looks similar to Frangipani*

CARE AND HANDLING

- Make sure the flowers are tight in the centre and not showing any yellow centres. There should be no sign of petal transparency. Avoid any blooms that look yellow – this is a sign of age.

- Handle with care. Hold the flower at the calyx. If the surface fibres of the petals are broken, the flower will develop brown lines in the petals.

- Before use, prepare a shallow tray with a sheet of cottonwool laid over it. Mix water with preservative and soak the cottonwool. Insert the stems through the cottonwool so they can drink. Leave them for one hour.

- Wired Gardenia flowers can be misted very lightly. Over-misting may induce petal browning.

- Gardenia can cause reactions in people who suffer from hay fever. Be aware of this when creating hand held arrangements.

COMMERCIAL HANDLING

- Gardenia can be kept in the cool room at temperatures of 6–8 degrees Celsius.

GARRYA

(gar-ree-ya) Common names: Silk Tassel; Curtain Bush

BOTANICAL VARIETIES Garrya elliptica FAMILY Garryaceae NATURAL SEASON Winter and spring COLOUR AVAILABILITY Lime green

CUT FLOWER LIFE SPAN 2 weeks (early season)

CARE AND HANDLING

- Cut branches in the garden using sharp secateurs.

- When purchasing, ensure that the flowers (catkins) are firm. Any pollen drop indicates age.

- Use preservative to assist the life span of the catkins.

- Recut 3–4 centimetres from the stem ends. Cut on a sharp angle.

- Do not bash the stem ends.

COMMERCIAL HANDLING

- Garrya can be placed in the cool room at a temperature of 6 degrees Celsius.

GENERAL USE

Garrya foliage is very hardy and its dark green leaves are silvery underneath. They are perfect to use in wedding and corsage work as they last well. The long catkins are truly magnificent and enhance any design with their cascading beauty. They can look lighter in some designs if all the foliage is removed. Garrya looks at its best flowing from the base of arrangements or bouquets or in modern designs.

WEDDING USE

Garrya is a very delicate looking, but strong flowing flower. Never use if it is mature as it will shed pollen. Garrya can be used in hand-tied, natural stemmed bouquets, bouquet holders or in wired bouquets.

CORPORATE USE

Garrya can be used in corporate designs when the flowers are tight. Do not use it late in its season as it pollinates and drops, causing a mess. Never use if it is mature as it will shed pollen.

GROWING CONDITIONS

The male of this species is the showy one. It produces catkins in winter and these lengthen up to 20 centimetres in spring. If male and female varieties are planted together the female will produce clusters of purplish/black berries. In good quality, deep soil, Garrya will grow into a tree. In poor soils it won't grow beyond a shrub. It thrives in either full sun or partial shade. It will tolerate pruning but dislikes any form of root disturbance.

HISTORY

Garrya is native to western America. It was named after Nicholas Garry by David Douglas. Garry assisted Douglas in his plant hunting across western America. Douglas sent the plant to the Royal Horticultural Societies Garden in 1834.

GELEZNOWIA

(gel-ez-no-wee-ya) Common name: Yellow Bells

BOTANICAL VARIETIES Geleznowia verrucosa FAMILY Rutaceae NATURAL SEASON Spring COLOUR AVAILABILITY Yellow, creams and orange
CUT FLOWER LIFE SPAN 7–10 days

GENERAL USE

Geleznowia is a good filler flower. It can be used in posies and bouquets as well as a secondary flower in all arrangements.

CORPORATE USE

Geleznowia can be used in corporate designs if most of the foliage is removed and the water supply is not interrupted.

GROWING CONDITIONS

Geleznowia plants are not easy to strike and they like a hot, sandy position. They must have excellent drainage. In ideal conditions they can grow from seed sown in autumn or spring.

HISTORY

Geleznowia is native to Australia. It was named after the Russian botanist Nikolai Zheleznov. Its species name, verrucosa, comes from the Latin term 'verrucosus', meaning 'warty'. This refers to the warty bumps on the stems.

CARE AND HANDLING

- Purchase when the flowers are half to fully open. Avoid bunches where the leaves show brown tips.
- Separate the stems for airflow.
- Recut 2–3 centimetres from the stem ends. Cut on a sharp angle.
- Do not bash the stem ends.
- Remove any leaves that will sit below the waterline.
- Use preservative to assist the open flowers to last.
- Replace the vase water every 2–3 days.

COMMERCIAL HANDLING

- Geleznowia can be placed in the cool room at temperatures of 6–8 degrees Celsius.

GENISTA *(jen-is-ta) Common names: Broom; Genet; Dyer's Greenwood*

BOTANICAL VARIETIES Genista tinctoria (Dyer's Greenweed), Genista sagittalis (Winged Broom) (about 40 species in this genus) FAMILY Fabaceae NATURAL SEASON Spring COLOUR AVAILABILITY White/cream to bright yellow CUT FLOWER LIFE SPAN Up to 5 days

CARE AND HANDLING

- Cut or purchase when a third of the flowers are open.

- Recut 2–3 centimetres from the stem ends. Cut on an angle.

- Keep it away from excessive heat.

- Genista is sensitive to ethylene so keep it away from cigarette smoke and ripening fruit.

- Use preservative.

GENERAL USE

Cream Genista (Broom) flowers can be dyed with food dye. The flowing sprays can be used in bouquets and sheaves. It is best to use them in a base where there is a water source. Genista is a good filling flower or outline flower when purchased or picked on longer stems.

WEDDING USE

Genista is a lovely bridal accessory flower. It can cascade from all type of bouquets. Do not use it if all the flowers are fully open.

CORPORATE USE

Genista is a pleasant accessory flower. Do not use it if the flowers are fully open or they will drop. It is best used in glass containers.

GROWING CONDITIONS

Genista can be grown from seeds that have been soaked in water for 24 hours. Plant in spring. It will survive in poor soil and full sun, and is hardy to frost. It can be tip-pruned to promote bushy flowering. Propagate by taking half hardened cuttings in summer.

HISTORY

Genista is native to the Mediterranean area. It is the source of the brilliant red permanent dye Turkey Red, also known as Adrianople Red. Turkey Red was very well known in 19th century domestic history. The Genista tinctoria variety yields a yellow dye that was used with woad to make a permanent green dye. Hence the terms Dyer's Greenwood, Dyer's Weed and Dyer's Broom.

GERBERA

(jer-ber-a) Common names: Transvaal Daisy; Barberton Daisy; African Daisy

BOTANICAL VARIETIES Gerbera jamesonii FAMILY Asteraceae NATURAL SEASON Spring COLOUR AVAILABILITY Dark and light pink, blue, red, burgundy, yellow, cream, gold, orange, mauve and purple (varieties with variegations) CUT FLOWER LIFE SPAN 7 to 21 days

GENERAL USE

Gerberas come in various sizes, from miniature to large, with stem lengths of 30–60 centimetres. Mini Gerberas are fashionable, but the larger sized varieties are waning in popularity. However, they have a good surface area and are a practical flower to use in all floral designs.

Hothouse Gerberas sometimes have trouble bringing the water up the stem and that is why they droop. To rectify this problem, they need to be wired. Internal wiring will shorten the life span of the flower, but for commercial competition work or special function designs, this method is recommended.

WEDDING USE

Gerbera flowers have a large surface area and come in a wide range of colours, making them popular for wedding designs. For use in bouquet holders they will need either internal wire support through the stem, or wire support that is pierced up into the calyx with the external wire running down the stem. Make sure the wire is not pierced through the head. For bouquet holder insertion the wire should be 2–3 centimetres longer than the stem. Gerberas should also be wired for use in hand-tied, natural stemmed bouquets. For wired bouquets, use the pierce and mount wiring method.

Miniature Gerberas can also be used in wedding designs. The petals may be removed, leaving the centre as a small, attractive 'button flower'. These can be used in hairpieces, buttonholes and in all forms of bouquets. Black-centred Gerberas with the petals removed look dramatic in modern bridal bouquets. If the stem is exposed, it can be sprayed with black-coloured floral spray paint, binded with black tape or covered with black fabric for a striking visual effect.

Gerberas can plug or airlock when used in floral foam. This can happen if the stem ends close over or seal themselves. It usually occurs when the foam is old or if the water levels drop.

CARE AND HANDLING

- Purchase when the flowers are fully open. The centres of the flowers should be round, not oval. There should be no sign of petal damage, particularly any creases or brown marks (creases will become brown lines on the petal surface).

- Do not purchase if the centres shows pollination or there are black/brown marks on the stem ends (these are signs of age)

- Recut 2–3 centimetres from the stem ends. Cut on an angle.

- Gerberas will plug or air-block easily so ensure the vase or container is clean and free from bacteria.

- Gerberas don't like deep water as they have tiny hairs on their stem that absorb water. If the hairs waterlog then this will eventually weaken the stem.

- Do not leave them out of water for more than 15 minutes.

- Preservative is essential. The vase water should be replaced every two days.

- Do not mist the flowers. If they are over-misted then the centres will rot.

COMMERCIAL HANDLING

- Often Gerbera growers will pack the flowers on cards for protection. Unpack with care. If you lie the flowers down, place your hand under the petals to protect them from bruising on the bench.

- Gerbera can be kept in the cool room at temperatures above 8 degrees Celsius.

- If purple edges appear on the petals it is a sign that the refrigeration was too cold or that the flowers were in the cool room for too long.

- When arranging Gerberas, have a clean container on your bench and stand them in it. Some florists damage Gerberas with handling and the bruising takes some time to be seen. Usually by the recipient!

- Always sell Gerberas with a water source.

- Most florists will assist the stem to stand by using a wire wound down the stem. The wire should be painted and not reach the water.

- Yellow, white and pale pink Gerberas are sensitive to fluoride in the water. Petal damage with brown marks appearing at the tips is a sign that they have been affected by fluoride.

- Gerberas are attracted to and will turn towards the light. Be aware of this, particularly if you place them in the cool room with the lights on.

CORPORATE USE

Miniature or full-sized Gerberas can be used in corporate designs. The yellow/orange Sundance variety last longer than other varieties, and red Gerberas lasts the shortest amount of time.

Gerberas need either internal or external wire support (see Wedding use). The wire should not reach the water. If used in floral foam they will last approximately five days in office conditions.

GROWING CONDITIONS

Gerbera enjoys full sun. It needs perfect drainage, with a mixture of sandy, loam leaf mould in the soil. It is frost sensitive and tender. Plant from autumn divisions.

HISTORY

Gerbera is native to South Africa. Both single and double hybrids have been derived from the original Barberton Daisy – a clumpy perennial with coarse leaves like a big dandelion. Gerbera was named in honour of the German naturalist Traugott Gerber.

In the language of flowers, the white Gerbera means 'innocence', orange means 'you're my sunshine' and yellow means 'I'll try harder.'

GLADIOLUS

(gla-dee-oh-las) Common names: *Sword Lily*

BOTANICAL VARIETIES Gladiolus hybrida FAMILY Iridaceae NATURAL SEASON Spring and summer COLOUR AVAILABILITY Purple, red, white, yellow, orange, green and numerous variegations and stripes CUT FLOWER LIFE SPAN Up to 14 days

GENERAL USE

Gladiolus is a solid, practical flower with a wide colour range and multiple uses. The flowers' popularity waned through the 1990s but they have recently had a resurgence.

These flowers can be cut into sections and used as a filling flower in arrangements (including sheaf arrangements) or even to base a wreath. If the flowers are placed horizontally in an arrangement the tips will grow upwards.

In years gone by florists used Gladioli stems to support other shorter flowers and raise their height in designs. Other strong flower heads, such as Sim Carnations, can be placed into Gladiolus stems and will absorb enough moisture to last through a function.

Sometimes Gladioli grow with their florets facing in different directions. These can be turned, using your index finger and thumb, to face the front (the top florets show where the front is). Any bent tips should be positioned inwards to the centre of the design rather than away from the centre.

The stems can be cut into sections between each floret for use in floral foam. The florets can also be used in wired work.

WEDDING USE

Gladiolus flowers are ideal for all types of wedding designs. The flowers are available in many colours and the white varieties look white (not cream) when held against white gowns. The florets can be wired singularly using the pierce and mount wiring method. The petals can be also wired singularly and formed petal by petal into a Gladioli Rose (also known as a Globellia, Glamellia or Glady Rose). These mix well with Roses to give a full look to wired bouquets.

There are many popular varieties of miniature Gladiolus. The Bride variety is a good substitute for Frangipani in bridal work.

CARE AND HANDLING

- Cut or purchase when the two base florets are partly open and showing strong colour. The next five or so florets should be showing colour.

- Look at the sheaths that cover the flowers. Avoid any that are brown tipped.

- Removing the top three florets will help open the top flowers.

- Recut 4–5 centimetres from the stem ends using secateurs. Cut on a sharp angle.

- Remove any leaves that will sit below the waterline.

- Wash any dirt from the stems before placing them in the vase.

- Use preservative to assist the buds to open and to ensure maximum life span.

- Gladiolus is a heavy drinker, so keep the vase water topped up.

- It is mildly sensitive to ethylene so keep it away from cigarette smoke and ripening fruit.

- The florets will wither from the base. Remove them as they die.

- Keep the flowers cool at all times.

COMMERCIAL HANDLING

- Gladiolus can be kept in the cool room at temperatures of 6–8 degrees Celsius.

- Gladiolus can be stored out of water, in the refrigerator. Refrigeration temperature should be around 2–4 degrees Celsius for storage. Avoid this process unless you are an expert.

- Burning on the edges of the florets as they open is a sign that the cool room was too cold.

CORPORATE USE

Gladiolus lasts well in corporate designs when used in bud form. They are especially good for adding height to the back of arrangements.

GROWING CONDITIONS

There are many varieties of Gladiolus. All varieties grow from flat corms. The best time for planting varies, depending on climatic conditions. Check with your local nursery.

In areas where frost can occur it is necessary to lift the corms in autumn. They like well-drained, fertile soil and full sun. The stalks may need staking.

HISTORY

Gladiolus is native to Central and South Africa. Its name was derived from the Latin 'gladius', meaning 'little sword'.

Mashed Gladiolus bulbs were once used to raise splinters and thorns and to reduce infection. It was believed that the dried seed pods, when crushed and added to goat's milk, were a deterrent against colic.

Red Gladiolus flowers are very popular for Chinese New Year and they also feature in arrangements (presented on bamboo stands) to signify 'good luck' for the opening of a new business in China and across Asia.

In the language of flowers, 'Gladiolus' means 'I'm so sincere' or 'generosity.'

GLORIOSA

(glor-ee-oh-sa) **Common names:** *Glory Lily; Cat's Claw* **BOTANICAL VARIETIES** Gloriosa superba, Gloriosa rothchildiana, Gloriosa simplex **FAMILY** Colchicaeceae **NATURAL SEASON** Late winter and spring **COLOUR AVAILABILITY** Bright yellow and red, orange and claret **CUT FLOWER LIFE SPAN** 2 weeks

GENERAL USE

Gloriosa flowers have reflex petals, which give the flowers a modern look, especially when hung upside down. It is best to remove the anthers as they will drop and may stain.

WEDDING USE

Gloriosa has a distinctive look. It can be used in hand-tied, natural stemmed bouquets as well as wired or bouquet holders.

CORPORATE USE

Gloriosa flowers are very dramatic and modern looking in corporate designs. They last well in office conditions. Make sure they are used fresh as the foliage will yellow over time.

GROWING CONDITIONS

Gloriosa grows from tuberous roots. The tendrils that extend from the leaves cling to other bushes and trees. Plant in early spring in deep, rich soil. Gloriosa is much harder to grow in colder climates as it likes humidity and dislikes frost.

HISTORY

Gloriosa is native to Uganda. It is the national flower of Zimbabwe. This flower was named in honour of Baron Z Rothschild, who brought the flower from Africa to exhibit it in England in the early 1900s.

CARE AND HANDLING

- Cut or purchase when at least one flower on the stem is open. The colour should be strong red and yellow, with no sign of any brown spotting. The leaves should be undamaged and glossy green.

- Avoid flowers that look transparent or foliage that has dark spots – this is a sign that the flowers have been refrigerated.

- Be careful when separating the stems as the tendrils can catch and damage blooms and buds. Tendrils can be cut off.

- Remove any leaves that will sit below the waterline.

- Recut 2–3 centimetres from the stem ends, using a knife or secateurs. Cut on a sharp angle.

- Preservative is essential.

COMMERCIAL HANDLING

- Never place in the cool room.

- If the flowers wilt they will revive quickly if bathed (immersed).

- Gloriosa flowers are best sold with a water source. Wrap with care so as not to damage the blooms.

GOMPHRENA

(gom-free-na) Common names: *Strawberry Fields; Globe Amaranth*

BOTANICAL VARIETIES Gomphrena globosa FAMILY Amaranthaceae NATURAL SEASON Spring and summer COLOUR AVAILABILITY Pink, mauve, yellow, orange, red and white CUT FLOWER LIFE SPAN 5–7 days

CARE AND HANDLING

- Do not cut or purchase if the flowers show yellow pollen or a yellow colour on the foliage.
- Choose flowers that have a strong, consistent colour.
- Separate the flowers for airflow around the stems and blooms.
- Remove any leaves that will sit below the waterline.
- Wash the stems and recut 2–3 centimetres from the stem ends. Cut on a sharp angle.
- Use preservative to assist the life span of the flowers.
- Change the water and preservative every two days.

COMMERCIAL HANDLING

- Do not place Gomphrena in the cool room.

GENERAL USE

Gomphrena flowers are generally available with stems lengths of 20–45 centimetres. They look very pretty in posy or cottage designs. The deeper pinks are the most popular to the floral designer. They can be used in floral foam. Do not use in airconditioned environments. They are not suited to corporate work.

GROWING CONDITIONS

These annual and perennial plants are grown from seed and take three months to flower. They like well-drained soil and should be planted 30 centimetres apart. Sew the seeds about two months before planting out. They prefer warmer weather.

HISTORY

Gomphrena is native to America, South America and parts of Australia. The genus name Gomphrena is derived from the Latin word 'gromphaena', meaning 'a type of Amaranth'. In the mid-1700s Carolus Linnaeus described 11 species of Gomphrena.

GREVILLEA

(gra-vil-lee-ya) Common names: Spider Flower

BOTANICAL VARIETIES Grevillea pteridifolia, Grevillea whiteana, Grevillea sessilis, Grevillea robusta, Grevillea 'Poorinda Queen' (a hybrid variety) (around 340 species in this genus and many hybrid cultivars) FAMILY Proteaceae NATURAL SEASON Spring COLOUR AVAILABILITY Red, orange, pink, yellow and white (many others) CUT FLOWER LIFE SPAN 5 days

GENERAL USE

Grevillea foliage is very popular in floral arranging. The flowers look very attractive when teamed with other native flowers but they are heavy drinkers, so the vase water must be topped up regularly. Grevillea is particularly spectacular for decorating work.

Grevillea flowers are not suitable for corporate designs as the older flowers will drop as they deteriorate. The foliage will last five days at best in office conditions.

GROWING CONDITIONS

Grevillea grows best in full sun. It likes rich, slightly acidic, well-drained compost soil that is part gravel. It does not mind dryness. This plant likes fertiliser and dislikes humidity. Propagation is from firm tip cuttings taken in summer. All Grevillea varieties attract birds.

HISTORY

Grevillea is native to Australia. It was named after Charles Greville (1749–1809), an 18th century patron of botany.

CARE AND HANDLING

- Cut or purchase when the lower flowers are open.
- Recut 2–3 centimetres from the stem ends, using secateurs. Cut on a sharp angle.
- Use preservative.
- Change the vase water and preservative every two days.
- Do not place in airconditioned or heated environments.
- Grevillea is very sensitive to ethylene so keep it away from cigarette smoke and ripening fruit.

COMMERCIAL HANDLING

- Do not place in the cool room. The foliage will become brown/black and shrivel on removal.

GYPSOPHILA

(jip-so-fil-a) Common names: Baby's Breath; Million Stars

BOTANICAL VARIETIES Gypsophila paniculata, Gypsophila repans (about 100 annuals and perennials in this genus) FAMILY Carophyllaceae NATURAL SEASON Spring, summer and early autumn (Gypsophila repans in summer only) COLOUR AVAILABILITY Pink (perennials), white (annuals) CUT FLOWER LIFE SPAN up to 7 days

CARE AND HANDLING

- Cut or purchase when a third of the flowers are open. Shake the bunch to check for any flower fall.

- Purchase STS-treated Gypsophila if possible.

- Avoid purchasing bunches with brown flowers as this indicates age. If they have been refrigerated, it may be a sign of fungal infection.

- Check the stem ends and make sure foliage looks green and fresh. Check that the water is clear.

- Separate the stems to create airflow around the flowers.

- Remove any foliage that will sit under the waterline.

- Use preservative.

- They are best placed in shallow water.

- Gypsophila is ethylene sensitive. Remove any dead flowers as these are a source of ethylene and will affect the living flowers if they remain.

- Never leave the flowers out of water or they will dry out very quickly.

- Do not mist the flowers as this can activate fungal disease.

COMMERCIAL HANDLING

- Do not place in the cool room.

GENERAL USE

Gypsophila is used widely in floral design. Its popularity comes and goes but it is a pretty filling flower when teamed with Roses in bouquets. It can be separated into small clusters for wedding work. An older person will consider it to be a 'cheap' flower.

WEDDING USE

Gypsophila was one of the most popular bridal flowers in the 1980s. It can look delicate when used in small quantities. It is a light, filling flower and can be used in hand-tie, natural stemmed bouquets, bouquet holders and wired bouquets. Million Stars is a smaller and tighter variety and when broken up, looks very delicate and lasts well.

CORPORATE USE

Gypsophila can be used as a filler flower in corporate designs, but it is essential to use bleach in the water as it will foul water if it is not changed regularly.

GROWING CONDITIONS

Gypsophila likes full sun with a well-drained, alkaline soil. It does not need a lot of water. It grows from seed. The annual varieties take ten weeks from seed to flowering and then die back. They are re-sown for continuous blooming through the warmer months. The perennial varieties are grown from spring cuttings of lateral shoots. Place these into peat or sand and plant out in early autumn.

HISTORY

Gypsophila is native to Eastern Europe. It was first cultivated in Great Britain in 1759 and introduced to America in the late 1800s. The name comes from the Greek word 'gypsum', meaning 'chalk loving' or 'lover of chalk'.

HEDYCHIUM

(hed-ik-ee-yum) Common names: Ginger Lily; Ginger Lily of India

BOTANICAL VARIETIES Hedychium gardnerianum, Hedychium coronarium (about 40 species in this genus) FAMILY Zingiberaceae NATURAL SEASON Autumn COLOUR AVAILABILITY Cream, red, orange, white CUT FLOWER LIFE SPAN 5 days

GENERAL USE

Hedychium flowers are tall and elegant. Although hardy in the garden, they are delicate as cut flowers. They make an elegant vase flower and give height to arrangements. Do not use them in corporate designs.

GROWING CONDITIONS

Hedychium needs rich soil with plenty of water during the growing season. It is easy to grow and some refer to it as being as prolific as a weed.

HISTORY

Hedychium is native to the Himalayas. The Hedychium gardnerianum variety is named after the late San Francisco ginger collector, Gardner Waters.

CARE AND HANDLING

- Purchase when the flowers are just starting to open on the spike. The spike should have a scent and undamaged leaves.

- Recut 3–4 centimetres from the stem ends, using a sharp knife or secateurs. Cut on a sharp angle.

- Remove any leaves that will sit below the waterline.

- Use preservative to assist the buds to open and retain their scent.

- Change the water and preservative daily to ensure maximum life span.

COMMERCIAL HANDLING

- Do not place in the cool room.

HELENIUM *(hel-ee-nee-yum) Common names: Sneezeweed*

BOTANICAL VARIETIES Helenium autumnale (many varieties and hybrid cultivars) FAMILY Asteraceae NATURAL SEASON Summer and early autumn COLOUR AVAILABILITY Cream, yellow/gold, crimson, red CUT FLOWER LIFE SPAN Up to 5 days

CARE AND HANDLING

- Cut or purchase when the flowers are half open. The leaves should be a strong green with no signs of yellowing.
- Remove any leaves that will sit below the waterline.
- Wash the stems to remove dirt particles.
- Recut 2–3 centimetres from the stem ends. Cut on a sharp angle.
- Preservative is needed to assist the flowers to open.

COMMERCIAL HANDLING

- Heleniums are summer flowers and should not be placed in the cool room.

GENERAL USE

Helenium flowers have a casual, field flower appearance and lend themselves to less formal floral arrangements, such as in the vase at home. They are not suitable for corporate designs.

GROWING CONDITIONS

Helenium likes moist, rich soil and enjoys full sun. The seeds should be sewn in autumn. Plant them 30–40 centimetres apart.

HISTORY

Helenium is native to North America. It was named after Helen of Troy who was collecting elecampane root when she was captured by Paris. It is also known in America as 'Helen's Flower'. The common name 'Sneezeweed' came from Native American Indians, who made a snuff from the flower to make them sneeze and rid their bodies of evil spirits.

HELIANTHUS *(hel-ee-yan-thas) Common names: Sunflowers*

BOTANICAL VARIETIES Helianthus annuus (Sunflowers), Helianthus multiflorus (Double Sunflower) (a genus of about 70 annuals and perennials) **FAMILY** Asteraceae **NATURAL SEASON** Summer and autumn **COLOUR AVAILABILITY** Cream, yellow/gold, bronze and brownish tones **CUT FLOWER LIFE SPAN** 7–10 days

GENERAL USE

Helianthus (Sunflowers) have a strong, large surface area. They are dramatic and look effective in decorating arrangements and modern designs. They can air block quite easily when used in floral foam.

CORPORATE USE

Sunflowers can be used in corporate designs where there is a constant water source. They must be conditioned and never left out of water. All foliage must be removed as it will not last. Never use Sunflowers for corporate arrangements if they show pollen in their centres.

GROWING CONDITIONS

Sunflowers are easy to grow. Scatter the black seeds across well-drained, manured soil, rake them in and water. These annuals grow up to two metres tall. Use snailbait to deter snails.

HISTORY

Heliathus is native to South America, particularly Peru. It was named after Prince Alexander Philipp Maximilian (1782–1867), ruler of the small state of Neuwied, Prussia (now in Germany). The prince was a naturalist and in 1832 while travelling in North America, he discovered a particular species of Sunflower, which were subsequently named Helianthus maximiliani. The species was officially described for science in 1835 by the distinguished German botanist at Gottingen, Professor Heinrich Schrader. The Sunflower was once the emblem of the Sun God of the Incas.

The flower is a source of honey and yellow dye. Pith from the Sunflower stem is used in the preparation of microscope slides. The seeds are the source of Sunflower Oil.

CARE AND HANDLING

- Cut or purchase when the flowers are half to three-quarters open. The centres should not show any visual pollination.

- The leaves should be a strong green colour. Avoid Sunflowers that have soft or yellow leaves or have had their leaves removed.

- Check that the flowers are perfect on strong stems.

- Remove any foliage that will sit under the waterline.

- Recut 2–4 centimetres from the stem ends, using a sharp knife or secateurs. Cut on a sharp angle. If possible, cut the stems under water to prevent air blockages in the stems.

- Do not bash the stems.

- Use preservative to assist in maintaining the open flowers.

- If the flowers droop completely, recut the stems and place them in boiling water. This process clears the blockage quickly, but the life span of the flower is halved.

COMMERCIAL HANDLING

- Helianthus dislike being out of water and shock easily. They must be sold with a water source.

- If the leaves start to droop, immediately recut the stems up to 6 centimetres, and place in deep water with preservative. Leave them for up to three hours.

Romantic flower meaning: worship (Sunflower Dwarf);
pride (Sunflower Tall)

HELICONIA *(hel-i-ko-nee-ya) Common names: Sexy Pink; Crab Claw; Lobster Claw; Parrot Flower* BOTANICAL VARIETIES Heliconia rostrata (Sexy Pink), Heliconia caribaea (Crab Claw), Heliconia psittacorum (Parrot Flower), Heliconia wagneriana (Lobster Claw) (a large range of species) FAMILY Musaceae NATURAL SEASON All year round COLOUR AVAILABILITY Red, orange, yellow, pink, green, scarlet, cream CUT FLOWER LIFE SPAN Up to 4 weeks

GENERAL USE

There are many different varieties of Heliconia. One of these, Crab Claw, has very long stems that are particularly good for decorating. The flowers are quite inconspicuous as they are contained within the colourful bracts.

WEDDING USE

Miniature Heliconia is suited to all types of wedding designs. Larger Heliconia can be split and wired in sections. The individual petals can also be wired or wrapped using bullion wire and can be used to trail from bouquets.

CORPORATE USE

Heliconia flowers are suited to corporate designs as they hardly drink as cut flowers. Even so, they will only last 5–7 days in heated or airconditioned environments. Remove the leaves as they will curl and brown after 3–4 days.

GROWING CONDITIONS

Heliconia grows in the tropics and flowers all year round in ideal growing conditions. It likes filtered sun and rich, humus soil. Keep it constantly moist.

HISTORY

Heliconia is native to the South American tropics. It is grown mainly in Central Mexico, South America and the Caribbean, and is flown to flower markets across the world. Heliconia is also related to the banana plant. In the wild it is a food source for Hummingbirds. The name Heliconia is derived from the Greek work 'helix', meaning 'spiral'.

CARE AND HANDLING

- Purchase when the flowers are fully developed as they will not open once cut from the plant. Avoid any flowers with brown tips – this is a sign of age.

- Recut 2–4 centimetres from the stem ends and stand them in deep water.

- Keep the flowers above 12 degrees Celsius. Lower temperatures may cause damage to the bracts. Never place them in airconditioned environments.

- Treat the flowers to a light misting every now and again.

- Preservative will have no affect on the flowers, but chlorine or bleach added to the vase water will help to protect against bacteria.

COMMERCIAL HANDLING

- Never refrigerate Heliconia. This will cause them to blacken.

- When the stock arrives from the grower or market, unpack the flowers and bathe them in tepid water for up to one hour. The stems can be recut before or after the bathing process. Advise the consumer to recut the stems again when they take them home.

HELLEBORUS

(hel-lee-bor-us) Common names: Christmas Rose; Winter Rose BOTANICAL VARIETIES Helleborus argutifolius (lime), Helleborus orientalis (pink to mauve/purple) (a genus of 15 species) FAMILY Ranunculaceae NATURAL SEASON Winter and early spring COLOUR AVAILABILITY White, pinks, burgundy, green, purple, cream, purple/black, yellow CUT FLOWER LIFE SPAN 7 days

Romantic flower meaning:

succour for anxiety (Christmas Rose)

CARE AND HANDLING

- Cut or purchase when the flowers are half to fully open. Avoid any flowers with browning on the petals – this is a sign of age.

- Place them in water as soon as possible.

- The heads can be 'bathed' or fully immersed in water. Leave them for up to 3 hours and they will completely firm up.

- Recut 2–3 centimetres from the stem ends. This is especially important if the stem ends have been seared or boiled by the grower.

- Use preservative.

COMMERCIAL HANDLING

- Helleborus can be kept in the cool room a temperatures of 2–5 degrees Celsius.

GENERAL USE

Helleborus comes in a fabulous range of colours and is a good flower for cottage designs. The centres of the flowers are suitable for drying. It is possible to buy them in bunches or by the head. In times past, Helleborus flower heads were used extensively by florists for wreath work. The flowers were wired and used in layers to cover or 'top' the wreath. Their popularity has waned due to the need to wire them. Also, they are not well suited to floral foam designs.

Helleborus changes character towards the end of winter, with some varieties becoming green with seed pods and forming a hard centre. These can be used in corsage or fine wired work.

Do not use Helleborus for corporate designs. The flowers will droop and dry out in airconditioning or heating.

WEDDING USE

Helleborus flowers should be bathed before using in wedding designs. They are only suited to wired bouquets, using the pierce and mount wiring method. White Helleborus have spots in the centres of the flowers and this can look effective in bouquets.

GROWING CONDITIONS

Helleborus tolerates humus rich soil and prefers to be in partial shade. It is hardy to frost.

HISTORY

Helleborus is native to southern Europe and western Asia. It is closely related to Ranunculus. It is poisonous when eaten but for centuries it was thought that it would cure madness and was used as a deterrent to witchcraft. It was also planted near house doorways to ward off evil spirits from entering the house.

Helleborus flowers are used in winter decorations across Europe, especially in Scandinavia.

HIPPEASTRUM

(hip-pee-yass-trum) Common names: *Barbados Lily*

BOTANICAL VARIETIES Hippeastrum hybrids FAMILY Amaryllidaceae NATURAL SEASON Late spring and summer COLOUR AVAILABILITY Red, pink, green, yellow, orange and white CUT FLOWER LIFE SPAN 10–14 days

GENERAL USE

Hippeastrum is often compared to the Amaryllis, but it is larger and has less trumpet-shaped flowers. Hippeastrum flowers look dramatic in arrangements, provided they are not overcrowded. They can be used in modern designs however they are best suited to arrangements where floral foam is not used as the stem fibres can choke in the foam.

The stems can be curled for visual affect in a clear vase. To do this, use a knife and cut up the sides of the stem from the base. The more the stem is cut, the larger the curl. The width of each curl is determined by the number of vertical cuts. Curled stems look very effective provided they are the only flowers in the vase.

For decorating without a water source, hang the flowers upside down. They will last up to a month in this position, because the moisture contained within the stems moves slowly towards the flowers with the pull of gravity.

Hippeastrum is not suited to wedding designs unless a water source is provided.

CORPORATE USE

Hippeastrum flowers can look spectacular in corporate designs, especially when the stems are curled for display in a glass container.

GROWING CONDITIONS

Hippeastrum is grown from bulbs. It is frost tender and likes a rich loamy mixture. Add sand and charcoal and if planting in pots, a layer of rocks underneath for drainage. Ensure that a third of the bulb is above the soil level. Plant in early spring.

CARE AND HANDLING

- Cut or purchase when the buds are in clear colour and some flowers are starting to open.

- Avoid split or rolled stems as this indicates they have been in water for some time.

- Recut 2–3 centimetres from the stem ends, using a sharp knife. Cut on a sharp angle.

- Use preservative in the water to extend the flower's life span.

- Replace the water and preservative every 2–3 days.

COMMERCIAL HANDLING

- These flowers can be kept in the cool room at temperatures of 6–8 degrees Celsius.

HISTORY

Hippeastrum is native to tropical Central and South America. The name Hippeastrum means 'horseman's star' in Greek, and was chosen for the name of this flower by Reverend William Herbert, Dean of Manchester, in 1837. The name is thought to refer to the shape of the flower's petals.

Despite its common name of Barbados Lily, this flower is not actually native to Barbados. Many still use the name Barbados Lily in reference to Amaryllis, as originally the species was classified in this genus.

HYACINTHUS

(hi-a-sin-thus) Common names: Hyacinth

BOTANICAL VARIETIES Hyacinthus orientalis (numerous species have been developed) FAMILY Liliaceae NATURAL SEASON Late winter and spring COLOUR AVAILABILITY White, cream, hot pink, light pink, mauve, purple, lemon CUT FLOWER LIFE SPAN 14 days

GENERAL USE

There are three main forms of Hyacinths: Dutch (with tight flower heads), Roman (with looser flower heads) and Multiflora (with very loose flower heads). Most Hyancinths sold today are the Roman variety. They are usually purchased with three stems per bunch.

Hyacinths can be internally wired for use in floral foam. It is best to make an insertion in the foam prior to placing the stem into the foam. If the stem softens while in the foam, this indicates age, and you may need to wind wire around the base of the stem to stop it splitting. Hyacinth stems can be cut into sections and used individually for wreath work.

WEDDING USE

Hyacinthus is a very popular bridal flower. Individual florets can be wired and used for corsages and they are particularly delicate looking in bridal bouquets. The florets are usually 'pipped' (removed) from the main stem, leaving a short stem on the actual flower that is used to fasten the wire. Use the hairpin wiring method (down the throat of the flower). Open the wire slightly and insert to the left, or right of the centre. Ease the wire down and the shorter end of the return wire is then inserted on the opposite side. This stops the wire from pulling through the flower. Use binding tape to airlock the flower.

The stems can also be wired internally. They may need to be wired around the stem base if being used in a bouquet holder.

Darker coloured Hyacinths should be distributed carefully in bouquets as the flowers will 'spot' in photographs.

Hyacinths are highly perfumed so should be used with caution for wedding designs that are being held or worn by a hay fever sufferer.

CARE AND HANDLING

- Cut or purchase when the top of the spike is tight in bud form. The base florets should be open in a complete circle around the stem.

- The flowers should have a strong fragrance and leaves should be green and firm.

- Recut 2–3 centimetres from the stem ends. Cut on a sharp angle.

- Wash the stem ends, as particles of dirt can be caught in the foliage that grows close to the ground.

- Do not mist the flowers with water as they can become transparent and also catch water in the centres of the florets, which can cause fungal infections.

- Do not add preservative or sugar to the water.

- Do not place them near any form of heating.

COMMERCIAL HANDLING

- Hyacinthus can be kept in the cool room at temperatures of 4– 6 degrees Celsius.

- Hyacinthus can be stored in the cool room without a water source. For storing, the cool room temperature should be lowered to 1–2 degrees Celsius. Do not attempt to store unless you are fully familiar with this practice.

Romantic flower meaning:

sports loving; discreet loveliness (white Hyacinthus)

CORPORATE USE

Hyacinths can be used in corporate designs, but if used in floral foam or vases they should be wired internally up the stem to prevent them from bending over. The florets must be tight or they will not last. They need a constant water supply. They will last for around five days in hospital arrangements if they have a water source, but will dry out in heated and airconditioned environments.

GROWING CONDITIONS

Hyacinthus can be grown in a glass container in plain water for one year. In the garden it is frost hardy and prefers an open, sunny position with well-drained humus soil. Plant the bulb tops level with the ground.

HISTORY

Hyacinthus is native to southern Europe. The name Hyacinth came from the Greek Hyakinthos, who, according to legend, was a very handsome young man who was loved by the god Apollo as well as Zephyrus, god of the west wind. Zephyrus saw Hyakinthos and Apollo throwing a discus, and in a fit of jealousy, blew a strong wind that caused the discus to mortally wound Hyakinthos. A flower grew from his blood, which Apollo named 'Hyacinth'.

Three to four centuries ago, Hyacinths were extremely expensive due to their wonderful perfume. It was a flower collected by the wealthy.

In the language of flowers, the blue hyacinth means 'constancy.'

HYDRANGEA *(hi-drayn-jee-ya)*

BOTANICAL VARIETIES Hydrandea macrophilla (rounded heads), Hydrandea paniculata (pyramid shaped flowers) (many varieties)

FAMILY Hydrangeaceae NATURAL SEASON Late spring, summer and early autumn COLOUR AVAILABILITY White, pink, mauve, blue, dark pink, burgundy

CUT FLOWER LIFE SPAN approx 10 days

GENERAL USE

Hydrangea colours are determined by the PH levels in their soil. The smaller heads make a great base for posies. For wreaths, the heads can be separated and wired. Hydrangea flowers can look beautiful in a house vase for up to one month, however they will burn in hot summer temperatures. Use them with caution at the very start of their season, as they may not have completely firmed up.

Hydrangea can also be dried. Use late season flowers, hang them upside down or place into shallow water or glycerine solution, out of direct sunlight.

WEDDING USE

Hydrangea flowers are mostly used as a base for wedding designs. It is best to use mid or late season flowers as these will be firmer and stronger than early season flowers. It is a good idea to bathe or dunk the heads into water prior to use, and only use them at the base of the design.

Hydrangea flowers will not last in natural stemmed bouquets on a hot day. For warmer weather it is best to use them in bouquet holders with a water source.

CORPORATE USE

Mid or late season Hydrangea flowers can be used for corporate designs. They are best used in a deep container with other flowers.

CARE AND HANDLING

- Cut or purchase when some of the flowers are open and in strong colour. The foliage should be firm and green and there should be no brown heads.

- Transfer the flowers to water quickly to prevent the buds from drooping.

- Recut 2–3 centimetres from the stem ends. Cut on a sharp angle.

- Gently crush the stem ends to open the fibres and help them to drink. Do not bash the stem ends as it will damage their inner fibres.

- Never leave these flowers out of water.

- Remove any leaves that will sit below the waterline.

- Hydrangea flowers can be lightly misted with water but they will become transparent if over-misted.

- Preservative is essential.

- If the heads are to be used in designs they may need to be soaked in water until they firm up, but do not leave in water for more than two hours or they will become transparent.

Romantic flower meaning: callous

GROWING CONDITIONS

Hydrangea grows best in humus rich, porous soil that is kept moist. Acidic soils produce blue flowers and alkaline soils produce more pinks, reds and purples. An old trick is to place rusty nails in the soil around the plant – this will change the properties of the soil and therefore change the colours of the flowers.

Hydrangea is frost hardy but lime intolerant. It is a deciduous plant that can be propagated from cuttings.

HISTORY

Hydrangea is native to Japan, although some varieties are also native to China and the Americas. The Oakleaf Hydrangea was first discovered and named by John Bartram in the latter half of the 1700s, while he was exploring southern Georgia and Florida.

The name Hydrangea is derived from the Greek 'hydro', meaning 'water', and 'angeon', meaning 'vessel'. The name also refers to the plant's need for plenty of water.

HYMENOCALLIS

(hai-men-oh-kal-las) Common names: Spider Lily; Spider Flower; Peruvian Daffodil; Filmy Lily BOTANICAL VARIETIES Hymenocallis narcissiflora (Peruvian Daffodil), Hymenovallis littoralis (Filmy Lily), Hymenocallis caroliniana (Spider Lily/Flower), Hymenocallis harrisiana FAMILY Amaryllidaceae NATURAL SEASON Late spring and summer COLOUR AVAILABILITY White (there is also a yellow variety called Hymenocallis amancaes) CUT FLOWER LIFE SPAN 4–5 days

GENERAL USE

Hymenocallis flowers are particularly delicate in appearance and their leaves are also very appealing. They make a beautiful vase flower but they are very sensitive to airconditioning and therefore not suited to corporate work. Arranged with their own leaves in a tall vase, these flowers make a lovely showpiece in any home.

GROWING CONDITIONS

Hymenocallis is a bulbous plant that likes tropical conditions. Plant the bulbs in early spring, in a semi-shaded position. With a good water supply, a clump of green thin leaves will quickly develop.

HISTORY

Hymenocallis is native to the Andes mountains of Peru and Bolivia. The name comes from the Greek 'hymen', meaning 'membrane' and 'kallos', meaning 'beauty'. It is believed that this refers to the membrane that unites the stamens. The bulbs of some varieties are used for medicinal purposes.

CARE AND HANDLING

- Cut or purchase when the flowers are in half bud form. Avoid yellow leaves – this is a sign of age.

- Remove any leaves that will sit below the waterline.

- Preservative is essential for maximum life span. It will also assist in maintaining the open flowers.

HYPERICUM

(hai-pe-ri-kam) Common names: St Johns Wart; Rose of Sharon; Berries; Aaron's Beard; Chinese Hypericum monogynum (Chinese) FAMILY Clusiaceae SUB FAMILY Hypericaceae NATURAL SEASON Spring and summer BOTANICAL VARIETIES Hypericum cerastioides (Aarons Beard) Hypericum perforatum (St Johns Wart), COLOUR AVAILABILITY Yellow (for flowers), red, lime, pink, coral, orange (for berries) CUT FLOWER LIFE SPAN 5 days for the flowers, 7–10 days for the berries

CARE AND HANDLING

- Cut or purchase when the flowers are half open. There should be no sign of yellowing on the leaves.

- The berries should be shiny, firm and plump when picked.

- Remove any foliage that will sit below the waterline.

- Recut 2–3 centimetres from the stem ends, using sharp secateurs. Do not bash stem ends.

- Use preservative to assist the flowers' life span.

COMMERCIAL HANDLING

- Hypericum can be kept in the cool room at temperatures of 6–8 degrees Celsius.

GENERAL USE

Hypericum flowers are very pretty and delicate looking. The berries, which grow after the flowers have bloomed, are very popular in all types of floral designs.

WEDDING USE

Hypericum flowers should not be used in wedding designs, but the berries can be used as long as they are very firm and are not used on the edges of the design (otherwise they can stain clothing).

The berries should be wired using the cross-wiring method to lock them into place. Fasten the cross wires under the berry. Make sure the berries are securely fastened so that they cannot fall off (the wire can be glued into the berry to prevent this).

Thin coloured wires can be used when the wire is to be featured in the design. When used in floral foam, they are best placed low in the foam.

CORPORATE USE

Hypericum flowers will not last in corporate designs, but the berries can be used. Make sure they have not been in a cool room prior to use or the foliage will burn when placed in heated or airconditioned environments.

GROWING CONDITIONS

Hypericum enjoys full sun and needs well-drained soil. It is very easy to grow. It requires a strong winter prune and this is a good time to cover the roots with mulch. Propagate by seeds in autumn, softwood cuttings in spring and half-hardened cuttings in summer.

HISTORY

Hypericum is native to China. In some states of Australia it is considered a noxious weed. Some forms of Hypericum are used in herbal anti-depressant treatments.

HYPOCALYMMA

(hai-poh-ka-lim-ma) Common names: White Myrtle

BOTANICAL VARIETIES Hypocalymma angustifolium, Hypocalymma robustum FAMILY Myrtaceae NATURAL SEASON Late winter and spring COLOUR AVAILABILITY White, pink/red CUT FLOWER LIFE SPAN 5 days

GENERAL USE

Hypocalymma flowers are very pretty and are ideal for bowl arrangements (especially for weddings). They cannot be used in corporate work as they dislike airconditioning.

GROWING CONDITIONS

Hypocalymma enjoys a semi-shaded position in well-drained soil. They grow best in a warm, dry summer and wet winter climates. Cut back after flowering.

HISTORY

Hypocalymma is native to Australia. Its name comes from the Greek word 'hypo', meaning 'under', and 'kalymma', meaning 'veil'. The name refers to the calyx of the flower, which falls like a veil or cape.

CARE AND HANDLING

- Cut or purchase when the flowers on the top third of the tip are half open (these flowers open from the tip down). There should be no sign of yellowing on the leaves.

- Recut 2–3 centimetres from the stem ends, using secateurs. Cut on an angle.

- Remove any leaves that will sit below the waterline.

- Use preservative to maintain the open flowers.

COMMERCIAL HANDLING

- Do not place in the cool room.

IBERIS *(ai-bur-iss) Common names: Candytuft*

BOTANICAL VARIETIES Iberis gibraltarica FAMILY Brassicaceae NATURAL SEASON Spring and early summer COLOUR AVAILABILITY White (unperfumed), pink, mauve, deep pink, green (across the varieties) CUT FLOWER LIFE SPAN 7 days

CARE AND HANDLING

- Cut or purchase when half of the flowers are open.

- Recut 2–3 centimetres from the stem ends. Cut on an angle.

- Remove all foliage that will sit below the waterline.

- Use preservative or domestic bleach in the water.

- Ensure that there is airflow around the stems. They must never be tightly packed into a vase.

- Iberis does not like to be placed in deep water.

- Change the vase water regularly.

- Iberis is sensitive to ethylene so keep it away from cigarette smoke and ripening fruit.

COMMERCIAL HANDLING

- Iberis can be kept in the cool room at temperatures of 6–8 degrees Celsius.

GENERAL USE

Iberis flowers have round, clustered heads and are generally used as posy or vase flowers. The miniature varieties are ideal for edging posies or Nosegays (small posies). Be aware that if Iberis is wired it will collapse within hours.

GROWING CONDITIONS

There are two common types of Iberis grown for bedding plants – Iberis amara and Iberis umbellata. The latter has a rainbow of colours. Both varieties will grow in average garden soil with drainage and can be sown in early spring. They are herbaceous perennials.

HISTORY

Iberis gibraltarica (white flowers, sometimes with a tinge of pink) is native to Gibraltar. Other varieties are native to Europe. Iberis is named after Iberia (a region of Spain), because many members of the genus come from the Iberian Peninsula.

IRIS

(ai-riss) Common names: Flag; Dutch Iris; Fleur-de-luce; Fleur-de-Lis

BOTANICAL VARIETIES Iris hybrids, Iris Professor Blaauw (popular Dutch Iris), Iris reticulata, Iris xiphium, Iris xiphioides, Iris crocea (Golden Iris), Iris ensata (White Japanese Iris), Iris unguicularis (Algerian Iris) (many more varieties) FAMILY Iridaceae NATURAL SEASON Late winter and spring COLOUR AVAILABILITY Purple, yellow, deep blue, pale blue, white and cream CUT FLOWER LIFE SPAN 5–7 days

GENERAL USE

Iris flowers are commercially available all year round and very popular to combine with other spring flowers. Do not combine with Narcissus unless they have been in a separate vase for half a day (Narcissus exudes a sap when freshly cut that kills Iris).

They are also ideal for other types of arrangements, including bouquets. Do not use for corporate designs as they will not last throughout the week.

WEDDING USE

Iris is a popular flower for hand-tied bouquets. The white/yellow Iris is suited to brides of more traditional taste. Iris can be used in all forms of bridal bouquets, but be aware that the Dutch Iris photographs darker than it really is.

GROWING CONDITIONS

Iris like well-drained soil in either full sun or slight shade. Its rhizomes should be partly exposed to the sun. The Japanese Iris grows best under water and can be planted in ponds or fountains.

HISTORY

Iris is native to the Mediterranean region. To the ancient Greeks Iris was the messenger of the Gods who communicated using rainbows. In the language of flowers, blue Iris means, 'you mean so much to me', and the yellow Iris means 'passion'.

Iris is the Fleur-de-lis of France. King Louis VII is supposed to have chosen the name and the emblem it represents when his country joined the Crusaders who were fighting the infidels and driving them out of the Holy Land. It is suggested that the Fleur-de-Louis eventually became the Fleur-de-Luce and then became the Fleur-de-Lis (sometimes *lys*). During this time, Iris flowers grew in profusion along the river Lys. It was also part of the coat of arms of the Medici family and therefore on the coat of arms of Tuscany and Florence.

CARE AND HANDLING

- Cut or purchase when colour is visible at the end of the sheath that covers the flower. Make sure the petals have not unfurled – the flower may not open if the head is too tight.

- Avoid flowers with brown tips – this is a sign of refrigeration burn.

- The leaf tips should be not be curled or dry looking.

- Recut 2–3 centimetres from the stem ends, making sure that the whitish parts of the stem are removed. Cut on a sharp angle.

- Remove any foliage that will sit below the waterline.

- Wash the stems to remove any dirt particles between the leaves.

- Do not use a preservative as Iris dislikes sugar. Instead, use cold water with chlorine added.

- Iris is only mildly sensitive to ethylene. Grey/black tips on the petals can indicate ethylene damage.

- Iris dislikes heating and airconditioning.

COMMERCIAL HANDLING

- If possible, avoid placing Iris in the cool room. When they are removed they open quickly, especially in the warmer months. It is better for Iris to acclimatise to its surrounding room temperature.

- Iris can be stored long term in the cool room if necessary (i.e. if there is a severe shortage of stock). They can be stored without a water source. The cool room temperature should be 1–4 degrees Celsius. Do not lie them down as the tips will curl upwards.

The top petals of the Iris are called 'standards' and the three downward petals are known as 'falls'.

IRIS (BEARDED) *(ai-ris)* Common names: *Flag; German Iris*

BOTANICAL VARIETIES Iris sibirica, Iris ensata, Iris laevigata, Iris barbata, Iris germanica, (over 200 species) FAMILY Iridaceae NATURAL SEASON Spring COLOUR AVAILABILITY All colours CUT FLOWER LIFE SPAN Up to 5 days

GENERAL USE

Bearded Irises are stunning in their colours and their delicate appearance. They can be displayed in the home, mainly as a vase flower (as the life span of the flower is limited), or used in decorations such as table centrepieces and wedding display bowls or urns. Bearded Iris foliage can be cut and arranged with the flowers.

GROWING CONDITIONS

There are two main groups of Iris: Rhizomatous and Bulbous. These are mostly herbaceous perennials. They have underground corms, tubers or rhizomes. Their rhizomatous rootstocks should be at least half-exposed at planting time.

Bearded Iris enjoys full sun and well-drained soil (preferably have lime content). To ensure continuous flowering the roots should be divided every two to three years. Some cultivars will spike up to 180 centimetres in height.

HISTORY

Bearded Iris is native to northern and southern Europe, northern and southern Africa and parts of Asia Minor. For centuries the Iris Florentina has been the source for the violet scented 'Irris-root'. The roots need to be at least two years in age before their full flavour develops. The dried rhizomes are fragrant.

The Egyptians, Romans and Greeks valued Orris for its perfumery purposes and the seeds were used in medicines. In medieval times Irris was used to keep acne at bay as well as inducing sleep, as well as a cure for ulcers.

CARE AND HANDLING

- Cut or purchase when the buds are showing colour.

- Recut 2–3 centimetres from the stem ends. Cut on an angle.

- Wash the stems and leaves to remove any particles of dirt prior to placing them in the vase.

- Place into cool water with preservative added. The preservative will assist the buds to open and improve the strength of their colour.

- Do not place Bearded Iris in direct sunlight.

- If the flowers are removed as they die, another two or three flowers may then develop from bud. Doing this will considerably increase the vase life of the flowers.

- Lightly mist the flowers to show them in their peak of beauty.

COMMERCIAL HANDLING

- Do not place in the cool room or the flowers will shock on removal and fade quickly, especially when exposed to a high temperature contrast.

ISOPOGON

(ai-sop-a-gon) Common names: Cone Flower; Cone Bush; Drumsticks

BOTANICAL VARIETIES A range of species including Sopogon cuneatus, Isopogen anemonifolius, Isopogon anethifolius (Drumsticks), Isopogon dubius (Rosy Cone Flower) and Isopogon formosus **FAMILY** Proteaceae **NATURAL SEASON** Late winter, spring and sometimes early summer **COLOUR AVAILABILITY** Pink, purple, yellow/orange **CUT FLOWER LIFE SPAN** Up to 3 weeks

GENERAL USE

Isopogon flowers are generally available in lengths of 30–60 centimetres. These flowers are not commonly used in arrangements but they are long lasting, visually striking and are also a good filling flower.

WEDDING USE

Isopogon flowers can be used in wedding designs. They are best used wired or placed into bouquet holders.

CORPORATE USE

Isopogon flowers can be used in corporate designs (including office and hospital arrangements), as long as the foliage is removed. They will dry out in airconditioned environments but will usually last five working days in an office environment.

GROWING CONDITIONS

Isopogon can be propagated from ripe seed sown in winter. It can also be raised from cuttings, struck in peat and sand. It likes acidic soil with sand and regular watering.

HISTORY

Isopogon is native to Australia. The flowers (cones) remain on the bush for some months and this is why they are known as Cone Flowers. The genus was named by Robert Brown in 1810. The name means 'equally bearded', which refers to the plant's hairy nut.

CARE AND HANDLING

- Cut or purchase when the outer flowers are opening. Bunches with brown tips or yellowing leaves should be avoided.

- Handle with care as these flowers are easily damaged.

- Remove any leaves that will sit below the waterline.

- Wash the stems.

- Recut 2–3 centimetres from the stem ends, using secateurs. Cut on an angle.

- The stem ends can be lightly crushed.

- The flowers will last longer with preservative in the water, but it needs to be changed every 2–3 days.

- Preservative will also assist the buds to develop.

- Keep these flowers cool.

COMMERCIAL HANDLING

- Do not place in the cool room.

IXIA

(ix-ee-ya) Common names: African Corn Lily

BOTANICAL VARIETIES Ixia maculata (approximately 50 species) FAMILY Iridaceae NATURAL SEASON Spring COLOUR AVAILABILITY White, yellow, bright pink CUT FLOWER LIFE SPAN 7 days

CARE AND HANDLING

- Cut or purchase when the flowers at the base of the spike are open.

- Recut and wash the stems.

- Preservative is helpful for extended life span.

- Ixia is ethylene sensitive, so keep it away from heat and ripening fruit.

COMMERCIAL HANDLING

- Ixia can be kept in the cool room at temperatures of 6–8 degrees Celsius. Make sure there is airflow around the flowers while they are in the cool room (to prevent mould growth).

GENERAL USE

Ixia is a good 'all round' cut flower. It can be used in posies, funeral sheaves and wreaths, and lots of other arrangements. Ixia flowers make a good outline as well as a filling flower for bouquets and wreaths.

WEDDING USE

Ixia flowers can be used in hand-tied, natural stemmed bouquets as a surround, but they are best used in bouquet holders with a water source. They can be cut into sections to use as a filler flower.

CORPORATE USE

Ixia is a pretty flower and suited to smaller vases in office decorating. They will start to dry out, but usually survive around five days in office conditions.

GROWING CONDITIONS

Plant Ixia in summer, after the soil is fertilised with blood and bone, or plant it in early autumn for spring flowering bulbs. It prefers a mild climate. Propagation is usually from offsets.

HISTORY

Ixia is native to South Africa. This genus is named after the African word for 'baboons', which eat the corms.

IXODIA

(iks-oh-dee-ya) Common names: South Australian Daisy; Mountain Daisy; Hills Daisy

BOTANICAL VARIETIES Ixodia achillaeoides (Ssp Alata) FAMILY Asteraceae NATURAL SEASON Spring and summer COLOUR AVAILABILITY White

CUT FLOWER LIFE SPAN 7 days

GENERAL USE

Ixodia is a good fresh flower to use in general floristry, as it is clustered. It is also very popular as a dried flower. To dry, hang the flowers upside down in a cool, dry and well-ventilated place. They do not lose their look as a dried flower, but can be decorated with coloured floral sprays for an interesting effect.

WEDDING USE

Ixodia flowers are best used dried for wedding designs, but may also be used fresh. Whether dried or fresh, they are a delicate filling flower for bouquets or table centrepieces.

CORPORATE USE

Ixodia can be used fresh or dried in corporate designs.

GROWING CONDITIONS

Ixodia grows in the wild and are very easy to grow in South Australian or Victorian gardens. It grows best in well-drained soil.

HISTORY

Ixodia is native to Australia and is most prevalent in South Australia. The name Ixodia comes from the Greek 'Ixodes', meaning 'sticky'. This refers to the plant's sticky foliage.

CARE AND HANDLING

- Cut or purchase when the flowers are open.

- The flowers close when in poor light, but will re-open with strong light (when they are in water).

- Recut the stems and remove any foliage that will sit below the waterline.

- Wash the stems to minimise their stickiness.

- Use preservative to extend life span.

COMMERCIAL HANDLING

- Do not place into the cool room or the flowers will dry.

KALMIA

(kal-mee-ya) Common names: Calico Bush; Mountain Laurel
BOTANICAL VARIETIES Kalmia latifolia (7 species in this genus) FAMILY Ericaceae NATURAL SEASONAL Late spring to summer COLOUR AVAILABILITY Pink (other varieties red and white) CUT FLOWER LIFE SPAN 7–9 days

CARE AND HANDLING

- Cut or purchase when the flowers are at least half open. The foliage should be strong and green with no sign of yellowing.
- Recut 2–3 centimetres from the stem ends. Cut on an angle.
- Remove any foliage that will sit below the waterline.
- Use preservative in the water if the water is not optimum quality.
- Keep it away from airconditioning.

COMMERCIAL HANDLING

- Kalmia can be kept in the cool room at temperatures of 6–8 degrees Celsius.

GENERAL USE

Kalmia is a lovely posy flower. It is sold in bunches and is a little sticky to handle. These flowers can be used in most floral arrangements. Their clustered appearance makes them a good filling flower for funeral tributes as well.

WEDDING USE

Kalmia is most suited to bouquet holders. The pink shades are delicate for a bride who wants some colour in her bouquet.

CORPORATE USE

Kalmia is suited to corporate work. Use the flowers in bud form, just as they are starting to open.

GROWING CONDITIONS

These evergreen shrubs are slow to grow out of their native environment. They like an acid-rich soil and enjoy part shade and humidity. They need a good water supply. Plant them in late spring or early autumn. They will survive frosty winters. They are related to the Rhododendron family.

HISTORY

Kalmia is native to the American mountains. It is named after the Finnish Botanist, Pehr Kalm. Peter Collinson introduced this species to Britain in 1734, however it did not actually flower until 1741 in Catesby's Gardens at Fulham. Michaux (senior) introduced Kalmia to France in 1790 and it was after this time that the species was introduced to Europe.

Kalmia has various uses throughout history. In medicine, the leaves, in a pulverised form, have been used to relieve cutaneous affections. The hardened wood was once used by Native American Indians to make utensils, small dishes and spoons.

KNAUTIA

(knor-tee-ya) Common names: Field Scabious; Blue Buttons; Gypsy Rose

BOTANICAL VARIETIES Knautia macedonica, Knautia arvensis (Blue Buttons) FAMILY Dipsacaceae NATURAL SEASON Summer

COLOUR AVAILABILITY Dark red or purple/red (Knautia macedonica), pale blue (Knautia arvensis) CUT FLOWER LIFE SPAN 2 weeks

GENERAL USE

Knautia flowers (relatives to Scabiosa) last very well as cut flowers. They are suited to most forms of floral design, particularly posies. Do not use these flowers in corporate work as they dislike airconditioning and will dry out.

WEDDING USE

Knautia flowers can be used with a water source for bridal work or the flower base can be used in fine wired work.

CORPORATE USE

The base of the Knautia flower, with petals removed, can be used in corporate designs, however do not use the whole flower as they will dry out in airconditioned environments.

GROWING CONDITIONS

Knautia enjoy full sun and well-drained soil that is slightly alkaline. The seeds can be sowed from seed in spring, or the plant can be propagated from autumn divisions. Water across summer and stake the plants for wind protection.

HISTORY

This plant is native to Eastern Europe. The name of the genus Knautia relates to Dr Knaut, a 17th century German botanist.

CARE AND HANDLING

- Cut or purchase when one third of the flowers are open.

- Separate the bunches to ensure adequate airflow around the flowers.

- Remove any foliage that will sit below the waterline.

- Recut 2–3 centimetres from the stem ends. Cut on an angle.

- Use preservative to assist the life span of the flowers.

COMMERCIAL HANDLING

- Do not place into the cool room as they will sweat, and the foliage will brown if they are not separated. This will cause shock on removal.

KNIPHOFIA

(nip-hoh-fee-a) Common names: Red-hot Pokers; Torch Lily

BOTANICAL VARIETIES Kniphofia uvaria, Kniphofia atlanta (Red-hot Pokers), Kniphofia Bees Lemon (Torch Lily), Kniphofia hybrid cultivars (nearly 70 species in this genus) FAMILY Asphodelaceae NATURAL SEASON Late winter, spring and summer COLOUR AVAILABILITY Red, yellow, pink, lime CUT FLOWER LIFE SPAN 2 weeks

CARE AND HANDLING

- Cut or purchase when the base florets are open and in good colour.

- If the florets have brown tips and are level angling downwards to the stem, this means they are older and should be avoided.

- Recut 2–3 centimetres from the stem ends, using a knife or secateurs.

- Use preservative.

- Kniphofia is ethylene sensitive so do not place outside.

- Do not place in airconditioned environments or it will dry out.

COMMERCIAL HANDLING

- There is no need to place in the cool room, but if wanting to slow respiration, the cool room temperature should be 6 degrees Celcius.

GENERAL USE

Kniphofia flowers are sold without foliage. If they are arranged horizontally they will bend, or turn upwards from their tips. The flowers die from the base upwards and these florets can be removed to extend the vase life of the remaining flowers.

WEDDING USE

Kniphofia is usually considered too large for bridal work, but miniature varieties are available. They are available in not only oranges and yellows, but also in lime green with lemon tops. These look particularly effective with native flowers or in modern bouquet designs.

CORPORATE USE

Kniphofia will last in corporate designs. Make sure they are very fresh because they will start to die off and brown at the base if used when they are already mature. These flowers die back from the base. If you allow the petals to brown and die, they will remove easily and leave a stem with clustered green seeds exposed. These green stems look dramatic in modern corporate designs.

GROWING CONDITIONS

Kniphofia is hardy and easy to grow. It likes good drainage, sun and some mulch. It can be propagated from root divisions or from seed sown after flowering. Water well before it blooms.

HISTORY

Kniphofia is native to east and south-east Africa. Kniphofia uvaria was the first Kniphofia variety to reach Europe in 1707. The genus Kniphofia is named in honour of Johannes Hieronymus Kniphof (1704–1763), a professor of medicine at Erfurt University in Germany who was renowned for his published work, *Botanica in Originali.*

LACHENALIA

(lak-en-nay-lee-ya) Common names: Soldier Boys; Soldier Lily; Cape Cowslip BOTANICAL VARIETIES Lachenalia aloides (Cape Cowslip), Lachenalia bulbifera (Soldier Boys) FAMILY Hyacinthaceae NATURAL SEASON Winter and spring COLOUR AVAILABILITY Yellow/green, red/gold, red/pink CUT FLOWER LIFE SPAN 7 days

GENERAL USE

Lachenalia flowers are very attractive, but as the flowers look downwards, they may appear (to the untrained eye) to be wilting. They are hard to get in some areas, but they last well and they can be used in most types of floral work. They make a pretty vase flower on their own.

GROWING CONDITIONS

Lachenalia needs well-drained soil. Plant in autumn and thin leaves will develop quickly. Pendulous spikes will follow. Keep it dry over summer. Propagate from offsets or by dividing established bulbous clumps. If planted in areas of heavy rainfall it is best to lift them it the ground over summer.

HISTORY

Lachenalia is native to Southern Africa. The genus is named after Werner de Lachenal (1739–1800), a professor of botany at Basel, Switzerland.

CARE AND HANDLING

*   Cut or purchase when the lower flowers are open and showing full colour.

*   Recut 2–3 centimetres from the stem ends. Cut on an angle.

*   Preservative is optional.

COMMERCIAL HANDLING

*   Do not place in the cool room.

LACHNOSTACHYS

(lak-nos-stay-ses) Common names: Lambs Tail

BOTANICAL VARIETIES Lachnostachys verbascifolia FAMILY Chloanthaceae (sometimes also included in Limiaceae family) NATURAL SEASON Spring COLOUR AVAILABILITY Grey/white LIFE SPAN 2 weeks

CARE AND HANDLING

- Cut or purchase when the flowers are open. The heads should look full and they should be upright and firm.

- Separate the bunches to ensure adequate airflow around the flowers.

- Recut 2–3 centimetres from the stem ends, using secateurs.

- Wash the stems to remove any dirt particles.

- Remove any foliage that will sit below the waterline.

- Preservative in the water is optional, however, bleach is required to keep the water clear.

- Do not stand in deep water but make sure the water is regularly topped up.

- Do not mist with water.

COMMERCIAL HANDLING

- Do not place in the cool room or the foliage will deteriorate rapidly. The stems will also waterlog in cool temperatures.

GENERAL USE

Lachnostachys is a textured flower that looks great with other native flowers. It can also be made to look soft and delicate if arranged with spring flowers. It is a good filler flower as well as an outline flower for arrangements. It will dry out in airconditioning.

WEDDING USE

Lachnostachys flowers and foliage can be used as a surround on hand-tied, natural stemmed bouquets. Lachnostachys can also be used in bouquet holders, or wired bouquets. Do not use this flower in hot weather.

CORPORATE USE

Lachnostachys is a good filling flower/foliage for corporate designs. Use bleach in the water to prevent the flowers/foliage fouling the vase water.

GROWING CONDITIONS

Lachnostachys grows in the wild and will tolerate mild weather. It requires water before flowering and will survive in poor quality soil. Separate the plant for replanting after flowering. Cut back the bush after flowering.

HISTORY

Lachnostachys is native to Western Australia. The etymology stems from the Greek word for 'blown or puffed 'up', as the calyx is enveloped in a cottony mass.

LATHYRUS

(la-thai-ras) Common names: Sweet Pea

BOTANICAL VARIETIES Lathyrus odoratus hybrids (there are over 100 species in this genus) FAMILY Fabaceae

NATURAL SEASON Late winter, spring and summer COLOUR AVAILABILITY Pink, mauve, yellow, cream, apricot, purple, maroon

CUT FLOWER LIFE SPAN 5–7 days

GENERAL USE

Lathyrus is a very pretty, dainty flower, ideal for posies and for the vase at home. It does not hold well as a wired flower as it requires a constant water source. It dislikes heat as a cut flower.

WEDDING USE

Lathyrus flowers look light and pretty when used in hand-tied, natural stemmed bouquets. They can be wired or wire supported for use in bouquet holders with a water source. Do not use these flowers in hot weather.

CORPORATE USE

If Lathyrus is used in bud form it will last well in corporate designs.

GROWING CONDITIONS

Lathyrus needs deep, rich soil in a sunny position. It likes lime and fertiliser enriched with phosphorus and potash. Cut back to ground level in autumn. Annuals are grown from seed and perennials are grown by division when dormant.

HISTORY

Lathyrus is a native species that grows from Sicily through to the Southern Balkans.

This flower was a favourite of Queen Alexandra in Edwardian times. British Victorian railway workers once planted these flowers with great popularity in gardens around railway stations, where many remain to this day.

CARE AND HANDLING

- Cut or purchase when the top buds are in full colour and starting to open. All leaves should be green.

- Strongly perfumed flowers are a sign of freshness.

- Shake the bunch to check for flower drop.

- Separate the bunches, but be careful with the delicate tendrils.

- Remove any foliage that will sit below the waterline.

- Recut 2–3 centimetres from the ends. Cut on an angle.

- Preservative is recommended.

- Lathryus flowers prefer to be in deep water and do not like being misted.

- Do not place in direct sunlight.

- Lathryus is sensitive to ethylene so keep it away from cigarette smoke and ripening fruit.

COMMERCIAL HANDLING

- Lathryus can be kept in the cool room at temperatures of 6–8 degrees Celsius.

Romantic flower meaning: delicacy

LAVANDULA

(la-ven-doo-la) Common names: *Lavender*

BOTANICAL VARIETIES Lavendula spica, Lavendula stoechas, Lavendula pterostoechas and hybrids (8 species of evergreen aromatic shrubs in this genus) FAMILY Lamiaceae NATURAL SEASON Spring and summer COLOUR AVAILABILITY Mauve, purple, white, pink LIFE SPAN 5–7 days

GENERAL USE

Lavendula is a very pretty flower to use in cottage style posies. If used in floral foam it should have wire support. If used in gift or corsage work, it will need a fine wire, hooked at the top, to be wound through the flower head and down the stem for support.

Lavendula can also be dried. Hang it upside down in a well-ventilated area. Remove all foliage, as any moisture dropping onto the heads will rot them.

WEDDING USE

Lavandula must be wire-supported for use in any bridal designs. Use fine wire. Hook the end and wind the wire down through the flowers. Stronger wire can be used to support the stem in a bouquet. The flower head will droop if the stems are not supported. This method works for hand-tied, natural stemmed bouquets, bouquet holders and wired bouquets.

Lavender is sweet smelling so be careful when using it in bouquets that will be held by hayfever or asthma sufferers.

Do not use Lavendula in corporate work. It dislikes heating and airconditioning and will droop in these environments.

GROWING CONDITIONS

Lavendula will grow in almost any moist soil. It enjoys a warm, sunny position. It can be propagated from tip cuttings in autumn or from half-hardened cuttings in autumn. It is best to deadhead the flowers regularly. Trim back but do not cut into the old, woody stems.

Lavendula makes a great hedge and there are many types to choose from, including French, English, Spanish, Dutch, and Italian.

CARE AND HANDLING

- Cut or purchase when flowers are open and in full colour.

- Avoid any dried heads.

- Recut 2–3 centimetres from the stem ends. Cut on a sharp angle.

- Wash the stems.

- Remove any foliage that will sit below the waterline. If the foliage is not removed it will foul the water very quickly.

- Use preservative to give the flowers extra strength.

- Keep cool as a cut flower, but do not place in airconditioned or heated environments.

COMMERCIAL HANDLING

- Lavendula can be kept in the cool room at temperatures of 6–8 degrees Celsius. Allow for conditioning time on removal.

- Bunches should be separated if placed in the cool room, as they are prone to moulding if they are packed too tightly.

HISTORY

Lavendula is native to many areas stemming from the western Mediterranean across to India. The name Lavender is derived from the Latin word 'lavare', meaning 'to wash'. This is a reference to the fact that the flower was used by the Romans to add a delicate scent to their baths.

Fleas are repelled by the scent of Lavender, and as such, it was once used by the French to successfully assist in stopping the spread of the bubonic plague.

Lavender remains a popular cottage garden plant for the English, where large tracts of land have been devoted to the growing of Lavender due to its popular use in perfumery.

Lavender is also popular for its many herbal properties, and Lavender oil is commonly extracted from the flower for use as an antiseptic and calmative. The dried flower can now even be purchased as a culinary spice.

LEPTOSPERMUM

(lep-toh-spur-mam) **Common names:** *Tea Tree; Lavender Queen; Pacific Beauty* BOTANICAL VARIETIES Leptospermum polygalifolium, Leptospermum scoparium hybrids (80 or so species in this genus) FAMILY Myrtaceae NATURAL SEASON Spring and early summer COLOUR AVAILABILITY White, lime, red, pink LIFE SPAN 5 days

GENERAL USE

These flowers are also grown in double cultivars and they look great in all floral designs. However, they do not last when out of water and the single flowers do not last when wired. The 'Pacific Beauty' (Leptospermum polygalifolium) is a great flower to use in large church-service bowls and function arrangements. Do not use Leptospermum in corporate designs as they dry and drop in heating and airconditioning.

WEDDING USE

Leptospermum flowers can be used in bouquet holders with a water source, or in hand held bouquets if kept in water until the time of the service.

GROWING CONDITIONS

These plants are drought hardy and they grow well in sandy soils. They are tolerant to wind and salt spray as they often grow near the beach. They can be propagated in summer. Place half-ripe cuttings into a sandy mix.

HISTORY

Leptospermum is native to Australia. Its name is derived from the Greek words 'leptos', meaning 'thin' and 'sperma' meaning 'seed' which is a reference to the small seeds of the plant.

The name Polygalifolium is derived from the Latin word 'folius', meaning 'leaf' as the leaves resemble the genus polygana. It has been said that Captain Cook once brewed a form of tea from the tiny leaves of Leptospermum, hence its common name, Tea Tree.

CARE AND HANDLING

- Cut or purchase when at least three-quarters of the flowers are open. If there are too many unopened buds then they may not open at all.

- Do not purchase late in the season as the flowers drop easily.

- Remove any leaves that will sit below the waterline.

- Recut 2–3 centimetres from the stem ends, using sharp secateurs. Cut on an angle.

- Use preservative.

COMMERCIAL HANDLING

- Do not place in the cool room.

LEUCADENDRON

(loo-ka-den-dran) Common names: Safari Sunset; Sylvan Red; Inca Gold; Christmas Cones; Multi-Cones; Yellow Tulip; Flame Tip; Silver Bush; Geelbos

BOTANICAL VARIETIES Leucadendron salignum (Geelbos), Leucadendron argenteum (Silver Bush), Leucadendron laureolum, Leucadendron orientale, Leucadendron salicifolium, Leucadendron macowanii, Leucadendron comosum, Leucadendron coniferum (there are many hybrids) FAMILY Proteaceae NATURAL SEASON Late winter, spring and early summer COLOUR AVAILABILITY Burgundy, yellow, orange, lime, red/burgundy and combinations of all LIFE SPAN 4 weeks

CARE AND HANDLING

- Cut or purchase straight stems. There should be no sign of burn tips at the ends of the bracts.

- Recut 2–3 centimetres from the stem ends, using secateurs or a sharp knife. Cut on an angle.

- Remove any leaves that will sit below the waterline.

- Preservative is optional but recommended.

- These flowers will drink heavily so ensure the water supply is always topped up.

- Keep cool as a cut flower.

- Containers should be scrupulously clean.

COMMERCIAL HANDLING

- In most cases there is little need to place Leucadendron in the cool room, but if necessary the cool room temperature should be 6–8 degrees Celcius.

- If necessary, Leucadendron can be stored long term in the cool room at temperatures of 2–4 degrees Celcius. Avoid storing these flowers if possible.

GENERAL USE

Leucadendron flowers are very popular, partly due to the fact that they last for so long as cut flowers. The flowers and bracts are available in short, medium and long stems. There are some 70 different varieties. They are now grown commercially to be available throughout the year.

They can be used in all forms of floral design. The silver leaf can be curled and it looks striking with Cymbidium Orchids in corsage work.

Leucadendron flowers can be dried if hung upside down in a well-ventilated area.

WEDDING USE

Leucadendron flowers are available in many colours and shapes. They are hardy and can be used in hand-tied, natural stemmed bouquets or bouquet holders as well as fully wired bouquets. They can be 'feathered' or split apart. The single bracts can be wired or tied on bullion wire for a trailing affect.

CORPORATE USE

Leucadendron flowers are ideal for use in corporate designs. Sometimes the foliage may dry in airconditioned or heated environments, so it is best to remove it before use.

GROWING CONDITIONS

Leucadendron plants enjoy humidity. They like well-drained soil and mulch, although it is best not to use animal manure around them. They are propagated from seed or cuttings.

HISTORY

Leucadendron is native to southern Africa. It is a cousin of the Protea.

LEUCANTHEMUM *(loo-kan-the-mum) Common names: Shasta Daisy; Ox-eye Daisy* BOTANICAL VARIETIES Leucanthemum superbum (Shasta Daisy), Chiffon, Leucanthemum vulgare (Ox-Eye Daisy) (30 or so species of annual and perennial Daisies) FAMILY Asteraceae NATURAL SEASON Summer COLOUR AVAILABILITY White, lemon LIFE SPAN Up to 14 days

GENERAL USE

Leucanthemums are used for general floral items. They quite often require internal wiring as the heads can be particularly weak. The single heads of Leucanthemums can be coloured using food dye. This process can take several hours (four hours minimum).

The Chiffon variety has frilly edged petals instead of the usual flat-layered petals of the other varieties. These can look interesting in floral designs.

WEDDING USE

Leucanthemum flowers should be internally wired for hand-tied, natural stemmed bouquets, or for use in bouquet holders. For wired bouquets they can be wired using the pierce and mount method.

These flowers can be dyed with food dye or coloured with floral spray paints and, of course, used in their natural white/cream colour.

CORPORATE USE

Leucanthemums will last five days in office conditions if used in bud form. Use preservative as they will foul the water if it is not changed regularly.

GROWING CONDITIONS

These plants are annuals and herbaceous perennials. They enjoy well-drained soil and should be kept moist. Propagate from seed, or separate clumps when they become too dense as they will multiply in the garden.

These plants make an excellent garden border. They can be moved after flowering. Cut back to ground level after flowering season.

CARE AND HANDLING

- Cut or purchase when two or three flowers are open. Look for round flowers with centres that are tightly packed together. Yellow leaves indicate age.

- Open the bunches to ensure there is adequate airflow around the flowers.

- Cut 2–3 centimetres from the stem ends. Cut on an angle.

- Remove any foliage that will sit below the waterline.

- Use preservative to assist the flowers to open and hold.

COMMERCIAL HANDLING

- Leucanthemum can be placed in the cool room at temperatures of 6–8 degrees Celsius. Airflow around the flowers is vital or else the foliage will blacken and mould.

HISTORY

Leucanthemum is native to Europe. It was originally bred by Luther Burbank, an American plant breeder. The hybrid of Leucanthemum lacustra and Leucanthemum maximum was first developed in the early 1900s.

The Shasta Daisy variety gained its name from the snowcapped Mount Shasta in the far north of California.

LEUCOSPERMUM

(loo-koh-spur-mum) Common names: *Pin Cushions; Catherine Wheel; Firewheel* BOTANICAL VARIETIES Leucospermum cordifolium (Pin Cushion), Leucospermum tottum (Firewheel Pin Cushion), Leucospermum lineare, Leucospermum conocarpodendron (many hybrids and around 50 species in this genus) FAMILY Proteaceae NATURAL SEASON Spring to early summer COLOUR AVAILABILITY Orange, red, yellow, lime LIFE SPAN Up to 14 days

GENERAL USE

Leucospermum flowers are very attractive and can be used in most designs. They have a dramatic appearance and they can feature in modern designs.

WEDDING USE

Leucospermum flowers can be split into sections for wedding designs. The lime Leucospermums are really effective in modern designs. They can be used in bouquet holders and wired bouquets, as well as hand-tied, natural stemmed bouquets.

CORPORATE USE

Leucospermum flowers will last well in corporate designs as long as they have a good water source.

GROWING CONDITIONS

Leucospermum plants like mulch, but not animal manure. Well-drained soil is best. The Leucospermum is not a self-pollinating species; rather it produces nectar to attract birds and Scareb beetles to the plant to assist in the pollination process.

HISTORY

Leucospermum is native to South Africa. The genus Leucospermum consists of 48 species that occur in southern Africa, with the majority occurring in the winter rainfall regions of the Western Cape. The genus Leucospermum is a member of the Protea family and the name is derived from the Greek word 'leukos', meaning 'white', and 'sperma' ('seed'); referring to the light-coloured seeds of many species.

CARE AND HANDLING

- Look for well developed, perfectly shaped flowers. Brown tips indicate age.

- The styles of each flower should be protruding straight out.

- Recut 2–3 centimetres from the stem ends, using a knife or secateurs. Cut on an angle.

- Do not bash the stem ends.

- Remove any leaves that will sit below the waterline.

- Preservative in the water is optional.

- If preservative if used, replace the water every two days.

LIATRIS *(lee-yat-ris) Common names: Blazing Star; Gayfeather*

BOTANICAL VARIETIES Liatris spicata FAMILY Asteraceae NATURAL SEASON Summer COLOUR AVAILABILITY Mauve/pink, purple, white

LIFE SPAN 1 to 2 weeks

CARE AND HANDLING

- The flowers on the spike open from the top downwards.
- Cut or purchase when the first buds have opened.
- They should have straight stems.
- Remove any leaves that will sit below the waterline.
- Recut 2–3 centimetres from the stem ends. Cut on an angle.
- Liatris will discolour water so preservative is recommended.
- Preservative will also assist the flowers to open.
- Replace the water and preservative regularly.

COMMERCIAL HANDLING

- Liatris foliage is subject to moulding, especially if placed in the cool room in tied bunches.

GENERAL USE

Liatris foliage will deteriorate before the flower. It is best to remove all foliage and substitute with a lasting foliage in the vase. The flowers are grown throughout the year due to their popularity. Liatris can be used in most floral work and they look very striking in modern designs. Due to their straightness, they are ideal for use in parallel designs.

WEDDING USE

Liatris flowers can be split into sections to shorten the flower or they can be used as a strong trail in bouquets. They will last well in any wedding design.

CORPORATE USE

Remove the foliage as it will dry out in corporate work. The flowers will start to dry but they should last five days.

GROWING CONDITIONS

These are hardy perennials. Well-drained soil is best, although Liatris is not fussy. It dislikes humidity and does well in mild areas. Propagate from seed or from division of the clumps. This can be done in autumn or spring. They generally grow up to 70 centimetres in height.

HISTORY

The Liatris is native to America. The plants are diuretic, with tonic, stimulant, and emmenagogue properties.

LILIUM (lil-ee-yam)

BOTANICAL VARIETIES See main text FAMILY Liliaceae NATURAL SEASON Summer (spring and summer for Asiatic varieties) COLOUR AVAILABILITY See main text CUT FLOWER LIFE SPAN 14–21 days

L. Auratum

L. Asiatic

L. Regale

LONGIFOLIUM (lon-gee-fo-lee-yam)

Common names: Christmas Lily (in the Southern Hemisphere); Easter Lily (in the Northern Hemisphere); Trumpet Lily; November Lily

BOTANICAL VARIETIES Lilium longifolium COLOUR AVAILABILITY White (perfumed)

ASIATIC

Common names: Tiger Lily

BOTANICAL VARIETIES Lilium asiatic hybrids (including Tiger Lily) COLOUR AVAILABILITY Orange with brown dots (Tiger Lily), all others in many colours and non-perfumed

LONGIFOLIUM X ASIATIC

Common names: L.A.

BOTANICAL VARIETIES Longifolium X Asiatic COLOUR AVAILABILITY White and highly perfumed

AURATUM

Common names: Oriental Lily; Rubrum Lily

BOTANICAL VARIETIES Lilium auratum, Lilium speciosum, Lilium stargazer (a popular variety), Lilium Casablanca (large blooms and beautifully perfumed), Lilium auratum rubrum, Lilium speciosum rubrum COLOUR AVAILABILITY Pink, white, lemon (red for Rubrum Lily)

REGALE

Common names: Regale Lily; St Joseph Lily

BOTANICAL VARIETIES Lilium regale (many hybrids) COLOUR AVAILABILITY Yellow throated white flowers (perfumed)

HEMEROCALLUS

Common names: Day Lily

BOTANICAL VARIETIES Lilium hemerocallus (many hybrids) COLOUR AVAILABILITY Original colours yellow and orange, now available in a wide range of other colours

Romantic flower meaning:

befriend me friend (Tiger Lily); purity (White Lily)

L. Asiatic

GENERAL USE

Liliums are very popular in floristry and with flower lovers. The larger heads are magnificent specimens with a strong scent. Be aware that Lilium (other than Asiatic) as a gift in hospitals or homes can be overpowering in perfume.

Several types of Lilies are deadly to cats. Easter Lily, Tiger Lily, Rubrum Lily and other members of the Liliaceae family can cause kidney failure if the cat eats the anthers or a leaf.

WEDDING USE

Liliums are always a popular choice for weddings. Make sure the anthers are always removed as they may stain a dress. Left on, they will also stain the flower itself. Do not refrigerate Lilies before use as room temperature is vital, otherwise the flowers can 'shock'. Casablanca Lilies and Longifolium X Asiatics can collapse if they are not conditioned correctly. Be careful during construction that you do not damage the petals as they will crease and bruise.

For wired work, cut the flowers from the stem and place them in shallow water. Use the pierce and mount method to wire the flowers when they are hard and strong. You can also tape some damp cottonwool on the stem end to lock in some moisture.

CARE AND HANDLING

- Lilium longifolium should be cut or purchased when they are in bud and showing clear white colour.

- Orientals, Asiatics and Longifolium X Asiatics should have one or two flowers opening on the stem.

- All foliage should be a strong green colour with no sign of yellowing.

- Avoid if the stem ends look dry or show any white markings – this is an indication that they have probably been stored. The stem ends should look clear in colour and texture.

- Avoid any flowers with visible veins – this is a sign of age.

- Avoid split Lily flowers, especially in Christmas Lilies. This can occur in the heat of summer.

- Always handle Liliums with care, as they will crease and bruise if they are placed on a bench or table for cutting or just to arrange. Run your hand under the flowers as you lay them down to protect the petals from damage.

- Remove any foliage that will sit below the waterline.

- Recut 3–4 centimetres from the stem ends, using a sharp knife.

- Remove the anthers from the stamens, or the pollen will stain the flower (as well as garments and tables). Be aware that by doing this, the life span of the flower is also marginally shortened.

- Preservative is not needed.

- Keep cool as a cut flower.

- They are very sensitive to ethylene, so keep them away from cigarette smoke and ripening fruit.

L. Auratum

Lilium is split into nine main divisions:
- *Asiatic hybrids*
- *Turks Cap or Martagon hybrids*
- *Candidum hybrids*
- *American species hybrids*
- *L. Longifolium and L. Formosanum hybrids*
- *Trumpet shaped Aurelian Lilies*
- *Oriental hybrids*
- *Other hybrids*
- *Species*

COMMERCIAL HANDLING

- Avoid refrigeration if possible, especially for Longifolium X Asiatic and Casablanca varieties. If refrigeration is needed, the cool room temperature should be 6–8 degrees Celsius.

- Be aware that due to their strong perfume, Liliums will react badly with Gladiolus, Roses and Carnations when all placed together in the cool room. The Liliums drain the moisture from these other flowers.

CORPORATE USE

Lilium flowers and foliage are hardy, but the anthers are the problem for corporate work. Many a florist has picked up a vase of open Lilies only to find yellow marks on their arms, clothing or even on their face. The pollen can stain. Use soap to remove from the skin. If pollen is visible on your clothing it is best to remove it by brushing fabric on fabric until the stain disappears. You can also use adhesive tape backed onto itself. Never use a wet cloth to remove the stains.

The only way to avoid anther stains is to remove the anthers before use for the flowers that are already open, and visit the client for a mid-week check to remove anthers in the rest of the blooms.

GROWING CONDITIONS

Lilium needs a sandy compost with leaf mould and charcoal. The soil can be acidic to neutral. It prefers full sun and needs to be watered regularly. Lilium will not grow in winter climates of less than 10 degrees Celsius. These flowers are bulbous perennials.

HISTORY

Lilium has been cultivated for over 3000 years, having ancestors from both Asia and the Middle East. The Madonna Lily is the oldest cultivated Lily on record. It was grown by the Cretans and Egyptians, centuries before the birth of Christ.

The Asiatic hybrids are a large group of Lilies that were originally bred in America in the 1950s. These hybrids have no scent.

The modern name 'Lily' is derived from the Ancient Greek word, 'leireon'. In Roman mythology, there is a story suggesting that the messy, staining pollen of the Lilium was imposed upon the flower by the goddess Venus, who was envious of the flower's beauty.

LIMONIUM

(lim-ohn-ee-yum) Common names: Statice; Misty; Sea Lavender; Marsh Rosemary; Emile BOTANICAL VARIETIES Limonium sinuatum (blue, yellow, white, pink), Limonium suworowii, Limonium satifolium (Sea Lavender), Linonium bonduelii (bright yellow), Limonium suworowii (Candlewick Statice), Limonium latifolium X bellidifolium (popular Misty Blue Statice) (around 150 varieties in the genus, mainly annuals and perennials) FAMILY Plumbaginaceae NATURAL SEASON Late spring, summer and early autumn COLOUR AVAILABILITY Blue-violet, yellow, white, pink LIFE SPAN 3 weeks

GENERAL USE

The Statice variety was a very popular funeral flower due to its colour, cost and the hardiness of the flower. Due to its association with funerals it was not sent as a gift flower. This has now changed and these days it is used in all kinds of floral designs, however, it is best not to give Limonium as a gift to an elderly person as it may cause offence.

The delicate Misty White and Misty Blue varieties are very popular in wedding bouquets and gift bouquets. However, in the height of its flowering season, this variety develops a smell like a tom cat's urine, so avoid the flower at this time! These varieties also drop their flowers at the end of the season, so again, avoid them at this time.

Limonium can be dried by hanging it upside down in a well-ventilated area. It will retain colour, but finer varieties will have some flower drop.

Limonium is available in field as well as hothouse varieties. Hothouse Limomium is longer and stronger and therefore there is a price difference between the two. The bunches are large and good value when purchased.

WEDDING USE

The Russian Statice, Misty Blue and Misty White varieties look great in bouquets. These flowers can trail, or they can be used in between main flowers. They give a light effect if they are not used in volume. The Emile variety looks similar but the heads are larger than the Misty varieties

These flowers are very easy to use in bouquet holders. Common Limonium can also be used in all bouquets. Be careful of using too much as it will dominate light colours and the Purple Statice will look almost black in photographs.

CARE AND HANDLING

- Cut or purchase when the majority of the flowers are fully open. The foliage should be deep green and fresh looking. Stems should be crisp with no sign of any discoloration.

- Do not purchase if the water is not clean. Any sign of slime indicates age.

- If purchased in sleeves remove immediately as Limonium will sweat in sleeves and foliage will deteriorate rapidly.

- Recut 2–3 centimetres from the stem ends. Cut on a sharp angle.

- Remove all foliage that will sit below the waterline.

- Wash the stems to remove particles of dirt.

- Shallow vase water level is best.

- Add chlorine or bleach to the water. If you put too much bleach in the water the stems will bleach but surprisingly the life span seems unaffected.

- Change the water every three days and add bleach or chlorine with each change of water.

- Do not mist the flowers as they are susceptible to grey mould.

- The foliage will yellow with age, particularly if placed in airconditioning.

COMMERCIAL HANDLING

- As a summer flower, Limonium dislikes the cool room and it will mould if left tightly bunched. The foliage will blacken and smell.

CORPORATE USE

Mixing bleach in the water is essential when using these flowers in corporate designs, as they will foul their water. Strip all excess foliage as it will yellow in heating or airconditioning.

In mid season, the Misty Blue and Misty White varieties emit an unpleasant odour, so avoid using it at these times. The smell they can develop is due to fungal infections, so keep airflow around them and this can often be avoided.

GROWING CONDITIONS

Limonium enjoys full sun and well-drained soil. This is a hardy garden plant and flowering continues all through summer. It can be grown from seed or seedlings and the best time to plant out is in autumn. Fertilise in spring. It is low growing, hardy to frost and tolerates most environments, including the seaside. Misty is a perennial, so cut it back in winter. Limonium sinuatum is primarily grown as an annual.

HISTORY

Limonium latifolum is native to both Russia and Bulgaria. Limonium sinuatum is native to the Mediterranean regions. Limonium bonduelli is native to Algeria whilst Limonium suworowii is native to Turkestan.

The common name 'Statice', is the Greek word for 'using to stand'. This is a reference to the spikes' ability to remain fresh looking for months on end. The name Limonium comes from the Greek word 'leimon', meaning 'meadow', a reference to the fact that the species often grow in salt marshes or meadows.

Limonium is popularly associated with funerals as it is often planted on or around gravesites, due to its ability to self seed and tolerate long periods of dry conditions.

LONAS

(loh-nas) Common names: Golden Ageratum; African Daisy

BOTANICAL VARIETIES Lonas annua FAMILY Asteraceae (alt. Compositae) NATURAL SEASON Late spring, summer and early autumn COLOUR AVAILABILITY Yellow/gold CUT FLOWER LIFE SPAN 5–7 days

GENERAL USE

Lonas is a clustered flower with no perfume, and is generally available with stem lengths of 30–50 centimetres. The flower will outlast the foliage. As a cut flower it can be used in a vase or in posies. They can be used in flower foam arrangements but will droop quickly if there is a lack of water. Do not use in wired work as they can wilt.

GROWING CONDITIONS

Lonas seedlings can be planted out in early spring. They enjoy full sun and will grow in any type of well-drained soil. These flowers form great borders in the garden.

HISTORY

Lonas is native to Northern Africa and Sicily.

CARE AND HANDLING

- Cut or purchase when the flower heads are showing strong colour but are still tight.

- Check the flowers for pollination in the flower centres and check there is no sign of yellowing on the foliage or a film on the stem.

- Recut 2–3 centimetres from the stem ends. Cut on an angle.

- Remove most of the foliage before use.

- Wash the stems to avoid dirt particles settling at the base of the vase.

- Use preservative or bleach into the water. Make sure the vase water is shallow.

- Lonas is sensitive to ethylene so keep it away from cigarette smoke and ripening fruit.

- Keep the flowers out of the heat.

- Ensure there is room in the vase for all flowers to have adequate airflow around the stems and blooms.

COMMERCIAL HANDLING

- Lonas can be kept in the cool room at temperatures of 6–8 degrees Celsius.

- These flowers will mould if they are tightly bunched.

LUNARIA

(loo-naa-ri-ya) Common names: Honesty

BOTANICAL VARIETIES Lunaria annua, Lunaria biennis (Honesty) FAMILY Brassicaceae NATURAL SEASON Flowers in spring, pods appear in autumn COLOUR AVAILABILITY Purple, pink, crimson, white LIFE SPAN 3–5 days (can also be dried)

CARE AND HANDLING

- Recut 2–3 centimetres from the stem ends. Cut on an angle.

- Remove any foliage that will sit below the waterline.

- Place the flowers into water with preservative added.

- The pods can be arranged without water.

GENERAL USE

Lunaria flowers are very pretty but do not last very long, plus, they are hard to find as cut flowers. They form stems of silver/cream and have circular seed pods. The dried pods are readily available for purchase and are extremely popular in dried arrangements. Handle with care as the pods are brittle and the surface area will tear. Lunaria also has attractive toothed foliage.

GROWING CONDITIONS

Lunaria is a biennial with non-perfumed purple, pink or white flowers. It is easy to grow in well-drained garden soil with full sun. Plant out seeds in early spring. The seed pods appear in late autumn.

Lunaria is very invasive plant and hard to remove from the garden. Lunaria variegate (crimson) is less invasive. It has white marked leaves. The seeds of Lunaria are hard to come by.

HISTORY

Popularly believed to have originated from China or Japan, this flower is actually native to the Mediterranean region. In South-East Asia the plant is commonly referred to as the 'Money Plant', as the seed pods have the appearance of silver coins. In Europe there was once a superstition that if horses walked on Lunaria, the plant held the power to cast off the horse's shoes. It is also said that Lunaria was once used to ward off madness.

LUPINUS

(loo-pin-us) Common names: Lupins; Russell Lupin; Texas Bluebonnet

BOTANICAL VARIETIES Lupinus varieties (mainly Russell Lupins), Lupinus texensis (Texas Bluebonnet) (around 200 species in this genus) FAMILY Fabaceae/Leguminosae NATURAL SEASON Spring to summer COLOUR AVAILABILITY Rainbow colours LIFE SPAN 5–7 days

GENERAL USE

Lupinus flowers can be purchased STS-treated. They will last much longer if treated but they are more costly to buy. The Russell Lupin variety is an elegant flower in vibrant colours. These flowers are best used in a vase rather than in floral foam, as the tips can fall in foam. Their vibrant colours and form will grace any vase and décor.

These flowers will last longer depending on growing climates; sometimes they can last up to two weeks, yet at other times only five days. Do not use in corporate work.

GROWING CONDITIONS

Lupinus is best planted in spring. It likes moist, well-drained soil and partial sun. Use a fertiliser high in phosphorous and add some lime to the compost in the soil. It will usually grow up to 80 centimetres tall.

It is best to propagate with cuttings taken from a piece of root stock. Do not allow all spikes to set seed. If you decide to sow seeds direct, the soil needs to be well prepared.

Lupinus holds a bacteria that lives in the nodules of its roots. If you turn it in the soil when it dies, it will add nutrients to the ground.

The most vibrant Lupinus in gardens are the perennial varieties. Russell Lupins in particular give a magnificent show of colours.

CARE AND HANDLING

- Cut or purchase when one third of the flowers on the spike are open and in full colour. The leaves should be firm and green, with no sign of yellowing.

- If purchased commercially, remove from the sleeve and separate for airflow around the flowers.

- Remove any foliage that will sit below the waterline.

- Wash the stems to remove any dirt particles.

- Recut 2–3 centimetres from the stem ends. Cut on an angle.

- Use preservative or bleach in the vase water.

- Change the water every 2–3 days.

- Lupinus is mildly sensitive to eth-ylene so keep it away from ciga-rette smoke and ripening fruit.

COMMERCIAL HANDLING

- Lupinus does not do well in the cool room and suffers on remov-al. If necessary to cool for a short time, the temperature should be 6–8 degrees Celsius.

HISTORY

Most varieties of Lupinus are native to northern America. In 1911, George Russell took the North American perennial Lupinus polyphyllus and crossed it with Lupinus laxiflorus, Lupinus lepidus and Lupinus mutabilis to produce brighter colours. Due to this mixed parentage, they did not last as long as the pure strain. After working on these breeds for years, he introduced the flower in 1937. Lupinus albus is native to souther Europe. As the flower was often found growing in poor soil, the ancient Romans incorrectly assumed that Lupinus robbed the soil they grew in of nutrients so that little else could grow. It is due to this belief that they named the flower 'lupis', latin for the word 'wolf', as they felt the flower damaged the ground as a wild animal might.

The Romans considered the seeds of the Lupinus albus a delicacy, and despite their bitter flavour, some Italians appreciate this acquired taste to this day. Lupinus is, however, poisonous if eaten in quantities.

LYCORIS

(lai-kor-iss) Common names: Spider Lily; Golden Hurricane Lily

BOTANICAL VARIETIES Lycoris aurea (Spider Lily, bright yellow/gold), Lycoris sanguinea (red), Licoris squamigera (pink, flushed with yellow) (around 18 bulbous perennials in this genus) FAMILY Amaryllidaceae NATURAL SEASON Late summer and early autumn

COLOUR AVAILABILITY Yellow/gold, red, pink/yellow LIFE SPAN 14 days

GENERAL USE

Lycoris flowers are sometimes confused with Nerines. They are a cousin to the Nerine genus, but they flower earlier than Nerines and have much longer stamens.

Lycoris flowers are lovely and arrange well in posies and bouquets. They are not long stemmed (usually around 30 centimetres in length). They can be used in small arrangements, table centrepieces and funeral designs. Single florets can be wired for wedding or corsage work. They are usually sold in bunches of ten.

GROWING CONDITIONS

Lycoris bulbs should be planted in shallow soil with the neck of the bulb above the soil. They often do not flower in their first season and the soil should be well mulched and well drained. Plant between summer and early autumn. Bulbs can be kept dry when dormant in summer but require moisture outside of this season.

HISTORY

Lycoris aurea is native to China, while Lycoris sanguinea and Lycoris squamigera are native to Japan. These ornamental flowers are very popular for decorative use at festivals and celebrations in China, where many legends surround Lycoris. In Japan, farmers often sow a strip of these plants along rice paddies so that in the warmer months, bright strips of Lycoris bloom, providing a startling visual decorative effect. Lycoris are also commonly used in Japan for funeral services.

CARE AND HANDLING

- Cut or purchase when the outer flowers are showing colour.

- Do not purchase if all flowers are open. Although they look like they are at their peak, they are actually past it and will not last very long.

- Recut 2–3 centimetres from the stem ends. Cut on an angle.

- Add bleach or preservative to the water.

- Lycoris is mildly sensitive to ethylene. Remove any spent flowers by pinching them off at the base and this will prevent their ethylene emissions from affecting the remaining flowers.

COMMERCIAL HANDLING

- Lycoris can be kept in the cool room at temperatures of 6–8 degrees Celsius.

LYSIMACHIA

(lai-si-mak-ee-ya) Common names: Loosestrife; Moneywort; Creeping Jenny BOTANICAL VARIETIES Lysimachia ephemerum (Loosestrife), Lysimachia punctata (Golden Loosestrife), Lysimachia nummularia (Creeping Jenny and Moneywort), Lysimachia vulgaris (yellow, bell-shaped flowers) Lysimachia Clethroides (small white blossoms) (a genus of around 150 species) FAMILY Primulaceae NATURAL SEASON Spring and summer COLOUR AVAILABILITY Yellow, white with pink/mauve centres LIFE SPAN 5–7 days

CARE AND HANDLING

- Cut or purchase when one third of the lower flowers are opening. The flowers open from the base upwards.

- Choose straight stems. The tips should be upright (they can be prone to wilting). The foliage should be green-grey with no sign of yellowing.

- If purchased commercially, remove from sleeves and open up bunches for airflow around the flowers.

- Recut 2–3 centimetres from the stem ends. Cut on an angle.

- Remove any leaves that will sit below the waterline.

- Wash the stems to remove particles of dirt.

- Add bleach or preservative to the water. Preservative may assist the buds to open.

- Lysimachia is mildly sensitive to ethylene so keep it away from cigarette smoke or ripening fruit.

COMMERCIAL HANDLING

- Do not place in the cool room.

GENERAL USE

Lysimachia ephemerum has pink/mauve centred white blooms. Lypsimachia punctata has yellow blooms. Both these varieties make lovely bouquet flowers, although the foliage dries out in airconditioning. Do not use in floral foam.

Lysimachia is usually purchased in bunches of ten (sometimes fifteen).

GROWING CONDITIONS

Lysimachia spreads very easily. It can be grown in constantly damp soil and even grown under water in ponds and bogs. Most species are grown from divisions in either autumn or winter. Some staking may be required. Propagate from division or from basal cuttings or layers.

HISTORY

This flower is native to Europe, however, the Lysimachia clethroides variety is native to China and Japan. The name 'Lysimachia' refers to King Lysimachus (the King of Macedonia) whose son, Agathocles, is said to have discovered the virtues of this herb.

The smell of Lysimachia repels both fleas and snakes and was used in medieval times to fend off vermin.

LYTHRUM *(Lith-ram) Common names: Purple Loosestrife; Spiked Loosestrife*

BOTANICAL VARIETIES Lythrum salicaria (35 species in this genus) FAMILY Lythraceae NATURAL SEASON Summer and early autumn COLOUR AVAILABILITY Bright pink/purple (most popular), mauve, crimson, red/violet LIFE SPAN 5 days

GENERAL USE

STS-treated Lythrum lasts quite well but flowers that have not been treated will shrivel and fall. It is a lovely vase flower to enjoy in the home but not one that is popular commercially. It should never be used in office decoration as it will drop and dry out in airconditioning.

GROWING CONDITIONS

Lythrum grows best in warmer climates, in soil that is constantly damp. Even in poorly drained areas, this plant performs well. The soil surface does need to be above water, and it can even be grown in a pot that has its base in a pond.

Cut back in autumn. Propagate by dividing the roots in autumn or spring. In warmer climates the seeds can be sown in early spring. In colder climates sow in autumn. This plant grows 60–120 centimetres in height. It is a herbaceous perennial related to *Lagerstroemia* (crepe myrtle).

HISTORY

This plant is native to southern Europe. The name Lythrum is derived from the Greek word 'lythron', meaning 'blood'.

CARE AND HANDLING

- These flowers open from the base of the spike upwards.

- Recut 2–3 centimetres from the stem end. Cut on an angle.

- Remove any foliage that will sit below the waterline.

- Bleach or preservative can be added to the water.

- Remove spent lower flowers from the stem to prevent their ethylene emissions from affecting the other flowers.

MATRICARIA

(mat-rik-ah-ree-ya) Common names: Feverfew; Golden Ball

BOTANICAL VARIETIES Matricaria eximia, Matricaria occidtalis FAMILY Asteraceae NATURAL SEASON Late spring and summer COLOUR AVAILABILITY Cream, yellow CUT FLOWER LIFE SPAN 7 days

CARE AND HANDLING

- Cut or purchase when half of the outer small petals in the yellow centre are open. There should be no sign of yellowing on the leaves.

- Wear gloves when handling, as direct contact with the leaves can cause skin inflammation.

- Remove any foliage that will sit below the waterline.

- Wash the stems to remove any dirt particles.

- Recut 2–3 centimetres from the stem ends, under water if possible as the stem ends tend to seal over in the air. Cut on an angle.

- Use bleach or preservative in the water.

- Replace the vase water every two days.

- Keep the flowers cool.

COMMERCIAL HANDLING

- Matricaria can be kept in the cool room at temperatures of 6–8 degrees Celsius.

GENERAL USE

These flowers are normally sold in bunches. They are a good vase flower as well as being suited to natural stemmed bouquet work. They have a strong perfume like Camomile.

GROWING CONDITIONS

Matricaria enjoys full sun and well-drained, moist soil. These flowers grow 30–60 centimetres in height. Take care with young children in the garden – if the leaves are sucked or chewed on, they can cause mouth ulcerations.

HISTORY

This plant is a native to Europe. It is a close relative of Chamomile (Matricaria recutita). As its name suggests, the herb Feverfew has been used traditionally for relief of fever.

MATTHIOLA (mat-ee-ohl-a) Common names: Stock; Gillyflower

BOTANICAL VARIETIES Matthiola incana hybrids (around 55 or so species in this genus) FAMILY Brassicaceae NATURAL SEASON Spring and summer COLOUR AVAILABILITY Red, purple, mauve, burgundy, yellow, cream, white, lime/white, pink, apricot CUT FLOWER LIFE SPAN 7–10 days

GENERAL USE

Matthiola has a wide range of floristry uses. The single florets can be used in wedding and funeral designs but usually are not, due to the time involved.

The longer stem variety (Column Stock) with larger heads, are more costly to purchase and are usually STS-treated (to last longer and withstand ethylene emissions).

Matthiola makes a lovely perfumed vase flower and looks delightful when combined with Erlicheer and Freesias.

GROWING CONDITIONS

Matthiola is a hardy perennial plant that grows best in full sun and neutral to alkaline soil. It likes some lime in the soil. It can be planted from seed. Although hardy, it is not an easy plant to grow as it will not grow where Matthiola has grown before.

WEDDING USE

Perfumed Matthiola florets can be wired and used individually in wired bouquets, hand-tied, natural stemmed bouquets, corsages and buttonholes. Do not use on a hot day as they may wilt.

CORPORATE USE

STS-treated Mathiola can be used in corporate designs if most of the flowers are in bud form (the lower flowers may be open). Column Stock is the strongest variety. Use preservative or bleach in the water.

HISTORY

Matthiola is native to the lands along the Mediterranean, such as Spain and Turkey. The genus is named after the Italian botanist Pier Andrea Mattioli (1501–1577).

CARE AND HANDLING

- Cut or purchase when the lower flowers on the spike are open. The pleasant perfume should be noticeable.

- Purchase STS-treated Matthiola if possible as they will last longer.

- Separate the flowers to make sure there is no sign of moulding. It is essential to have air flow around these flowers.

- Cut off the roots if they are still attached. Cut on a sharp angle.

- Wash the stems to remove any particles of dirt.

- Remove any foliage that will sit below the waterline

- Use preservative, otherwise the water will foul quickly.

- Change the water and preservative daily.

- Remove the lower blooms as they die, to prevent their ethylene emissions affecting the remaining flowers.

COMMERCIAL HANDLING

- Matthiola can be kept in the cool room at temperatures of 6–8 degrees Celsius, but make sure the water is changed daily and the flowers are not bunched tightly together, or the foliage will mould.

- Matthiola can be stored (long term) out of water in the cool room, at 2 degrees Celsius.

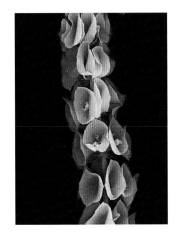

MOLUCELLA

(mol-u-chel-la) Common names: Molucca Balm; Bells of Ireland; Irish Bell Flower; Shell Flower BOTANICAL VARIETIES Molucella laevis FAMILY Limiaceae NATURAL SEASON Winter, spring and early summer COLOUR AVAILABILITY Lime/green CUT FLOWER LIFE SPAN Up to 4 weeks

CARE AND HANDLING

- Molucella has nettle-like leaves and these are generally removed by commercial growers. If not, remove them to show the beauty of the stem.

- Cut or purchase when the flowers are a strong lime green. Yellowing or white centres are a sign of age. The stems should be hollow and strong.

- Remove the packaging as soon as possible after purchasing, as they deteriorate without full air circulation.

- Keep the flowers in water at all times to prevent the tips from wilting.

- Recut 2–3 centimetres from the stem ends. Cut on an angle.

- Add bleach or preservative to the vase water.

- The calyxes of the flowers should sit above the waterline.

- Keep cool as a cut flower.

COMMERCIAL HANDLING

- Molucella can be kept in the cool room at temperatures of 6–8 degrees Celsius.

GENERAL USE

Molucella flowers are actually quite inconspicuous. The shell-looking calyxes are often mistaken for the flowers.

These flowers are extremely popular in floral design work. They can be cut into sections or used as a longer stem to give structure to a design. Single florets can be used in wired work provided the flower (calyx) is conditioned. These flowers are long lasting, however, if more mature in age, the white stamens will start to drop. Note that Molucella tips will turn to the light – this should be considered when creating arrangements.

Molucella can be dried by hanging it upside down in a well-ventilated area.

WEDDING USE

Molucella florets can be wired individually using the pierce and mount or hairpin wiring methods. They can look very delicate in corsages, buttonholes and hairpieces. The stems can be cut into sections and used in bouquet holders, and they can be wired. (If wired, use with caution in hot weather.)

CORPORATE USE

Molucella is useful in corporate designs. If used in floral foam a constant water source is vital or they will quickly droop and shrivel. They are very thirsty so use a deep container.

GROWING CONDITIONS

Molucella plants enjoy full sun, in moist, moderately fertile, well-drained soil. The plants will grow up to 70 centimetres in height. Sow the seeds in early spring. A balanced fertiliser can be used every month or so.

HISTORY

Molucella is native to Syria. Molucella is small genus of aromatic herbs that was first introduced to Britain in 1796 by Sir Joseph Banks.

MUSCARI *(mus-ka-ree) Common names: Grape Hyacinth*

BOTANICAL VARIETIES Muscari armeniacum, Muscari botryoides (bulbous perennials, around 30 species in this genus) FAMILY Hyacinthaceae NATURAL SEASON Late winter and spring COLOUR AVAILABILITY Blue/purple CUT FLOWER LIFE SPAN 7–10 days

CARE AND HANDLING

- Cut or purchase when the little flowers are in full colour.
- Recut 1 centimetre from the stem ends. Cut on an angle.
- Wash the stems to remove any dirt particles.
- Preservative is optional.

GENERAL USE

Muscari flowers are used in table centrepieces, small arrangements, funeral flowers and posies.

WEDDING USE

This flower is pretty in hand-tied, natural stemmed bouquets. If used in bouquet holders it is best to wire support the stems with fine wire wound through the flowers. They can also be wired internally.

GROWING CONDITIONS

Best to plant in clumps in early autumn. They are dormant in summer and lose their stringy leaves. They like rich, well drained soil that is well prepared. They can be lifted and divided in summer.

HISTORY

Muscari is native to Central and south Eastern Europe and has been cultivated for more than 400 years. Muscari is derived from the Latin word 'muscus'. This is a reference to the scent of some of the species.

MYOSOTIS

(mai-yoh-soh-tas) Common names: *Forget-me-not; Scorpion Grass*

BOTANICAL VARIETIES Mysotis alpestris, Mysotis sylvatica, Mysotis dissitiflora (around 50 species of annuals, biennials and perennials in this genus)

FAMILY Boraginaceae NATURAL SEASON Late winter and spring COLOUR AVAILABILITY Pale pink, baby blue to dark blue

LIFE SPAN 3–5 days in ideal conditions

GENERAL USE

Mysotis is a very pretty garden flower and delightful when mixed with spring bulb flowers like Daffodils, Hyacinths and Jonquils in posies. They look gorgeous mixed with Cecile Brunner Roses or Mignonette Sprays in small vases.

Mysotis flowers have a limited life span; however, their aesthetic beauty makes up for this. Do not use these in wedding designs as they will not last out of water.

GROWING CONDITIONS

Mysotis plants are grown easily from seed. They are of annual and perennial nature. The soil should be moist and rich in compost. Plant in a semi-shaded position with morning sun. Pull up the annuals and cut back the perennials.

When the plants grow old, shake them over paper laid on the ground, and you will collect enough seeds to plant for the following year.

HISTORY

Mysotis is originally native to China, but can now be found worldwide. The flower has a longstanding romantic connection, perhaps owing to the origin of its common name. Legend has it that long ago, as a German knight attempted to gather a posy of these flowers along a riverbank for his lady, he fell into the river and was swept away by a strong current. As he vanished under the water his partying words were the plea to 'forget me not!'

CARE AND HANDLING

- Make sure the roots have been removed and wash the stems to remove any dirt particles.

- Recut 2 centimetres from the stem ends and then place the stems into water immediately.

- Remove any foliage that will sit below the waterline.

- Use preservative.

- Keep the flowers cool.

Romantic flower meaning: constant love

NANDINA

(nan-dee-na) Common names: *Sacred Bamboo, Heavenly Bamboo*

BOTANICAL NAME Nandina domestica FAMILY Berberidaceae SUB FAMILY Nandinoideae NATURAL SEASON Spring

COLOUR AVAILABILITY White flowers, red/flame berries CUT FLOWER LIFE SPAN 14 days

CARE AND HANDLING

- Cut the spikes when the tiny white flowers are open.

- Remove any foliage that will sit below the waterline.

- Recut 2 centimetres from the woody stem ends, using secateurs. Cut on an angle.

- Preservative is not needed.

GENERAL USE

Nandina spikes, usually 15–30 centimetres long, are very hardy and can be cut into sections for use in a variety of floral designs. The berries can also be used, as long as they are young and not fully coloured (older, fully coloured berries will drop and stain).

The green or flame-coloured foliage of the Nandina is also very hardy and it too can be used in floral designs. It will last for weeks provided it is not cut too young.

WEDDING USE

Nandina flowers and berries can be used in wedding bouquets. Nandina foliage, with its strong red/green colours, is also a popular choice for bridal work in late winter and spring.

CORPORATE USE

Nandina foliage can be used in corporate work. The berries may also be used if they are tight in formation.

GROWING CONDITIONS

These plants are quite easy to grow. They prefer well-watered soil but they will adapt to dryness once established. They will grow in sun or shade and can grow up to three metres in height. The flame-coloured foliage develops in autumn and winter, but it does need sun to do so, or else it will remain green.

HISTORY

Native to Asia, Nandina domestica grows naturally in Japan, China and south-east Asia through to Eastern India. This plant is said to be the most commonly used plant in Japan. The dwarf form of this plant, Nandina domestica nana, has also proven very popular in Australian gardens.

NARCISSUS

(nah-si-suss) Common names: Daffodil; Jonquil; Erlicheer; Paperwhite

BOTANICAL NAMES Narcissus, Narcissus tazetta (Paperwhite and hybrid Daffodil), Narcissus papyraceus (Jonquil), numerous cultivars FAMILY Amaryllidaceae NATURAL SEASON Late winter and spring COLOUR AVAILABILITY White, cream, lemon, yellow, yellow/orange CUT FLOWER LIFE SPAN 5–7 days

GENERAL USE

Narcissus is a lovely flower to use in the vase at home, especially when arranged with other spring flowers. These flowers look fabulous in posies and they have a pleasant perfume. The Erlicheer variety also has a lovely perfume and is becoming increasingly popular.

In floral design work, Narcissus often needs to be wire supported so that the heads look upwards. Wire internally, bypassing the seed box, and reinserting the wire at the base of the flower. Be aware that wiring will shorten the flower's life span (as air can penetrate into the stem). For use in floral foam, make sure the flowers are at their freshest. If the stems weaken or split, this means the flower is older and should not be used.

All Narcissus varieties dislike any form of heating. Never use in corporate, office or hospital arrangements as they will dry out completely.

WEDDING USE

The Erlicheer variety can be used in wedding bouquets. They can also be wired singularly (using the pierce and mount wiring method) for corsages, buttonholes and hairpieces. Some of the double varieties like White Marble can be used for basing bouquets. Do not use Narcissus on a hot day as it may start to shrivel.

CARE AND HANDLING

- Cut or purchase when most of the flowers are in bud but showing strong colour. It's best if at least one flower (or bell) is open. They should feel strong in the stem and under the flowers.

- Avoid buying Narcissus later in the season when all the buds are open. Once the petals have bent back from the trumpet (known as the gooseneck) their life span is very limited.

- Recut 2–3 centimetres from the stem ends. Cut on an angle.

- Wash the stems to remove any particles of dirt.

- Narcissus needs to be conditioned on its own. When picked, the stems exude a sap that is detrimental to other flowers. After picking, place the stems in a container of water for 3–4 hours and then transfer them to the vase. By this time the amount of sap exuded is minimal. It is suggested to wait up to 24 hours before mixing with Anemones, Carnations, Freesias, Tulips and Roses.

- Wash your hands if you pick Narcissus – the sap can cause skin irritation.

COMMERCIAL HANDLING

- Narcissus can be kept in the cool room at temperatures of 6–8 degrees Celsius. Only place in the cool room if the buds are tight. They last better out of the cool room at room temperature.

- Narcissus can be stored (long term) in the cool room, out of water, at temperatures of 2–4 degrees Celsius. Store them vertically, as the heads will turn upwards if stored horizontally.

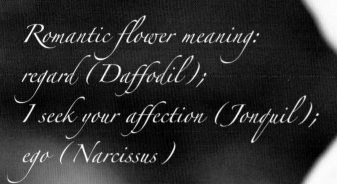

Romantic flower meaning:
regard (Daffodil);
I seek your affection (Jonquil);
ego (Narcissus)

GROWING CONDITIONS

All varieties of Narcissus can be planted from bulbs in late summer to early autumn. All flowers have six petals with a central trumpet that encases the stamens. They are fine in average soil, provided it is well drained. If drainage is poor, plant the bulbs on a layer of sand. If winters are cold, these bulbs can be left in the garden.

All Narcissus varieties are dormant during summer and if the soil is not well drained, they can rot if there is too much rain. They enjoy full sun but if grown in hot climates, some shade is best.

Water well after flowering as this will make good bulbs for the next season. Make sure they are not waterlogged. Divide every three years.

HISTORY

Narcissus is native to Southern Europe, Northern Africa, and Asia Minor.

The name perhaps stems from the Greek myth that tells the tale of Narcissus, the hero who once drowned in his own reflection and wasted away to a flower. Narcissus tazetta were often used by the Ancient Egyptians to decorate funeral wreaths.

NELUMBO

(ne-lum-boh) Common names: *Lotus Pods; Sacred Lotus of the Nile*

BOTANICAL NAME Nelumbo lutea, Nelumbo nucifera (Sacred Lotus) FAMILY Nelumbonaceae NATURAL SEASON Spring and summer COLOUR AVAILABILITY Green when fresh, brown when dried LIFE SPAN 2 weeks

GENERAL USE

It is very difficult to purchase Nelumbo flowers but the internal pods are very popular. They are usually sold in bunches of five.

Lotus pods look very effective in modern designs, particularly if they are placed to look upwards. When fresh green pods are use in floral foam, it is best to internally wire inside the stem to support the neck. This will marginally affect their life span, but if the are not wired and they flop, their life span is cut short dramatically and the arrangement is visually spoiled.

Nelumbo can be dried. Shake out the seed pods and hang them upside down in a well-ventilated area. Dried pods are popular in silk and dried arrangements.

WEDDING USE

Fresh Nelumbo, with its lime green colour and soft texture, will enhance most modern bouquets. They will need wire support and can be used in all types of bouquets.

CORPORATE USE

Dried, brown Nelumbo can be used in corporate designs. They can also be used fresh, but the green pods will need wire support or they will droop.

GROWING CONDITIONS

Nelumbo grows in mud under the water and is a giant of the Waterlily family. It is ideal for ponds or lakes. It grows from rhizomes.

CARE AND HANDLING

- Fresh pods should be lime green with no missing sections on the surface, no cracks, and no sign of brown blemishes. They should be soft to the touch.

- If they are being sold in a plastic sleeve, peel back the sleeve and check the necks for strength. A weak neck is a sign of water blockage.

- Remove the sleeve immediately after purchase.

- Recut and place into deep water with preservative added.

- Nelumbo is mildly ethylene sensitive so keep it away from cigarette smoke and ripening fruit.

- Do not place in airconditioned environments.

- If the heads droop, recut the stems and wrap the heads tightly so they are forced to stand. Place into deep water with preservative. Leave for two hours and they will firm up.

COMMERCIAL HANDLING

- Do not place in the cool room.

Romantic flower meaning: rejected love

HISTORY

Nelumbo is native to southern China, America, North Australia and India. To this day, the Lotus is held in great esteem in Egypt, China, Japan, India and Tibet. The Hindus believe that the Lotus symbolises Central India, while the leaves symbolise its surrounding provinces.

In the Orient, the plant is sacred in Buddhism, as it is believed that Buddha was born in a Lotus blossom. Buddhists believe that as this magnificent flower is able to grow from dirty mud in undrinkable water, it symbolises purity and perfection over wickedness.

The seeds and rhizomes of the Lotus are edible. The Egyptians made bread from the seeds, by grinding them into flour and adding milk or water.

NERINE (na-reen) Common names: Guernsey Lily; Cape Colony Nerine; Jersey Lily

BOTANICAL NAMES Nerine bowdenii, Nerine sarniesis (Guernsey Lily), Nerine undula FAMILY Amaryllidaceae NATURAL SEASON Late autumn, winter and early spring COLOUR AVAILABILITY White, pink, crimson, red, red/orange CUT FLOWER LIFE SPAN Up to 14 days

GENERAL USE

Nerine flowers can be used in all forms of floral work. The brown sepal casing on the lower exterior of the Nerine flower should be removed before use. Do not mistake this casing for dead petals – it is a normal feature of the Nerine flower and does not indicate age or lack of freshness.

WEDDING USE

Nerine is a popular bridal flower in late winter and spring. Both the florets and the clustered stems may be used. The florets can be wired singularly using the pierce and mount wiring method (do not use the hairpin wiring method as this will damage the anthers), and used for fine wired work such as tiaras, corsages, hairpieces and cake tops. The clustered stems can be used in bouquet holders, as well as in hand-tied, natural stemmed bouquets and wired bouquets. White Nerines mix well with Azaleas.

CORPORATE USE

Nerines will last in corporate designs, provided they start the week in bud form.

GROWING CONDITIONS

Nerine is grown from bulbs. It prefers light and sandy, well-drained soil, with full sun exposure. The flower spikes pop up in early spring. Feed and keep moist during flowering. Reduce water when the plant dies back in spring.

HISTORY

Nerine is native to Southern Africa and Europe. It is named after the Greek mythological water nymph. Botanists discovered Nerine on Guernsey Island in the 17th century (where it had grown after bulbs washed ashore following a shipwreck). This discovery resulted in the flower's common name, Guernsey Lily. Occasionally it is referred to as the Jersey Lily, after the actress Lily Langtree, who was from Jersey Island.

CARE AND HANDLING

- Cut or purchase when one flower on the spike is open.

- Recut 2–3 centimetres from the stem ends. Cut on an angle.

- Use bleach or preservative in the water.

- Do not mist, as the water can sit in the throats of the flowers and cause them to rot.

- Nerine is mildly sensitive to ethylene, so pinch out spent flowers as they age to prevent their emissions from affecting the other flowers.

COMMERCIAL HANDLING

- Nerine can be kept in the cool room at temperatures of 6–8 degrees Celsius.

NIGELLA *(nai-jel-la) Common names: Love-in-the-Mist; Devil-in-a-Bush* BOTANICAL NAME Nigella damascena varieties (around 15 species of annuals in this genus) FAMILY Ranunculaceae NATURAL SEASON Late spring/early summer COLOUR AVAILABILITY Blue, mauve, pink (Devil-in-a-Bush), red, purple and white LIFE SPAN 7 days

CARE AND HANDLING

- Cut or purchase when the petals are not flexed flat and the flowers are in full colour. The foliage should be green and fresh looking.

- Wash the stems and recut 2–3 centimetres from the stem ends.

- Remove any leaves that will sit below the waterline.

- Place in water immediately. These flowers air block easily.

- Use shallow water with preservative added.

- Change the vase water every 2–3 days.

- Nigella flowers need conditioning time when cut or left out of water.

- Keep cool as a cut flower.

COMMERCIAL HANDLING

- Do not place in the cool room as the low temperatures will cause mould and the flowers will droop upon removal.

- These flowers suffer from vessel blockage and must be kept in water at all times.

GENERAL USE

Nigella is generally available with stem lengths of 30–70 centimetres, and can be used in most forms of floral work, except for designs made in floral foam.

The centres, or seed capsules, can be purchased commercially, or the petals may be removed from the flower to reveal the seed capsules. These can be used in delicate wired work.

Nigella will not last in corporate designs as the foliage will yellow and the flowers will dry out and collapse.

GROWING CONDITIONS

Nigella belongs to the Buttercup family and it is an annual plant. It performs well in normal soil conditions and likes a sunny position. It can be sown from spring to summer and will flower within weeks of germination. Once established, it will seed regularly.

HISTORY

Nigella is native to Southern Europe and has been grown in European gardens for centuries. It is used traditionally as both a condiment and healing herb in Southern Europe and the near East.

Romantic flower meaning: uncertainty (Love-in-the-Mist)

NYMPHAEA

(nim-fee-ya) Common names: Water Lily; Egyptian Lotus; Blue Lotus

BOTANICAL NAMES Nymphaea gigantee (Australian Water Lily), Nymphaea capensis (Blue Lotus), Nymphaea tuberosa, Nymphaea rubra, Nymphaea alba (many more varieties) FAMILY Nymphaeaceae NATURAL SEASON Spring, summer and early autumn COLOUR AVAILABILITY Red, white, yellow, gold, mauve, purple, cream CUT FLOWER LIFE SPAN 14 days

GENERAL USE

Nymphaea flowers have internal cells in the stems. These cells do not block easily and the flowers are often purchased out of water, either in boxes or bunches of five or ten. Nymphaeas are popular to float in ceramic bases or they are traditionally used as the top flowers on wreaths (known as topping flowers).

Nymphaea flowers will open and close. The outer sepal casing controls this. If the sepals are removed the petals will peel back. Some florists will 'crack' these flowers. This means cracking the sepals to keep the flower open. This method horrifies Water Lily enthusiasts but it keeps the flower open for floral design!

Some floral designers apply wax under the base of the flower head as another method for keeping the flowers open. Professional floral wax spray can be used or you can drip candle wax.

Another method employed by some floral designers is to cut a circle of cardboard with a hole in the centre and place the stem through the hole, so that the circle becomes a collar to hold up the petals.

WEDDING USE

Nymphaea flowers were very fashionable in the 1940s. Today, they are used in a variety of bridal designs, including hand-tied natural stemmed bouquets and float bowls. For bouquets, the flowers should be wired using the pierce and mount wiring method. Avoid using these flowers in temperatures above 35 degrees Celsius.

CORPORATE USE

Nymphaea can be used in corporate decorating, but only for float bowls.

CARE AND HANDLING

- Check the flowers. There should be hardly any sign of pollination. Browning in the centres indicates age.

- Recut 2–3 centimetres from the stem ends. Cut on an angle.

- Use preservative.

Romantic flower meaning: chastity and virtue

GROWING CONDITIONS

Nymphaea requires still water to grow properly. Do not grow it in pools with fountains or cascading water as the flowers will spot and damage. These plants should be planted 40–45 centimetres beneath the water surface. They will develop extensive roots.

HISTORY

Nymphaea is native to both Egypt and areas of Asia and Australia. The flowers were once used in ancient Egypt for funeral wreaths. The Nymphaea plant has also been used for culinary purposes. As the seeds contain oil, protein and starch, Asians, Africans and Europeans consumed them in times of food shortages. The dormant tubers were ground down and then boiled or roasted as a potato might be. The leaf stalk of Nymphaeas gigantean can be peeled and eaten raw or roasted, and is still often eaten by Indigenous Australians.

ONCIDIUM (on-sid-ee-yum) Common names: Dancing Ladies; Golden Shower

BOTANICAL VARIETIES Oncidium sphacelatum, Oncidium sultamyre, Oncidium varicosum FAMILY Ochidaceae NATURAL SEASON Most of the year COLOUR AVAILABILITY Yellow CUT FLOWER LIFE SPAN 4 weeks

CARE AND HANDLING

- Buy or cut when the lower flowers are open.

- Avoid flowers with any curling or translucency in the blooms – this is a sign of age or refrigeration.

- Recut 2–3 centimetres from the stem ends. Cut on an angle.

- Use preservative if the vase water is not optimum quality.

- If the flowers flag they can be bathed in water to revive them. Submerge for no longer than 30 minutes.

COMMERCIAL HANDLING

- Never place these tropical flowers in the cool room.

GENERAL USE

Oncidium is a member of the Orchid family. It has several branches to each stem and is usually sold with five stems to a bunch. The stems are often sold with attached water vials or small plastic bags filled with cotton wool. They need a constant water source.

These flowers can be separated from the stem to use in bouquet holders and other floral designs. If they are wired as single blooms their life span is limited.

WEDDING USE

Oncidiums are suited to all forms of bridal work but in hot weather they are best used unwired and with a constant water source. When wired and without water, they will just last the evening, provided it is not too hot.

CORPORATE USE

Oncidiums must be fresh to last in corporate designs, so make sure the supplier has not handled them. These Orchids give a good show with the number of small blooms on each stem.

GROWING CONDITIONS

Oncidium is popular in hanging baskets where they will flow and cascade and show the meaning of their common name 'Dancing Ladies'. Propagate them by division.

HISTORY

Oncidium is native to South America.

ORCHID *(or-kid)*
FAMILY Orchidaceae

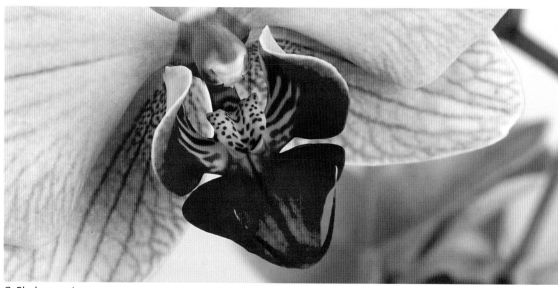

O. Phalaenopsis

CATTLEYA
Common names: Corsage Orchid

BOTANICAL VARIETIES over 40 species NATURAL SEASON Spring and autumn
COLOUR AVAILABILITY White with yellow centres, mauve with purple centres, purple, lime, pink, yellow, lemon, burgundy, red CUT FLOWER LIFE SPAN 7–10 days

Cattleya flowers must be handled delicately. Mist lightly, if at all, as they can become transparent. Brown spots may develop if they are bruised or get too wet.

CYMBIDIUM

BOTANICAL VARIETIES Around 52 species NATURAL SEASON From late summer in hothouses, from winter to late spring in natural conditions COLOUR AVAILABILITY White, pink, red, orange, yellow, cream, lime, purple, mauve and many other colours CUT FLOWER LIFE SPAN Up to 8 weeks

In Australia, these flowers are generally available from May to November. They come in a fabulous colour range with some spotting of colour near the throat.

PAPHIOPEDILUM
Common names: Slipper Orchid

BOTANICAL VARIETIES Around 77 species NATURAL SEASON Winter and spring
COLOUR AVAILABILITY Green, burgundy, red/orange, lime/yellow CUT FLOWER LIFE SPAN Up to 6 weeks

Paphiopedilum is an exotic looking Orchid that can be grown outdoors. It is traditionally used in corsage work.

PHALAENOPSIS
Common names: Moth Orchid

BOTANICAL VARIETIES Around 60 species NATURAL SEASON Late spring and summer
COLOUR AVAILABILITY White, pink, lavender, yellow CUT FLOWER LIFE SPAN Up to 4 weeks

The fronds of these Orchids are visually effective in display work. They dislike airconditioning.

O. Cymbidium

DENDROBIUM
Common names: Singapore Orchid

BOTANICAL VARIETIES Numerous species NATURAL SEASON Spring
COLOUR AVAILABILITY White, pink, lavender, yellow, lime CUT FLOWER LIFE SPAN Up to 6 weeks

The Singapore Orchid is actually a hybrid variety of the Vanda Orchid. They are grown throughout the year in ideal conditions and available in a wide variety of colours. They have numerous floristry uses.

If they become limp, they can be revived by fully immersing them in water for up to 30 minutes.

VANDA

BOTANICAL VARIETIES Vanda tessellata (many hybrids) NATURAL SEASON Winter
COLOUR AVAILABILITY Wide range of petal and throat colours CUT FLOWER LIFE SPAN Up to 4 weeks

Although Vanda Orchids naturally flower in winter, they are available nearly all year round through hothouse cultivation. Vanda Orchids should be firm and unmarked with no sign of the veins in the petals. Their stems can be recut. Preservative is recommended.

VANDOPSIS

BOTANICAL VARIETIES A genus of around 4 species NATURAL SEASON Late spring and summer
COLOUR AVAILABILITY Brown/red CUT FLOWER LIFE SPAN Up to 4 weeks

Vandopsis is a finer version of Vanda Orchid and is mainly exported from Singapore to all over the world.

O. Phalaenopsis   *O. Dendrobium*

GENERAL USE

Orchids are an ever-popular flower for the vase at home as well as for professional designs.

Orchids must be firm before use in wired bouquet work. To firm them up, cut each bloom from the main stem, leaving a short stem on each flower. Place them around the edges of a shallow dish filled with water. Leave for one hour. Singapore Orchids can also be bathed (fully immersed) to firm them up.

WEDDING USE

Orchids are very popular and long lasting in bridal designs. The most delicate and expensive variety is the Cattleya Orchid.

Orchids with strong stems can be wired using the pierce and mount method. Fine-stemmed Orchids can be wired with the hairpin method (down the throat of the flower). Cymbidium Orchids should never be hairpin wired as they can bleed.

Phalaenopsis Orchids can be wired with the hairpin method, using a piece of wire covered in white binding tape. In a Phalaenopsis Orchid you will see two openings for the insertion of the wire.

CORPORATE USE

Orchids are suited to corporate work, including office, restaurant and foyer designs.

HISTORY

Many species of Orchid originated in South America, but the Vanda and Vandopsis varieties are native to South East Asia.

Traditionally, herbalists gathered these flowers for their root, as they were packed with carbohydrates and alkaline alkaloids and were prized for their curative powers.

CARE AND HANDLING

- When any variety of Orchid starts ageing, the flower will show some transparency and begin to show veins and wrinkles. When purchasing, look for fresh blooms with no sign of age.

- No Orchid should be refrigerated.

- Use preservative in the water.

- Light misting is recommended

- If the flowers soften, this usually means they have air blocked. Recut 5–10 centimetres from the stem ends.

ORNITHOGALUM

(or-nith-og-a-lam) Common names: Arab's Eye; Star of Bethlehem; Chincherinchee; Nap at Noon; Summer Snowflake BOTANICAL VARIETIES Ornithogalum arabicum, Ornithogalum narbonense, Ornithogalum dubium (orange), Ornithogalum thyrsoides (white Chincherinchee), FAMILY Hyacinthaceae NATURAL SEASON Spring (Ornithogalum thyrsoides) Spring and early Summer (others) COLOUR AVAILABILITY White with a black centre, or orange (Arabs Eye, Ornithogalum dubium), White but available in all colours due to commercial dyeing (Chincherinchee) LIFE SPAN up to 25 days

GENERAL USE

The Arab's Eye variety of Ornithogalum is used mainly in posies and bouquets. These flowers can also be used successfully in natural designs. The longer, angular stems are dramatic in modern arrangements. The flowers are lightly perfumed.

The Chincherinchee variety of Ornithogalum is a very hardy, practical flower, usually available with a stem length of 60 centimetres. These flowers are long lasting and reliable. They can be used in all aspects of floral design and are resilient to heating and airconditioning.

WEDDING USE

Both the Arab's Eye and Chincherinchee varieties of Ornithogalum are good, hardy wedding flowers. They are best used in bouquet holders. They can also be used in hand-tied, natural stemmed bouquets, and are great filling flowers. Chincherinchee can be coloured with food dye to match the colours of a bridal gown.

CORPORATE USE

Ornithogalum flowers are suited to corporate designs, and if properly prepared for use, will last a full 25 days in most conditions. Use the flowers in bud form with the lower flowers open.

GROWING CONDITIONS

Ornithogalum plants grow best in well-drained soil and full sun. They should be kept moist during growth season and kept dry when they are dormant. They are very hardy in warmer climates.

HISTORY

Ornithogalum has its origins in both Africa and the Mediterranean. It has been suggested that the name is derived from the Greek 'ornis', meaning 'bird', and 'gala', meaning 'milk'. This flower is known in South Africa as 'Tjenkenrientjee'. This is where the common name 'Chincherinchee' is phonetically derived from.

CARE AND HANDLING

- Cut or purchase the Arab's Eye variety when the flowers are starting to open.

- Cut or purchase the Chincherinchee variety when some of the lower flowers are open. Chincherinchee has green flowers that open from bottom up and develop into cream/white flowers on one spike.

- Recut 2–3 centimetres from the stem ends. Cut on an angle.

- Wash the stems to remove any particles of dirt.

- Place into water. Preservative is optional.

- These flowers do not need any conditioning time.

- The colour of Chincherinchee can be changed by putting the stems into food dye of any colour. Within two hours, the colour will have been drawn up into the flower and the new colour will remain throughout the life of the flower. This does not appear to lessen the life of the flower at all.

COMMERCIAL HANDLING

- Ornithogalum can be kept in the cool room at temperatures of 6–8 degrees Celsius.

- It can be stored (long term) in the cool room at a temperature of 2 degrees Celsius. It can be stored out of water.

OZOTHAMNUS *(oh-zoh-than-nas) Common names: Rice Flower, Wild Rice*

BOTANICAL VARIETIES Ozothamnus obcordatus (yellow Rice Flower), Ozothamnus diosmifolius (Rice Flower), Ozothamnus ledifolius (white flowers opening from red and pink buds) FAMILY Asteraceae NATURAL SEASON Late spring and summer COLOUR AVAILABILITY Yellow, white, pink, red CUT FLOWER LIFE SPAN 5–7 days

CARE AND HANDLING

- Cut or purchase when blooms are in full colour.

- If they are purchased commercially, always remove from sleeves. Open bunches for air flow around the flowers.

- Remove any foliage that will sit below the waterline.

- Recut 2–3 centimetres from the stem ends. Cut on an angle.

- Use bleach or preservative or else the water will foul within days.

- Change the water daily.

- Keep them cool as a cut flower.

- Ozothamnus is sensitive to ethylene, so keep it away from cigarette smoke and ripening fruit.

COMMERCIAL HANDLING

- Do not place in the cool room.

GENERAL USE

Ozothamnus is sold in bunches with stem lengths of 30–80 centimetres. The flowers will outlast the foliage. Do not use in office decorations as heating and airconditioning will both dry the flowers and the foliage.

GROWING CONDITIONS

Ozothamnus need well-drained soil and direct sunshine. It grows up to 80 centimetres in height. Do not confuse this plant with Pimelea nitens, as it is also known by the common name of Rice Flower.

HISTORY

Ozothamnus is native to Australia and New Zealand. These flowers are grwon commercially and exported across Asia.

PAEONIA

(pee-oh-nee-ya) Common names: Peony; Tree Peony

BOTANICAL VARIETIES Paeonia lactiflora hybrids (30 species in this genus) FAMILY Paeoniaceae NATURAL SEASON Late spring COLOUR AVAILABILITY Pink, white, flecked, lemon, light pink, dark pink, burgundy, red CUT FLOWER LIFE SPAN Up to 14 days

GENERAL USE

In previous times, Paeonia stem ends were scalded or burnt after being cut (as with Roses). Today it is generally accepted that this method is not necessary, and they can simply be recut and conditioned before use.

Most varieties of Paeonia are thornless. They are usually sold in bunches of five stems. These flowers will open into a great show of beauty. Most varieties have a lovely perfume, although a few have an unpleasant perfume.

Use the open Paeonia lower in the design if you are using two or three flowers. These flowers look truly magnificent en mass in wedding arrangements or funeral casket tributes.

WEDDING USE

The Paeonia is a truly beautiful bridal flower. For bouquets, they are best used in bouquet holders, as they need a constant water source. If they are to be used in a wired bouquet, put some damp cottonwool on the stem end and bind it with floral tape. If used in hand-tied, natural stemmed bouquets, use other flowers to support them. It is best to make these up on the day of the wedding.

CORPORATE USE

Paeonia flowers can be used in office decorating, but only if they commence the week in bud form, showing some colour.

CARE AND HANDLING

- Cut or purchase when the bud blooms are showing colour.

- Check the foliage is undamaged and strong in colour. The stems should look crisp and clean.

- Remove any foliage that will sit below the waterline.

- Recut 2–3 centimetres from the stem ends and place them in conditioning solution for 3–4 hours, then transfer to the vase.

- Use bleach in the water to prevent bacteria growth. Preservative is optional.

- If they flag due to air embolisms, revive by placing them in boiled water for 30 seconds.

COMMERCIAL HANDLING

- Paeonia can be kept in the cool room at temperatures of 6–8 degrees Celsius.

Romantic flower meaning: bashfulness

GROWING CONDITIONS

There are two main types of Paeonia: the tree species and the herbaceous perennials. Both enjoy colder winters and do best in cold areas in rich, well-drained soil, heavy with compost and manure. Afternoon shade is desirable. They will tolerate summer sun if they are kept well watered. Once they are established, they dislike disturbance.

Paeonia can be propagated from root division in autumn (include the roots and dormant buds). Use a sharp knife and cut carefully.

HISTORY

This flower finds its origins in Western China, Tibet, Siberia and Mongolia. Only one strain originated in Southern Europe.

A wide range of varieties were developed in the 19th century. James Kelway hybridised Peonies in the 1860s, and by the turn of the century there were 300 single and double varieties.

The flower is named in honour of 'Paeon', who was a physician to the gods in Greek mythology. The Chinese often refer to Paeonia as the 'King of Flowers'.

It is documented that during the 15th century in England, the roots were worn around the neck or arm to ward off evil spirits.

PAPAVER

(pap-av-a) Common names: *Iceland Poppy; Oriental Poppy; Opium Poppy*

BOTANICAL VARIETIES Papaver croceum (Iceland Poppy), Papaver orientale (Oriental Poppy), Papaver somniferum (Opium Poppy) (over 50 species of annuals and perennials in this genus) FAMILY Papaveraceae NATURAL SEASON Late winter to early spring (Iceland Poppies), early summer (Oriental Poppies) COLOUR AVAILABILITY Red, scarlet, purple, yellow, orange, white, gold, mauve CUT FLOWER LIFE SPAN 5 days

GENERAL USE

Papaver flowers are vibrant in colour with a delicate, paper-thin appearance. Some varieties are scented. They are generally available with stem lengths of 30–70 centimetres, and look beautiful when arranged simply in the vase at home. They will turn towards the light.

Papaver pods are visually effective in floral designs, with the Opium pod variety being particularly striking. The flowers will not last in office decorations but the pods will.

WEDDING USE

Papaver can be used in hand-tied, natural stemmed bouquets. Support them with other flowers and keep them in water until the time of the service. Do not them use on a hot day.

The pods of Papaver orientale look fabulous when used in bridal work for corsage or hairpiece designs.

GROWING CONDITIONS

These plants are annuals and herbaceous perennials. The Iceland Poppy enjoys a cool climate and blooms from late winter to early spring. The Oriental Poppy blooms in early summer. All Poppies enjoy well-drained soil and full sun.

Propagate the perennials by root cuttings in either autumn or winter. Once established, do not disturb them. They will die back after flowering.

Poppies can swamp other less vigorous plants so be aware of this when planting.

CARE AND HANDLING

- Cut or purchase when 1–2 flowers are opening and the rest of the buds are showing some colour. Avoid flowers that show pollination in the centre.

- Poppies exude a milky sap when first picked, and their stems will seal over from drinking. They can be scalded with boiling water to prevent this leakage.

- Wear gloves when handling, as the sap of Poppies can cause minor irritation to the skin.

- If picked from the garden, place the flowers into a separate vase with conditioning solution for up to 24 hours. Then recut and place in the display vase with preservative added.

- If purchased, recut 2–3 centimetres from the stem ends and place into vase water with preservative added (to assist buds to open).

COMMERCIAL HANDLING

- There is no need to place Papaver in the cool room as they flower in late spring and summer and dislike the cold.

Romantic flower meaning:

consolation (red); wild extravagance (scarlet); solace (white)

HISTORY

The Papaver orientale variety, commonly known as the Oriental Poppy, is native to Armenia, however most other varieties are native to both Europe and Northern Africa.

Poppies have a long documented history. These flowers were grown as ornamental plants in Mesopotamia, centuries before the birth of Jesus Christ; and evidence of Papaver has been uncovered in the Egyptian tombs.

Perhaps the biggest evolution for Papaver, particularly the Orientale variety, occurred in 1906 when the salmon pink variety, 'Mrs Perry' was introduced.

Nowadays, Poppy has a strong association with war remembrance. This connection has been attributed to the 9th century poet Homer, who once compared a hanging Poppy bud to a dying soldier.

PENSTEMON *(pen-stem-an) Common names: Beard Tongue*

BOTANICAL VARIETIES Penstemon davidsonii and Penstemon hybrids FAMILY Scrophulariaceae NATURAL SEASON Spring COLOUR AVAILABILITY Blue/mauve, pink, orange, gold, crimson CUT FLOWER LIFE SPAN 5–7 days

GENERAL USE

Penstemon is purchased in bunches. It is considered an old fashioned flower. It is used mainly for posy work, particularly cottage style posies. It also makes a lovely vase flower for the home.

GROWING CONDITIONS

Keep the soil fertile and well drained. A gravel soil is ideal. These flowers enjoy part sun but need wind shelter. Propagate from divisions or cuttings.

HISTORY

Penstemon is native to America and Mexico. Hundreds of hybrids have been developed in Europe since the 1800's. It is said that the roots of Penstemon were used by native Americans for relief from toothache.

CARE AND HANDLING

- Separate the bunches to allow for airflow around the flowers.
- Remove any foliage that will sit below the waterline.
- Recut 2–3 centimetres from the stem ends. Cut on an angle.
- Penstemon should be placed in shallow water, with bleach or preservative added.
- Change the water every 2 days.
- Penstemon is mildly sensitive to ethylene, so keep it away from cigarette smoke and ripening fruit.

COMMERCIAL HANDLING

- Do not place in the cool room.

PHLOX

(floks) Common names: Wild Sweet William; The Pride of Texas

BOTANICAL VARIETIES Phlox paniculata and Phlox drummondii (a genus of 67 annuals and perennials) FAMILY Polemoniaceae NATURAL SEASON Late spring and summer COLOUR AVAILABILITY White, red, scarlet, purple, pink, violet CUT FLOWER LIFE SPAN 5–7 days

CARE AND HANDLING

- Cut or purchase when at least half of the florets are open and in full colour.

- Phlox are prone to flower drop so check them carefully. Any sign of flower drop indicates that the flowers are old.

- Recut 2–3 centimetres from the stem ends. Cut on an angle.

- Remove any leaves that will sit below the waterline.

- Use some bleach in the water. Preservative is optional.

- Do not place in heated or airconditioned environments.

- Phlox is sensitive to ethylene, so keep it away from cigarette smoke and ripening fruit.

COMMERCIAL HANDLING

- Do not place in the cool room.

GENERAL USE

Phlox is a pretty flower when used in traditional work such as posies or bouquets. These flowers are pleasantly colourful in any vase.

Do not use them in office decorations as they will droop or dry out.

GROWING CONDITIONS

Phlox will grow in dry conditions provided it does not dry out. A sandy, light, well-drained soil is best and it does not like chalky or clay soils.

Phlox can grow from seed or seedlings and it is best to enrich the soil with compost. Older clumps can be divided in autumn. It grows 30–50 centimetres in height.

HISTORY

Phlox is native to North America, with the particular varieties listed above being native to Texas. Phlox was first sent to England in 1745. The word 'phlox'' is Greek for 'flame'.

PHYLICA

(fil-ic-a) Common names: Flannel Bush; Golden Phylica

BOTANICAL VARIETIES Phylica plumose (150 species of evergreen shrubs) FAMILY Rhamnaceae NATURAL SEASON Autumn, winter and early spring

COLOUR AVAILABILITY Green, yellow CUT FLOWER LIFE SPAN 14 days

GENERAL USE

Phylica is a good, hardy cut flower. It can be used in floral foam or in wired work. When arranging in the vase, make sure the flowers have airflow around them.

WEDDING USE

Phylica has clustered heads that can be cut into single stems, or wired for corsages.

If used in wedding bouquets, it is best to use in bouquet holders as there is a water source. Wire support each stem. If used in hand-tied bouquets, use a strong foliage or flower as a surround. A wire support is still advisable.

CORPORATE USE

Phylica is suitable for office work but the foliage will start to dry out by the end of the week. Mix with other strong foliages to camouflage the Phylica foliage.

GROWING CONDITIONS

Phylica likes humid conditions and well-drained soil. Acid content in the soil is best. These plants can be propagated from seed or autumn cuttings of shoots that are half-ripened.

HISTORY

Phylica is native to South Africa. Strangely, it is common belief that this flower is both an Australian native and a member of the Protea family, however this information is incorrect.

CARE AND HANDLING

- Cut or purchase when the blooms (bracts) are open. Check that the foliage is not browning.

- Remove any leaves that will sit below the waterline.

- Recut 2–3 centimetres from the stem ends. Cut on an angle.

- Preservative is not needed, but a small amount of bleach in the water will help to fight off bacteria.

- Keep cool as a cut flower.

- Phylica is mildly sensitive to ethylene, so keep it away from cigarette smoke and ripening fruit.

COMMERCIAL HANDLING

- Do not place in the cool room.

PHYSOSTEGIA

(fai-soh-stee-ia) Common names: Gallipoli Heath; The Obedience Plant BOTANICAL VARIETIES Physostegia virginiana, Physostegia purpurea FAMILY Libiateae NATURAL SEASON Summer and autumn COLOUR AVAILABILITY Purple and pink CUT FLOWER LIFE SPAN 5–10 days

CARE AND HANDLING

- Purchase STS-treated Physostegia if possible. Untreated Physostegia is highly sensitive to ethylene.

- Cut or purchase when 3–4 florets are open on the spike. The foliage should be strong, crisp and a dark green.

- Check for any flower drop.

- Recut 2–3 centimetres from the stem ends. Cut on an angle.

- Remove any leaves that will sit below the waterline.

- Use bleach or preservative in the water.

COMMERCIAL HANDLING

- Physostegia can be kept in the cool room at temperatures of 6–8 degrees Celsius. Make sure the bunches are separated.

GENERAL USE

Physostegia is usually sold in bunches. These flowers can be used in all designs. They were once strictly associated with funerals as they were used in funeral wreaths and never used in gift floral work. This association is not valid today.

GROWING CONDITIONS

These plants will self-seed. Spring and summer is the best time for planting by seed and late autumn is the best time for planting from propagated divisions. They need an acid soil and enjoy half to full sun.

Keep Physostegia moist during the growing season and cut the plants back after blooming in autumn. If you stake the stems during growth and then remove the stakes, the stems will stay where you placed them – this is why the plant is also known as the 'Obedience Plant.'

HISTORY

Physostegia is native to North America.

PIERIS (pee-rus) Common names: Andromeda; Bog Rosemary; The Lily-of-the-Valley Bush; Pearl Bush

BOTANICAL VARIETIES Pieris japonica, Andromeda compacta (pink), Andromeda polifolia FAMILY Ericaceae NATURAL SEASON Foliage all year, flowers in spring COLOUR AVAILABILITY Pink (mildly perfumed), white, green, cream CUT FLOWER LIFE SPAN 5-7 days

CARE AND HANDLING

- Cut or purchase when flowers are half open.
- Recut 2–3 centimetres from the stem ends.
- Use preservative.
- The flowers will drop as they age.
- Do not use in airconditioned environments.

COMMERCIAL HANDLING

- Do not place the flowers in the cool room or they will drop.

GENERAL USE

Pieris is ideal for cottage style posies or for the vase at home.

WEDDING USE

Pieris can be used in wedding work such as cascading designs and table centrepieces. The single blooms can be used for cake sprays, hairsprays and corsages. They can also be used in wired bouquets, bouquet holders and hand-tied bouquets. Use them in bud form as older flowers can drop. Wire with a small hairpin at the top of the flower and wind down through the flowers using a fine wire to support the heads for single stem use. This stops them falling.

CORPORATE USE

Pieris can be used in bud form for corporate designs, although it will only last five days in most office environments.

GROWING CONDITIONS

Pieris needs an acidic soil in full sun or partial shade. It is suited for peat beds or acidic rock gardens. It can be propagated from suckers or seed or by dividing rooted runners or cuttings. The plant produces umbels of white, pink or white/pink bell shaped flowers.

HISTORY

Pieris is native to eastern and southern Asia, Japan and the temperate regions of the Northern Hemisphere. In arctic climates Andromeda polifolia grows naturally in peat bogs. The botanical variety name Andromeda is a reference to the Greek goddess of the same name who, in Greek mythology, was once rescued from a sea monster by Perseus.

PLUMERIA

(ploo-mare-ree-yaa) Common names: *Frangipani; Temple Flower; Pagoda Tree; Graveyard Tree* BOTANICAL VARIETIES *Plumeria rubra (yellow or pink flowers)* FAMILY *Apocynaceae* NATURAL SEASON *Spring and summer* COLOUR AVAILABILITY *Cream with lemon centre, pink, deep pink (highly fragrant)* CUT FLOWER LIFE SPAN *5–7 days in water, 3–4 days out of water*

GENERAL USE

Plumeria (Frangipani) flowers are imported to colder climates. Florists should unpack them immediately and follow the conditioning process described under Care and Handling. Do not use these flowers unless they are conditioned.

Plumeria can be used in a range of floral designs. The stems, when wired, must be air-sealed using binding tape.

WEDDING USE

Plumeria is very popular in wedding work. The yellow centres are the most popular, but do not underestimate the beauty of pink Frangipani!

Because these flowers are picked without stems, they are best suited to fully wired bouquets. They should be wired using the pierce and mount method, and soaked in shallow water before wiring to firm them up. If mixed with other flowers that need a water source, they can be arranged in a bouquet holder.

It is also possible to use Plumeria in hand-tied bouquets, mixed with other flowers. The flowers should be wired, with the wire inserted in between the other flowers as a camouflage.

Plumeria is also used as a Lei flower.

GROWING CONDITIONS

Plumeria will only grow in warm, frost-free locations. They prefer well-drained soil and full sun.

CARE AND HANDLING

- Plumeria flowers are pinched from the branch. Do not crush the flower or it will bruise.

- These flowers will bruise when the fibres of the flower are damaged. Be careful not to press on the petals when handling them. The flowers can be touched gently by running your fingers down the flower towards the petals.

- To prepare for use, place a sheet of cottonwool in a shallow tray and add water. Recut 2 millimetres from the stem end and place the end of the flower through the cotton wool into the water. This process gives the flowers conditioning time. They should not be removed until you are ready to use them.

- Do not mist them – this may cause spotting.

- Preservative is optional.

COMMERCIAL HANDLING

- Do not place in the cool room.

HISTORY

Plumeria is native to Central and South America and is also found in tropical environments. Southern states of Australia regard this flower as a somewhat exotic species but in the northern states, where they are more prolific, they are viewed as commonplace.

Frangipani is often referred to as the 'tree of life' because it has the ability to continue to flower even when not in the ground. The flower owes its common name to the legend that tells of an Italian man, Frangipani, who once created an exquisite perfume by combining volatile oils. Frangipani gained instant fame when the Queen consort 'Catherine de Medici' claimed his perfume to be her favourite fragrance.

In Asia, Frangipani are commonly referred to as 'Temple Flowers' as they are often planted near temples and used as an offering to the gods. The flower is a symbol of immortality for Buddhists and for this reason is commonly planted near graves.

The milky sap of Frangipani is poisonous as it has glucosides and alkaloids and is therefore dangerous if swallowed. The Amazonians applied this sap to the external skin, as it has medicinal qualities.

POLIANTHES

(pol-ee-an-theez) Common names: Tuberose

BOTANICAL VARIETIES Polyianthes Polyianthes tuberosa FAMILY Agavaceae NATURAL SEASON Late summer and early autumn COLOUR AVAILABILITY white/cream CUT FLOWER LIFE SPAN Up to 14 days (if spent florets are removed)

GENERAL USE

Polianthes is a perfumed flower, cream in colour. The spiked stems can be used in most floral designs. Be cautious of using these in table centrepieces as the perfume can upset the bouquet of good wine.

Some floral designers remove the top buds to promote even opening of the flowers. If you need to open buds, place the stems in warm water. The spikes open from the base upwards.

WEDDING USE

Polianthes florets can be wired as single blooms for wedding work. Use the pierce and mount wiring method. These flowers are well suited to corsage, hairpieces, cake tops and delicate bouquets.

CORPORATE USE

Polianthes can be used in corporate designs if they start the week in bud form. These flowers die from the base upwards. Organise a mid-week visit to see if any lower florets need removal.

GROWING CONDITIONS

Polianthes plants like sun, but also part shelter. Prepare the soil well before planting and plant the tubers into damp earth in spring. The soil needs to be well fertilised and lime free. Good drainage is essential. The planting should be shallow. Do not water again until leaves appear.

Polianthes tubers only bloom once. The flowered tubers should be discarded and the offsets can be separated and stored. They may take up to two or three years to flower.

HISTORY

Polianthes is native to Mexico. The Chinese in Java use the flowers in vegetable soup. The flower is the principal ingredient of the Tuberose Flower oil used in high quality perfumery.

CARE AND HANDLING

- Cut or purchase when three or four florets are open at the base.

- Strong perfume is a sign of freshness.

- Recut 2–3 centimetres from stem ends. Cut on an angle.

- Remove any leaves that will sit below the waterline.

- Polianthes is sensitive to ethylene, especially from the wilted flowers on the stem. Remove any spent blooms daily and the remaining blooms will last longer.

- Use preservative.

Romantic flower meaning: illicit pleasures

POLYGONATUM

(pol-ee-gon-ah-tam) Common names: Solomon's Seal

BOTANICAL VARIETIES Polygonaum multiflorum (50 species in this genus) FAMILY Convallariaceae NATURAL SEASON Spring and early summer COLOUR AVAILABILITY white CUT FLOWER LIFE SPAN Up to 12 days

CARE AND HANDLING

- Recut 2–3 centimetres from the stem ends. Cut on an angle.
- Remove any leaves that will sit below the waterline.
- Wash the stems to remove any dirt particles.
- Use preservative.
- Do not place in airconditioned environments (it will dry out).
- Keep cool as a cut flower for maximum life span.

COMMERCIAL HANDLING

- Polygonatum can be kept in the cool room at temperatures of 6–8 degrees Celsius.

GENERAL USE

Polygonatum flowers are graceful, with a lovely arching formation. They also have a lovely scent. They are particularly good to use at the base of large arrangements and cascading table centrespieces. They are also elegant as a surround flower in bouquets. These flowers can be used in most floral designs.

WEDDING USE

Polygonatum flowers are well suited to hand-tied natural stemmed bouquets. Do not use on a hot day.

CORPORATE USE

Polygonatum foliage will last in an office environment, but the flowers will only last in an office where the heating and/or cooling system does not have direct fans blowing onto the flower.

GROWING CONDITIONS

Polgonatum is a herbaceous perennial that thrives in average, well-drained soil. This plant is ideal to grow in shady spots in the garden. It is grown from long, tuberous bulbs. Plant out in autumn. The rhizomes should sit just below the soil level. It will shoot in spring – the leaves stand out like pairs of wings and the flowers form from arches, along which grow green tipped bells.

Polgonatum likes sub-zero temperatures to commence annual dormancy. Keep moist when growing in full sun in summer. The flowers grow up to 60 centimetres in height.

HISTORY

Polgonatum is native to Europe. It is said that the root stock resemble King Soloman's seal.

PROTEA

(proh-tee-ya) **Common names:** *King Protea; Pink Ice; Pink Mint; Peach Protea; Princess Protea; Sugarbush; Repens; Rose Sugarbush; Honey Protea; Bot River Protea; Queen Protea* **BOTANICAL VARIETIES** *Protea cynaroides* (King Protea), *Protea nerifolia* (Pink Ice, White Mint and Pink Mint), *Protea magnifica* (Woolly-bearded Protea and Queen Protea), *Protea grandiceps* (Peach Protea and Princess Protea), *Protea repens* (Sugarbush, Repens and Honey Protea), *Protea compacta* (Bot River Protea), *Protea exima* (Ray Flowered Protea), *Protea scolymocephala* (Rose Sugarbush), *Protea eximia* (Broad Leaved Sugarbush) (there are about 100 species) **FAMILY** Proteaceae **NATURAL SEASON** Winter and spring **COLOUR AVAILABILITY** Lime, pink, cream, red/pink, white (*Protea repens*) **CUT FLOWER LIFE SPAN** Up to 4 weeks

GENERAL USE

Proteas are popular cut flowers. They can be dried and removal of the bracts leaves a most attractive husk. These can be sprayed with wood lacquer to give more shine if desired.

The fresh or dried bracts can be wired in little bundles and used around the edge of posies. This gives a feathered effect. These flowers retain shape when dried but fade in colour. If using the stems in foam, they need to be cut on a very sharp angle because they are knotty. Sometimes King Protea may need to be shaved up the base of the stem to lessen its width.

The leaves of King Protea can be used to cover floral foam with a pleasing visual effect. They last well, except when in airconditioning as they will dry and turn brown.

WEDDING USE

Protea is heavy in appearance, but can be cut into sections for more delicate use in wedding designs. If they are cut in half they will brown on the tips in four to five hours, but if the bouquet features natives, this can look quite effective.

CORPORATE USE

Always remove all leaves – they will not last very long at all in office conditions. The flower will last for ages and will eventually dry. Be aware they are very thirsty so the vase water levels must be checked daily.

GROWING CONDITIONS

Protea likes sandy soil, preferably acidic, with perfect drainage and full sun. It enjoys winter rainfall and the contrast of dry, windy summers. It prefers a sloping ground.

CARE AND HANDLING

- Cut or purchase when the bracts are starting to open. Pink Ice should have a circular opening 3–4 centimetres wide at the top, and the bracts in the King Proteas should be reflexing backwards.

- The leaves should be perfect and a strong green in colour. Avoid any marks or browning on the leaves.

- Recut 2–3 centimetres from the stem ends, using secateurs or a knife. Cut on a sharp angle.

- Remove any foliage that will sit below the waterline.

- Do not bash the stems.

- Do not spray or mist Proteas as they are prone to fungal disease.

- These flowers are very thirsty so ensure an adequate water supply.

- Use bleach in the water as Proteas will turn water brown. It is best to change the vase water every second day.

- Preservative is recommended.

- The flower will usually outlast the foliage. The foliage is not resilient to airconditioning and will turn brown within days.

COMMERCIAL HANDLING

- Do not place in the cool room or the leaves will blacken. Protea compacta, Protea nerifolia (Pink Mink and Pink Ice) and Protea exima are the varieties most prone to leaf blackening.

HISTORY

While there are varieties native to Australia, New Zealand, South America and Malaya, the main variety of Protea originated in Africa.

The Protea is the national flower of South Africa and is named after the Greek sea god, Proteus, the servant of Poseidon.

It is interesting to note that ancestors of the Protea family have been discovered in fossils dating back millions of years.

PTILOTUS

(tai-loh-tas) Common names: Mulla Mulla; Woody Bears

BOTANICAL VARIETIES Ptilotus obovatus, Ptilotus exaltatus (Wooly Bears, Pink Mulla Mulla) (around 100 annual and perennial herbs in this genus) FAMILY Amaranthaceae NATURAL SEASON Spring to early summer COLOUR AVAILABILITY White/grey, white/pink CUT FLOWER LIFE SPAN 7 days

GENERAL USE

Ptilotus flowers have reddish stems and exude a perfume. The flowers have a fluffy, feathery appearance. They are an excellent filling flower for floral designs and their texture is compatible with Banksias, Leucandendrons and any native flowers.

GROWING CONDITIONS

Ptilotus needs well-drained soil and full sun. It enjoys sandy soil and plenty of humus. Water from late winter until it blooms. It grows in desert areas and does not do well in a nurtured environment or in cold winters.

Seed germination is not always easy, but these plants can be grown from short lengths of fleshy roots, propagated in sandy mix.

HISTORY

Ptilotus is native to Australia.

CARE AND HANDLING

- Cut or purchase when the flower heads are starting to open. They should be showing colour and the stems should be strong.

- Recut 2–3 centimetres from the stem ends. Cut on an angle.

- Remove any foliage that will sit below the waterline.

- Preservative is recommended.

RANUNCULUS *(ran-unk-yoo-las)* Common names: *Turban Buttercup; Buttercup; Crow's Foot* BOTANICAL VARIETIES Ranunculus asiaticus (over 400 species in this genus) FAMILY Ranunculaceae NATURAL SEASON Late winter and spring COLOUR AVAILABILITY Wide colour range CUT FLOWER LIFE SPAN 5 days

CARE AND HANDLING

- Cut or purchase when flowers are in bud and showing full colour. Check there is no yellowing on the leaves.

- Recut 2–3 centimetres from the stem ends. Cut on an angle.

- Wash the stems and place into deep water. Use bleach or preservative in the water.

- These flowers will foul water if it is not changed daily.

- Keep away from heat, direct sunlight and airconditioning.

- Do not use in corporate office designs.

- Do not mist as this will cause the flowers to deteriorate.

- Keep cool as a cut flower.

COMMERCIAL HANDLING

- Avoid placing Ranunculus in the cool room if possible.

GENERAL USE

Ranunculus is a pretty vase flower, with the black or green flower centres giving it a striking look. It can be used in posies or simple natural stemmed bouquets, or wired for funeral wreath work. The petals will drop after five days (on average). Do not use in hospital arrangements as they will not last in that environment.

GROWING CONDITIONS

Ranunculus can be grown from seed. It grows best in cool climates, in a sunny position and moist soil enriched with compost. These plants are slow growing.

HISTORY

Ranunculus is a native to the Northern hemisphere. The name is derived from the Latin word for 'little frog'.

In the language of flowers, Ranunculus means 'radiant charm'. Ranunculus are believed to be the 'Lilies of the Field' referred to in the Bible, in which these flowers are said to have outshone King Soloman himself.

All Ranunculus varieties are poisonous to livestock.

Romantic flower meaning: radiant charm

RESEDA

(res-ee-da) Common names: Mignonette

BOTANICAL VARIETIES Reseda odorata FAMILY Recedaceae NATURAL SEASON Spring COLOUR AVAILABILITY Mauve, yellow, white, yellow, gold, crimson, orange CUT FLOWER LIFE SPAN 5–7 days

GENERAL USE

Reseda is an old fashioned flower. It is not strong out of water and will wilt quickly. It is ideal for cottage posies and it has a lovely fragrance. Do not use in office decorations as it will dry out quickly.

GROWING CONDITIONS

Sow Reseda in lightly raked, well-drained soil. Good humus will assist growth. Sow in autumn, mild winters or spring. Deadhead this plant regularly.

HISTORY

Reseda is native to Northern Africa. The emperor Napoleon once sent the seeds of this flower from Egypt to Josephine, who grew them at Malmaison. They then became a fashionable flower across Europe, with their popularity lasting well into the 19th century.

CARE AND HANDLING

- Cut or purchase when the flowers are half open.

- Check that the foliage is crisp and strong. There should be no visible film on the stems.

- Separate the bunches for air circulation.

- Recut 2–3 centimetres from the stem ends. Cut on an angle.

- Remove any foliage that will sit below the waterline.

- Add bleach or preservative to the water. Change the water every two days.

- Reseda is sensitive to ethylene, so keep it away from cigarette smoke and ripening fruit.

COMMERCIAL HANDLING

- Do not place in the cool room. The foliage will foul the water and deteriorate quickly.

RHODODENDRON

(roh-doh-den-dron)

BOTANICAL VARIETIES Rhododendron species (a genus of over 800 species) FAMILY Ericaceae NATURAL SEASON Late winter and spring COLOUR AVAILABILITY Pink, green, purple, red, white, lemon, yellow, mauve (also flecked varieties) CUT FLOWER LIFE SPAN 7 days (provided they are not in direct sunlight)

CARE AND HANDLING

- Cut or purchase when the florets are half to three quarters open. The leaves should be strong and dark green.

- Remove any leaves that will sit below the waterline.

- Wash the stems to remove any particles of dirt.

- Recut 3–4 centimetres from the woody stem ends. Cut on a sharp angle.

- Do not the bash the stem ends.

- Use bleach or preservative in the water.

- Do not place these flowers in direct sunlight.

GENERAL USE

Rhododendron is highly attractive when used as a vase flower as well as in made up floral work, wreath work and in large wedding arrangements. The leaves can be used to base floral items.

Some varieties are perfumed. They are usually sold in bunches.

The florets may be wired for fine work, but they do not last well.

GROWING CONDITIONS

Rhododendron grows best in humus-rich acid soil and light shade. It dislikes full sun in warmer climates. Remove spent flowers after flowering.

HISTORY

Most species of Rhododendron are native to China, Tibet and Nepal, however there are some species that are native to New Guinea and North America.

This flower is the national flower of Nepal.

In the language of flowers, Rhododendron means 'beware'. The name Rhododendron is appropriately derived from the Greek word for 'tree rose', a reference to the similarities in the appearance of the two flowers.

Romantic flower meaning: danger

ROSA *(roh-za) Common names: Rose*

BOTANICAL VARIETIES Rosa hybrids FAMILY Rosaceae NATURAL SEASON Spring, summer and autumn (garden varieties), all year round (hothouse varieties) COLOUR AVAILABILITY All colours CUT FLOWER LIFE SPAN 14 days (if kept in excellent condition)

GENERAL USE

Before arranging Roses, remove the outer casing petals and if desired, strip the stems of their thorns. Pick off larger thorns by hand and remove smaller ones with a towel (see page 25 for instructions). You may also use a rose stripper or knife, but be aware that these tools can partly remove the outer fibres of the stem, which allows air to dry the stem and shorten the flower's life span. It is advisable to only remove the thorns that will sit below the waterline.

There are many varieties of Roses and lots of different ways to use them in floral design. Rose hips (the seed pods of Roses) can be used in wired floral designs. For wreath designs, open Roses can be held in a design by cross wiring through the base of the head. This stops them from opening further.

Mature Roses can be opened for more surface area. The petals are peeled over the thumb and they will hold open. If they are too fresh, the petal will bounce back.

Spray Roses are available through the local season and all year for glasshouse varieties. They will not last as long as other varieties, as they open more quickly.

Cecile Brunner is a very delicate, tiny Rose that is ideal for posies and wired corsage construction.

Rose stems are available in several standard lengths (in centimetres): 20, 25, 30, 35, 40, 45, 50, 55, 60, 65, 70, 80 and 90.

Do not use Roses for corporate arrangements as they will dry out in office conditions.

CARE AND HANDLING

- Roses should always be sold with a water source. Ask for this if it is not supplied.

- Cut or purchase when the blooms are in bud but showing strong colour. In winter choose buds that are half open, as they may not continue to open if they are too tight.

- Feel the buds to make sure they are firm. Look at the stem ends – they should not be dark or dry looking as this is a sign of age. Make sure the foliage is unmarked and strong. Roses suffer from Botrytis (grey mould) and marked foliage is a warning sign of this.

- When cutting Roses, take a bucket of water with you to place the flowers in as soon as they are cut.

- Remove any foliage that will sit below the waterline. The thorn ends can be removed using a towel, but it is best to leave them on as removing them can cause infection.

- Recut 2–4 centimetres from the stem ends. Cut on an angle. Recut under water if possible to ensure air cannot get into the stems. If cutting out of water, make sure the transition into the vase water is quick.

- Preservative in the water is recommended.

- See the advice on pages 36–37 for reviving wilted Roses.

Champagne Rose is a popular wedding Rose but do not use it when it's fully open as it will not last. It needs to be half open on the wedding day.

COMMERCIAL HANDLING

- Roses can be kept in the cool room at temperatures of 6–8 degrees Celsius.

- The outer sepal casing of petals is generally removed for commercial use of Roses. These are removed using the index finger and thumb, pinched from the base. This makes the Rose look perfect. For a natural design leave the lime marked petals in place.

WEDDING USE

The Rose is the most popular bridal flower. It is also very temperamental and needs to be handled and prepared very carefully for bridal work.

Roses need to be in top condition for use in bridal designs. If the centres are visible they may not last through the whole day. Make sure they at the optimum opening stage. Clean off the outer petals if necessary. The centre of the rose should be tight when gently pinched between the thumb and forefinger.

Arrangements made up with Roses should be kept in a water source until the time of the ceremony.

For fully wired bouquets, Roses should be properly conditioned and then wired using the pierce and mount wiring method.

For natural stemmed bouquets and bouquet holders, use the support wiring method (down the side of the stem). Insert the wire into the calyx and place it down the flower stem.

Remember, wires should never be seen in the stem holding area. They should only reach the tie point of the bouquet. Also make sure that the wire does not penetrate into the flower head or brown pin marks may appear as the flower opens.

GROWING CONDITIONS

Roses are tolerant of a wide range of soils and conditions. They grow best in damp, but free draining humus, rich soil, in full sun. Prune them in summer for another flowering and prune hard in early winter. Always cut out dead growth.

Romantic flower meaning:
awakening love (bud of White Rose); happy love (Bridal Rose); Passion (Red Rose); freshness (Damask Rose); love (Rose); ambassador of love (Cabbage Rose)

HISTORY

The Rose originated in China. The first Rose was cultivated 5000 years ago, and to this day the Rose remains the most popular flower in the world. There are currently around 250 species and tens of thousands of cultivars in existence.

Chinese Roses first appeared in Europe in the late 18th century. Parson's 'Pink China' and Slater's 'Crimson China' both arrived in 1789. Pink China became the ancestor of many of the new categories of Rose in the 19th century.

Rosa gallica and alba were among the first rose species to yield an extensive range of cultivars.

Rosa officinalis, the European Rose, dates from the 13th century and was grown in France for the purpose of perfumery.

The crossing of Noisettes with Bourbons produced the Tea Rose and in 1808, the first tea-scented Rose was received from China by Sir Abraham Hume. This variety was named 'Hume's Blush' in his honour.

In 1837 the first Hybrid Perpetual was raised in France. It was called 'Princess Helene' and was followed by some 400 cultivars.

The Romans were extravagant with their use of Roses and Cleopatra was known to have once covered an entire chamber with rose petals (up to 40 centimetres deep) to welcome Caesar.

The Rose is the national flower of England and features in English heraldry. Rose oil is one of the most highly valued oils in the world.

SALVIA *(sal-vee-ya)* Common names: Sage; Gentian Sage

BOTANICAL VARIETIES Salvia farinacea, Salvia clevelandii (many cultivars) FAMILY Lamiaceae NATURAL SEASON Summer to autumn COLOUR AVAILABILITY Blue/mauve, pink, purple, scarlet CUT FLOWER LIFE SPAN 5–7 days

GENERAL USE

Salvia is purchased in bunches. It is considered old fashioned flower. It is used mainly for posy work, particularly cottage style posies and is a pretty vase flower.

These flowers can also be used for function arrangements as long as they're fresh. Salvia flowers will drop within days if picked when they're too open.

Do not use Salvia flowers in corporate designs. They will not last in heated or airconditioned environments.

GROWING CONDITIONS

Salvia needs fertile, well-drained soil, rich in humus and ideally, lime. This plant enjoys part sun and dislikes heavy, wet soils. Grow Salvia from seed in spring, or propagate from softwood cuttings taken from the previous growing season.

HISTORY

Salvia is native to the Americas. It is named for the Latin word 'salvia', meaning 'to heal'. Salvia is the largest genus in the Lamiaceae family, with over 900 species.

CARE AND HANDLING

- Separate bunches to allow air-flow around the flowers.

- Recut 2–3 centimetres from the stem ends. Cut on an angle.

- Remove any foliage that will sit below the waterline.

- Use bleach or preservative in the vase with shallow water and change the water every two days.

- Salvia is mildly sensitive to ethylene, so keep it away from cigarette smoke and ripening fruit.

COMMERICAL HANDLING

- There should be no need to place Salvia in the cool room, but if absolutely necessary, it can be placed in temperatures of 6–8 degrees Celsius.

SANDERSONIA

(san-dur-soh-nee-ya) Common names: Christmas Bells; Chinese Lantern Lily; Golden Lantern Lily BOTANICAL VARIETIES *Sandersonia aurantiaca* FAMILY Colchiacaceae CUT FLOWER LIFE SPAN 5 days COLOUR AVAILABILITY Orange to yellow/orange NATURAL SEASON Summer

CARE AND HANDLING

- Cut or purchase when up to one half of the bells are open on each branch. The leaves should be a glossy green and the bells should be strong. Avoid yellow leaves.

- The stems will seal over quickly when out of water so keep in a water source at all times.

- Remove any leaves that will sit below the waterline.

- Recut 2–3 centimetres from the stem ends and then lightly crush the ends. Cut on an angle.

- Use preservative.

- Change the water and add preservative regularly.

- Keep cool as a cut flower.

COMMERCIAL HANDLING

- Do not place in the cool room.

GENERAL USE

Sandersonia is an attractive vase flower, especially when combined with flowers of contrasting colours. They are bright and have a relaxed look about them.

Do not use Sandersonia flowers in airconditioning as it will dry them out. They are not suited to wedding bouquets.

GROWING CONDITIONS

Sandersonia grows in warm climates and prefers rich, well-drained soil. It grows from tubers, as well as offshoots taken in early spring.

HISTORY

Sandersonia is native to South Africa, where it is commonly known as the Christmas Bell. The flower was named after Mr John Sanderson (1820–1891), who discovered the plant in South Africa in 1851. It was the botanist William Jackson Hooker (1785–1865) who named the flower after its finder.

SCABIOSA

(skai-bee-oh-sa) Common names: Pincushion Flower, Egyptian Rose

BOTANICAL VARIETIES Scabiosa atropurpurea, Scaniosa caucasica (Pincushion Flower) FAMILY Dipsacaceae NATURAL SEASON Spring and summer COLOUR AVAILABILITY Blue, white, purple, cherry/red, crimson CUT FLOWER LIFE SPAN 7–10 days

GENERAL USE

Often considered a cottage type flower, Scabiosa is suited to most floral work. It is particularly attractive as a vase flower and popular in bouquets and posies. It dislikes airconditioning, which tends to dry the tips of the flower.

For modern designs, all petals may be removed, leaving just the centres on the stem. The stems will sometimes curve – this is a feature that a floral designer can use to complement a design. Towards the end of the season the flower colour will fade.

WEDDING USE

These flowers are delicate and should not be used on a hot day. They are best used in the inner perimeter of bouquets, with stronger flowers around them for support.

CORPORATE USE

Scabosia in half open bud form will last five days in corporate designs.

GROWING CONDITIONS

Scabiosa needs alkaline, well-drained soil. Plant it from seed in autumn. This flower will last well and gives a strong show in the garden over the warmer months.

HISTORY

Scabosia is native to South Western Europe. In the Middle Ages, it was thought to cure Scabies. The word 'scabie' means 'to itch' and thus the flower was named for its itch-curing properties. The first Scabiosa to be known in Northern Europe was introduced by botanist Carolus Clusius, known in France as Charles de L'Ecluse (1526–1609).

CARE AND HANDLING

- Cut or purchase when the flowers are open and the centres look tight.
- Check the bunches for any flower drop.
- Recut 2–3 centimetres from the stem ends. Cut on an angle.
- Remove any leaves that will sit below the waterline.
- Preservative is recommended.
- Scabiosa is sensitive to ethylene, so keep it away from cigarette smoke and ripening fruit.

COMMERCIAL HANDLING

- If necessary, Scabiosa can be kept in the cool room at temperatures of 6–8 degrees Celsius. The bunches must be separated or the foliage will discolour and mould. Avoid the cool room if possible, as the temperatures may cause the petal tips to burn.

SCILLA

(sil-la) Common names: Bluebell; Squill; Jacinth; Peruviana Lily; Wild Hyacinth; Persian Lily BOTANICAL VARIETIES Scilla hyachinthoides, Scilla mischtschenkoana, Scilla sibirica (Siberian squill), Scilla campanillata FAMILY Hyacinthaceae NATURAL SEASON Autumn and spring COLOUR AVAILABILITY Blue, purple/pink, pink/red and white CUT FLOWER LIFE SPAN 5–7 days

CARE AND HANDLING

- Cut or purchase when lower flowers are starting to show colour.

- Recut 2–3 centimetres from the stem ends. Cut on an angle.

- Scilla is a bulb flower. Cut the white bulb section off the stem. This will help the stem to absorb water more efficiently.

- Add preservative.

- The florets will start to die from the base up – when this happens they should be removed, to give further vase life to the remaining florets.

COMMERCIAL HANDLING

- Do not place in the cool room as this will affect their life span.

GENERAL USE

Scilla is a good posy flower and can be used in most floral designs. Ensure a constant water supply. These flowers look similar to Dwarf Agapanthus or an English Bluebell. Do not use Scilla in corporate designs.

WEDDING USE

Scilla is a pretty flower to use in casual, hand-tied, natural stemmed bouquets or bouquet holders. Use wire to support the stems.

GROWING CONDITIONS

Scilla grows from an onion-like bulb. It benefits from mulching and will grow in full sun, or partial shade. It is easy to grow and once established, prefers to be left undisturbed.

HISTORY

Scilla comes from Southern Europe, Asia Minor and Southern Africa. The word 'scilla' is Latin for 'squill'. Extracts from Scilla bulbs have a medicinal history for use as diuretics and expectorants.

Romantic flower meaning: constancy (Bluebell)

SEDUM *(se-dum) Common names: Stonecrop; Iceplant; Liveforever*

BOTANICAL VARIETIES Sedum spectabile (Iceflower) and varieties, Sedum sexangulare (Stonecrop), Sedum purpureum (Liveforever) FAMILY Crassulaceae NATURAL SEASON Summer and autumn COLOUR AVAILABILITY Brown, yellow, crimson CUT FLOWER LIFE SPAN 7–10 days

GENERAL USE

Sedum is an interesting flower and due to its mass is best used low in a design. Do not use in wedding work as the flowers will not hold without a constant water source. These flowers will last five days in office decorations.

GROWING CONDITIONS

Sedum will grow in poor soil. All varieties can be grown from cold weather divisions. In warmer weather, small stem cuttings can be struck. Sedum has succulent leaves and can be grown on slopes and over rockeries. It is amazingly persistent and can regenerate from any fragment of its composition. This trait, along with its robust appearance, accounts for its common name, 'Liveforever'.

HISTORY

Sedum is native to the Northern Hemisphere with one variety native to Peru and parts of Mexico. The name is derived from the Latin 'sedo', meaning 'to sit', and refers to the plant's low flowering habit.

CARE AND HANDLING

- Cut or purchase when the flowers form a dense mass of colour. The leaves must not show any sign of yellowing.

- Recut 2–3 centimetres from the stem end. Cut on an angle.

- Remove any leaves that will sit below the waterline.

- Preservative is recommended.

COMMERCIAL HANDLING

- There is no need to place in the cool room. As a summer flower they dislike the cold.

SERRURIA *(se-roo-ree-ya) Common names: Blushing Bride*

BOTANICAL VARIETIES Serruria florida FAMILY Proteaceae NATURAL SEASON Spring COLOUR AVAILABILITY Pink and white (also known as sugar and spice)

CUT FLOWER LIFE SPAN 7–14 days

CARE AND HANDLING

- Avoid bunches that have drooping heads.

- Recut 2–3 centimetres from the stem ends. Cut on an angle.

- Remove any leaves that will sit below the waterline (the leaves are quite small).

- For maximum life span, keep the flowers cool.

COMMERCIAL USE

- Serruria can be kept in the cool room at temperatures of 6–8 degrees Celsius.

GENERAL USE

Serruria is a lovely flower to use in wired work. When wiring, make sure that the stem end is sealed with binding tape.

WEDDING USE

This tiny bridal Protea is delicate in texture and can be used in hand-tied, natural stemmed bouquets, bouquet holders or fully wired bouquets. Sometimes the stem will need a wire support as the heads are heavy.

CORPORATE USE

Serruria will last well in corporate designs. Usually the stems are quite short, so these flowers are best placed in groups, close to floral foam, with other flowers that give height and structure to the design.

GROWING CONDITIONS

Serruria likes a temperate climate with good drainage and sunshine. After the long flowering season give the plant a trim. This flower grows up to 60 centimetres in height.

HISTORY

Serruria is native to South Africa. It was named in honour of James Serrurier, an 18th century Dutch professor of botany who worked at the University of Utrecht.

SOLIDAGO

(sol-li-dah-go) Common names: Golden Rod; Golden Wings

BOTANICAL VARIETIES Solidago canadensis FAMILY Asteraceae NATURAL SEASON Summer COLOUR AVAILABILITY Golden yellow

CUT FLOWER LIFE SPAN 7–10 days

GENERAL USE

Solidago foliage will dry out before the flowers, so it is best to remove all foliage before using it in arrangements, especially for airconditioned offices or homes. The flowers will just last one week in these drying conditions.

Solidago is a great filler flower in most forms of floral work. It is a nice flower for use in natural stemmed bouquets.

WEDDING USE

Solidago is a delicate filling flower and can be used in all forms of bouquets. It is ideal for trails. Use in half bud form. It is also attractive in corsages and buttonholes, and in small pieces as an accessory flower.

CORPORATE USE

Solidago can be used in corporate designs, in bud form. Remove all foliage before use.

GROWING CONDITIONS

Solidago enjoys rich garden soil, supported with light stakes as it grows. To propagate this flower, divide off older clumps. It will grow up to 70 centimetres in height.

HISTORY

Most varieties of Solidago are native to North America. The Cherokees thought that this flower had medicinal qualities. They used a leaf tea for many conditions and prescribed a root tea for neuralgia. They chewed the plant's roots to cure a sore mouth.

CARE AND HANDLING

- Cut or purchase when half of the flowers are in strong colour. The foliage should be green, strong and unmarked.

- Always remove from sleeves and separate bunches.

- Remove any foliage that will sit below the waterline.

- Recut 2–3 centimetres from the stem ends. Cut on an angle.

- Preservative is recommended.

- Solidago is sensitive to ethylene, so keep it away from cigarette smoke and ripening fruit.

COMMERCIAL HANDLING

- These flowers dislike the cool room as they are a summer flower. They can be stored at a low temperature but only if absolutely necessary.

SOLIDASTER *(sol-ed-as-tah)*

BOTANICAL VARIETIES Solidaster luteus (a cross between Aster and Solidago) FAMILY Asteraceae NATURAL SEASON Late summer and autumn COLOUR AVAILABILITY Yellow CUT FLOWER LIFE SPAN 7–10 days

CARE AND HANDLING

- Cut or purchase when half of the yellow flowers are open. The heads should be undamaged and there should be no sign of yellowing on the leaves.

- Recut 2–3 centimetres from the ends. Cut on an angle.

- Remove any foliage that will sit below the waterline.

- Preservative in the water is recommended.

GENERAL USE

Solidaster is a good posy flower and an attractive vase flower. It can be used as a filling flower in most floral designs.

GROWING CONDITIONS

Solidaster will grow in any soil condition. It enjoys full sun and must be kept well watered. It is propagated only by division.

HISTORY

Solidaster is native to North America. Being a hybrid, Solidaster got its name from its parents' names, 'Aster' and 'Solidago'. The plant first appeared in 1909 in France, as the result of an experiment.

STACHYS *(stak-iss) Common names: Lamb's Tongue; Lamb's Ears; Dusty Miller*

BOTANICAL VARIETIES Stachys byzantina (around 300 species in this genus) FAMILY Lamiaceae NATURAL SEASON Spring

COLOUR AVAILABILITY Pink with silver grey CUT FLOWER LIFE SPAN Up to 5 days for flowers; 3 weeks for foliage

GENERAL USE

Stachys flowers are attractive and will last sufficiently in a vase, but it is the foliage that is used the most. The silver/grey leaves are plush looking and textured, and are excellent to base a floral design.

GROWING CONDITIONS

Stachys grows best in colder climates. Most soil conditions will suit the Stachys, but the soil should be moist. This flower is planted easily from the division of older plants. Stachys is often planted to form a garden border.

HISTORY

Stachys is native to Europe. Around the world and for centuries, it has been used for its medicinal properties on a wide variety of ailments. Whilst it has some medicinal uses that are constant, Stachys is viewed by herbalists as a panacea.

CARE AND HANDLING

- Cut or purchase when only the flowers at the base of the spike are open.

- Do not purchase if the foliage is water-logged.

- Recut 2–3 centimetres from the stem ends. Cut on an angle.

- Remove any foliage that will sit below the waterline as it will deteriorate quickly when immersed.

- Preservative in the water is recommended.

- Stachys is mildly sensitive to ethylene, so keep it away from cigarette smoke and ripening fruit.

CARE AND HANDLING

- Cut or purchase when there are one or two flowers open on the cluster. They should have a strong scent (this is a sign of freshness).

- Make sure there are no visible spots or creases on the petals.

- Recut one centimetre from the stem ends.

- Preservative is recommended.

- Do not mist as these flowers are susceptible to spotting. Also, any water that sits in their throats may cause them to rot.

- Stephanotis is sensitive to ethylene, so keep it away from cigarette smoke and ripening fruit.

COMMERCIAL HANDLING

- These flowers are usually packed in airtight containers by the growers, with either 25 or 50 pieces per container. When they are removed from the box they can be placed in a shallow dish to absorb water, but they must never float or they will become transparent.

- Floral designers can keep them in the cool room, in airtight containers, prior to being used. They should be conditioned on removal, (sit stems in conditioning solution for 30 minutes) before use.

GENERAL USE

Stephanotis flowers grow in clusters. They are waxy in appearance and have a strong perfume. These flowers are a classic wedding flower and were used widely throughout the 20th century in this medium.

Always stand these flowers in a jar rather than lying them down on the bench. This will help to prevent bruising.

Do not use Stephanotis in corporate designs.

WEDDING USE

Stephanotis is one of the most glamorous wedding flowers. They have a stunning texture and are beautiful when combined with Gardenias in bouquets.

Stephanotis flowers are mainly used in wired bouquets. They are also used for corsages, hairpieces, caketops and a wide range of other wedding designs. These flowers need to be wired down the throat (hairpin method) with a fine wire.

If they do not feel firm sit their bases in shallow water for 30 minutes before using. They should be kept sealed in a plastic container until they are ready to be used.

GROWING CONDITIONS

Stephanotis requires well-drained soil, and is best fertilised with rotted organic matter. It is struck from spring cuttings and it must be struck in heat. This plant needs a warm position, not below 18 degrees Celsius. Stephanotis is a natural climber.

HISTORY

Stephanotis is native to Madagascar. The genus name 'Stephanotis' has Greek origins. It is made up of two words: 'stephonos', meaning 'crown', and 'otos', meaning 'ear'. The name refers to its appearance, which faintly resembles a 'crown of ears'.

STEPHANOTIS (stef-a-noh-tas) Common names: Waxflower; Madagascar Chaplet Flower BOTANICAL VARIETIES Stephanotis floribunda FAMILY Asclepiadaceae NATURAL SEASON Spring, summer and early autumn COLOUR AVAILABILITY White CUT FLOWER LIFE SPAN 5 days (maximum)

STRELITZIA

(stre-lit-zee-ya) Common names: Bird of Paradise

BOTANICAL VARIETIES Strelitzia reginae FAMILY Musaceae NATURAL SEASON Late autumn, winter, spring and early summer in humid climates, or spring to summer in cooler climates COLOUR AVAILABILITY Blue, green, white/blue, orange CUT FLOWER LIFE SPAN 3 weeks

CARE AND HANDLING

- Cut or purchase when the first floret (or crest) is visible out of the split green sheath. Do not purchase if the flower is enclosed, as it may not open.

- There are three flowers in each sheath. If the sheath is tight you will need to force it open with your fingers. You can then lift the flowers into view, bringing them out of the sheath.

- Be careful when handling – the sap is poisonous and should not come into contact with your mouth.

- Recut the stems using a knife. Cut on an angle.

- Do not split or bash the stems.

- These flowers are thirsty and prefer lukewarm water.

COMMERCIAL HANDLING

- Do not place in the cool room. The tips will brown with refrigeration.

GENERAL USE

Strelitzia is generally available with stem lengths of 50–100 centimetres. They like humid conditions. Their leaves can also be used in designs.

WEDDING USE

Strelitzia is best used in dramatic hand-tied natural stemmed bouquets. The flowers can be taken apart and wired into sections for modern wired bouquets. Wear gloves when doing this, as the sap can cause skin irritation.

CORPORATE USE

These flowers will last five days in corporate designs, but some burning on the tips will usually occur within this time. There are three flowers in each sheath and the enclosed flowers will brown in office environments.

GROWING CONDITIONS

Strelitzia likes a warm, open position with good drainage. In late winter you can split the base of the plant and plant it elsewhere. This plant is hardy and drought tolerant. Its root system is invasive and this must be kept in mind when deciding where to plant it.

HISTORY

This flower is originally from South Africa. It was named after the wife of King George the third, Queen Charlotte, who was from Mechlenberg-Strelitz in Northern Germany. Sir Joseph Banks introduced the plant to the British Isles and he named the plant after Queen Charlotte. The common name 'Bird of Paradise' is named, literally, after the bird, as the flowers resemble the bird's beak and plumage.

SYRINGA

(si-rin-ga) Common names: *Lilac*

BOTANICAL VARIETIES Syringa vulgaris, Syringa persica (white) (over 20 species) FAMILY Oleaceae NATURAL SEASON Late winter and spring COLOUR AVAILABILITY Pink, purple, mauve, primrose yellow, red/violet, white CUT FLOWER LIFE SPAN 5–7 days (does not last as well in late season)

GENERAL USE

Syringa is usually sold with five stems per bunch, with stem lengths of 30–60 centimetres. These are lovely flowers for the vase at home. They are also an excellent choice for table centrepieces, provided there is not expensive wine on the table as the scent of the flowers can upset the bouquet of the wine.

Syringa can be used for a cascading effect as well as a filler flower in floral designs. The flowers usually last longer than the foliage, so for formal arrangements the foliage can be discarded and replaced with another foliage such as leather fern.

WEDDING USE

Syringa is not hardy as a cut flower, but it will survive in a hand-tied bouquet if the bouquet is kept in water until the time of the ceremony. In bouquets it is best used with other flowers, such as Roses, for support. The flower can be cut into sections.

CORPORATE USE

Syringa flowers can be used in corporate designs, although they are not ideal for use in office conditions. The foliage will not last and must be completely removed before the flowers are used. It is also advisable to use these flowers with another strong flower to support them. After about four days in office conditions their tips will start to dry.

GROWING CONDITIONS

Syringa grows best in cold climates, in humus loam and an acid rich soil that is treated with a ration of lime. Spent flowers should be dead-headed. You can propagate from early summer and tip the cuttings that are struck in a sandy soil.

CARE AND HANDLING

- Cut or purchase when at least half of the flowers are open and have a strong scent. The foliage should be strong. Beware if the foliage has been removed by the florist, as this is a sign that it is older stock.

- These flowers suffer from flower drop later in the season. Gently shake the bunch to check for this.

- Recut 2–3 centimetres from the stem ends, using secateurs. Cut on a sharp angle.

- Bashing the woody stem ends will damage the fibres. They can be lightly crushed instead.

- Place in shallow water, in a spotlessly clean vase. Check the water levels daily and top up if necessary.

- Preservative is optional. Some experts believe that preservative will maintain the flowers' perfume, but this is debatable.

- Syringa is sensitive to ethylene, so keep it away from cigarette smoke and ripening fruit.

- Keep the flowers cool, but do not place in airconditioned environments.

COMMERCIAL HANDLING

- Do not place in the cool room.

Romantic flower meaning: charity (Lilac Field);
first love (Lilac Purple); youthful innocence (Lilac White)

HISTORY

Syringa is native to Europe and North Eastern Asia. It was introduced into European gardens from Ottoman gardens. It is generally believed that Ogier Ghiselin de Busbecq, the Roman Emperor's ambassador, supplied Lilac slips to botanist Carolus Clusius, around 1562. Syringa is the state flower of the American state of New Hampshire.

TAGETES

(tag-et-ees) Common names: Marigold; Aztec Marigold; African Marigold; French Marigold; Irish Lace; Signet Marigold BOTANICAL VARIETIES Tagetes patula (French Marigold), Tagetes erecta (African Marigold), Tagetes tenuifolia (Signet Marigold) (over 50 species) FAMILY Asteraceae NATURAL SEASON Late spring, summer and early autumn COLOUR AVAILABILITY Yellow, orange, flame, cream and variegations CUT FLOWER LIFE SPAN 5–7 days

GENERAL USE

Some find the smell of Tagetes flowers to be unpleasant. For this reason, they are best not to be used in corporate decorating, table centrepieces or bridal work.

They can be used in funeral work such as wreaths and sheaves as they are a good filling flower with strong colour presence. Their colours are suited to modern décor, beach houses and casual outdoor living, as they are not considered a select flower.

GROWING CONDITIONS

Tagetes requires well-drained soil, sun, moisture and humus for solid flowering. It is very easy to grow from seed. In warmer climates it can be sown at any time throughout the year. The Tagetes minuta variety is sometimes planted between vegetable crops to ward off pests. The oil it contains is reputed to repel vermin as well as flies.

HISTORY

Tagetes is native to Mexico. It was taken to Spain in the 16th century, and had earlier been taken to Northern Africa.

Tagetes has many uses. The petals were once used as a substitute for Saffron and are used in salads, or cooked. Tagetes oil (extracted by steam) is used by aromatherapists to help with fungal and parasitic issues. Medicinally, this flower has been used to facilitate the flow of mucus and loosen congestion, and has been used on sores, cuts and bunions. Australian soldiers that fought in the Boar War brought these plants back to Australia.

In the language of flowers, Tagetes means 'desire for riches'. It is considered a cheaper type of flower and was once referred to as the 'poor man's flower'.

CARE AND HANDLING

- Cut or purchase when the flowers are half to fully open. The foliage should be strong green in colour with no sign of yellowing.

- Open the bunches for air circulation.

- Remove any leaves that will sit below the waterline.

- Recut 2–3 centimetres from the stem end. Cut on a sharp angle.

- Use bleach or preservative in the water and change every 2 days.

- Do not place in heated or airconditioned environments – this will dry out both the flowers and foliage.

COMMERCIAL HANDLING

- These flowers can be kept in the cool room at temperatures of 6–8 degrees Celsius. Allow conditioning time on removal.

- Separate the bunches – if they are left in bunches in the cool room the foliage will blacken and mould.

TELOPEA

(tel-oh-pee-ya) Common names: *Waratah*

BOTANICAL VARIETIES Telopea speciosissima, Telopea oreades (Gippsland Waratah) FAMILY Proteaceae NATURAL SEASON Spring COLOUR AVAILABILITY Red, pink, white CUT FLOWER LIFE SPAN 4 weeks

Note: *There is a variety of flower known as Alloxylon that looks like Telopea but in a more fragmented form. The foliage is similar and hardy and it is sold commercially. These flowers last well and as a cut flower, prepare in the same way as Telopea.*

GENERAL USE

The Telopea is a large flower and can be used in modern or traditional designs. They are usually placed down the axis of an arrangement in graded sizes, or placed low in a design. The weight of these blooms means you must consider the scale, or sizes, of the flowers you use with them, as they are very dominant in size and colour.

CORPORATE USE

These large flowers are suited to corporate designs but they require a good water source. They dislike airconditioning. They will just last a week in office conditions if the centres are tight and fresh.

GROWING CONDITIONS

Telopea is difficult to grow and needs a lot of mulching over sandy, damp loam. It can be grown from seed or spring cuttings.

HISTORY

Telopea is native to Australia. The Telopea speciosissima is the floral emblem for the State of New South Wales. Of the Protea genus, there are only four species in Australia. The flower's common name, 'Waratah', is an Aboriginal word. There are a number of Aboriginal stories about Waratahs. One mythological story explains that the flower was a symbol of the love of Krubi and Bahmai, two lovers separated by war. The leaves were a symbol of Bahmai's spear, and the flaming red flowers were said to have sprouted from Krubi's tears.

CARE AND HANDLING

- Cut or purchase when there are very few florets open. The centres should look very tight and the foliage should be unmarked and a deep green.

- A blue tinge of colour can indicate age or refrigeration.

- The stems are woody. Do not bash them, but recut 2–3 centimetres from the stem ends, using secateurs. Cut on an angle.

- Remove any leaves that will sit below the waterline.

- Preservative is not needed.

- Telopea is very sensitive to ethylene, so keep it away from cigarette smoke and ripening fruit.

COMMERCIAL HANDLING

- Do not place in the cool room.

THRYPTOMENE

(thrip-toh-meen) Common names: Heath Myrtle

BOTANICAL VARIETIES Thryptomene saxicola (40 species in this genus) FAMILY Myrtaceae NATURAL SEASON Late winter and spring COLOUR AVAILABILITY Cream, pink CUT FLOWER LIFE SPAN 5–7 days

CARE AND HANDLING

- Cut or purchase when only a third of the flowers are open.

- Shake the stems to check for flower drop.

- Some growers will place Thryptomene under hessian or damp newspaper, as this flower also drinks through its heads. Do not buy them in this manner, as their vase life will be shortened.

- Remove any fine foliage that will sit below the waterline.

- Recut 2–3 centimetres from the stem ends. Cut on an angle.

- Keep cool as a cut flower.

- These flowers should be misted to help them drink.

- Preservative is recommended.

COMMERCIAL USE

- Thyrptomene can be kept in the cool room at temperatures of 6–8 degrees Celsius.

- Florists should inform customers that this flower will dry and drop as it ages.

GENERAL USE

Thryptomene is a delicate flower. It can be used in all types of floral designs, including large floral foam arrangements and bouquets. These flowers can be coloured with floral spray colours or food dye.

Do not use in office decorations as they will dry out quickly in heating or airconditioning.

WEDDING USE

In days gone by this flower was thought of as a cheap flower associated with wreaths, and even though these days it is used in all types of designs, some will still not use it in bouquets.

When it is used, it should be placed sparingly for a delicate look. It can be wired in small sprays for corsage work.

Do not use Thryptomene on a hot day as it can dry out. It is best used in bouquet holders with a water source.

GROWING CONDITIONS

Thryptomene grows best in well-drained, moderately fertile, neutral to acidic soil. It enjoys full sun in a temperate climate.

HISTORY

Thryptomene is native to Australia. It is a relative of the Tea Tree (Leptospermum). This plant is listed as being found at Mount Olga by Ernest Giles, during his exploration expeditions in Australia.

TILLANDSIA

(til-land-zee-a) Common names: Spanish Moss; Pink Quill; Airplant

BOTANICAL VARIETIES Tillandsia usneiodes (Spanish Moss), Tillandsia lindenii (Pink Quill), Tillandsia crispa (Airplant) Tillandsia cyanea Family Bromeliaceae NATURAL SEASON Spring, summer and autumn COLOUR AVAILABILITY Grey, pink, lemon, orange, purple CUT FLOWER LIFE SPAN 3–4 weeks

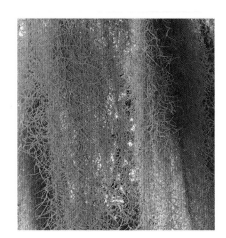

GENERAL USE

Tillandsia flowers (Spanish Moss and Airplant varieties) are popular in many floral designs. Their texture and dramatic layered flowers particularly complements modern designs. They can be used in both corporate and wedding work.

GROWING CONDITIONS

Tillandsia gains nutrients and water through its leaves. It can grow in leaf mould and sand and it attaches itself to trees. It only grows in tropical temperatures.

HISTORY

Tillandsia is native to North and South America. It is named for the Swedish physician Elias Tillands, and is the largest genus in the Tillandsioidae subfamily. There are over 500 known species of Tillandsia, and more are being discovered every year.

Tillandsia has developed an ability to take all its food and water through specially designed cells without needing any roots, making it one of the world's most amazing plants.

CARE AND HANDLING

- Tillandsia cyanea should have tight layered flowers when fresh.

- The flower colours of all varieties should be strong and vibrant.

- Recut the stem ends and place into water with preservative.

COMMERCIAL HANDLING

- Do not place in the cool room.

TRITELEIA

(tri-ta-lah-lee-ya) Common names: Queen Fabiola; Ithuriel's Spear; Trumpet Lily

BOTANICAL VARIETIES Triteleia laxa (a genus of 15 species) FAMILY Alliaceae SUB FAMILY Themidaceae SEASON AVAILABILITY Spring and early summer COLOUR AVAILABILITY Blue/mauve CUT FLOWER LIFE SPAN 5–7 days

CARE AND HANDLING

- Cut or purchase when 4–6 flowers are open.

- Look for buds that are showing full colour.

- Avoid any shrivelled flowers.

- Recut 2–3 centimetres from the stem ends. Cut on an angle.

- Remove any leaves that will sit below the waterline.

- Keep cool as a cut flower.

- Use bleach or preservative in the water.

- Triteleia is sensitive to ethylene. Remove spent blooms to avoid their ethylene emissions affecting the remaining blooms.

COMMERCIAL HANDLING

- Do not place in the cool room.

GENERAL USE

Triteleia is a pretty, light flower to use in posies and bouquets. It is not suitable for office decorating, as airconditioning will, cause the lower flowers to die while the buds are opening.

GROWING CONDITIONS

Triteleia will grow in most soils, but good drainage is needed. It can be grown in full sun, or fairly deep shade, and is suited to most climates other than tropical. The Triteleia bulb blooms in December and then goes dormant, requiring a dry summer rest.

HISTORY

This flower is native to Oregon, United States. Triteleia laxa is the Latin name for Ithuriel's Spear. The common name comes from the spear of the angel Ithuriel (angel of justice) who has the power to reveal deception. In religious stories, when Satan, disguised as a snake, whispered into Eve's ear, he was pricked by Ithuriel's spear and was thus revealed as 'Satan'.

TULIPA

(too-lip-a) Common names: Tulip; Turban Lily; Parrot Tulip

BOTANICAL VARIETIES Tulipa hybrids FAMILY Liliaceae NATURAL SEASON Late winter and spring (available commercially from glasshouses all year round) COLOUR AVAILABILITY Wide range including variegations CUT FLOWER LIFE SPAN 7–10 days

GENERAL USE

Tulipas (Tulips) are an elegant vase flower and are also suitable for wiring in arrangements. Use green wire (either painted or covered) to insert at the base of the head and follow down the stem.

Tulips can be fully opened for wreath work. Place your thumb under the petal and arch the petal over it. This gives maximum surface area.

When mixing Tulips with Narcissus that has been freshly cut from the garden, first place the Narcissus in a separate vase for up to 24 hours. This allows time for the sap in the Narcissus stems to expel. After this, it can be safely arranged with the Tulips.

Tulips can grow up to 20 centimetres from the time they are picked to the end of their cut flower life span. Be aware of this possibility when creating arrangements.

WEDDING USE

Tulips are a very popular choice for bridal bouquets. They can be used in bouquet holders, hand-tied bouquets or wired bouquets.

In wired bouquets, they should be wired using the pierce and mount method. This will prevent them from growing and opening once they are made up into the bouquet.

If you want the flowers to open up once they are in the bouquet, use them in bouquet holders or in hand-tied natural-stemmed bouquets and make sure they have a water source. When used in bouquet holders they must be wire supported from the head and down the stem. Make sure they are kept in the dark (covered with cloth) if made the day before the wedding, or they will grow towards the light.

CARE AND HANDLING

- Cut or purchase when Tulips are in bud and showing colour. The stems should be strong and the foliage undamaged, and strong green in colour.

- Avoid any bunches with yellowing on the foliage.

- Avoid any bunches with transparent, discoloured or weak edges on the blooms – this is an indication that they have been sitting in the cool room for too long.

- Remove any leaves that will sit below the waterline.

- Wash the stems to remove particles of dirt.

- Recut 2–3 centimetres from the stem ends and place into water.

- Do not use preservative in the water. A little bleach is optional.

- Tulipas are directional and will move toward the light, and will continue to grow as cut flowers. This can be prevented by piercing the top of the stem (about two centimetres below the flower head) with a pin. Though this will shorten the life span of the flower.

- If heads bend over, they can be revived by wrapping them in coned paper (to support the stems and heads) and placing them in deep water. Leave for up to three hours, then unwrap and place them back in the vase.

COMMERCIAL HANDLING

- Tulipas can be kept in the cool room at temperatures of 6–8 degrees Celsius.

- For use in floristry, wire support is often necessary especially when using in bouquet holders and floral foam.

Romantic flower meaning: fame (Tulip);
declaration of love (Tulip Red); unrequited love (Yellow Tulip)

CORPORATE USE

Tulips are not ideal for use in office conditions, however, they are often requested by clients. If used, they should start the week in bud form and be prepared to make a mid-week visit to replace them if necessary.

GROWING CONDITIONS

Tulip needs rich, limed, well-drained soil and plenty of sunshine. It prefers climates where there is a cold winter; otherwise the bulb will not flower again. Tulip enjoys full sun from late autumn to early spring. Plant 15 centimetres deep and lift the bulbs after the foliage dies back. Store bulbs in an airy place.

HISTORY

This flower is native to Turkey. The name originates from the Turkish word for 'turban'. The Tulip was first introduced to Vienna in 1544 by O De Busbecq, the Austrian Ambassador to the Sultan of Turkey. Tulips became all the rage in Europe and the Dutch embraced them with great passion.

By 1644 new colours were being produced in Holland, and many fortunes were made through the trade of valuable rare bulbs. In the early 18th century though, Hyacinths became the popular fashion and the Tulip was delegated to second position.

VERONICA *(vur-on-ik-a)* Common names: *Blue Feather Flower*

BOTANICAL VARIETIES Veronica gentianoides, Veronica virginica, Veronica spicata, Veronica scrophulariaceae, Veronica pinnata (over 250 species in this genus, annuals and perennials) FAMILY Scrophulariaceae NATURAL SEASON Late winter, spring and summer COLOUR AVAILABILITY a wide range of colours CUT FLOWER LIFE SPAN 5–7 days

GENERAL USE

Veronica is a garden type cut flower and the purple varieties are appealing when mixed with pink flowers. They make a lovely cottage-style vase flower for the home. Their foliage is hardier than the flowers and can be mixed into different arrangements.

Veronica flowers are not suited to office decorating and they dislike airconditioning.

GROWING CONDITIONS

Veronica needs good quality, well-drained soil and plenty of sunshine. It is raised from seed.

HISTORY

Veronica is native to Europe, East Asia and North America.

CARE AND HANDLING

- Cut or purchase when the flowers are showing colour from the base and about one third of the flowers are open.

- Open the bunches and check there are no yellowing leaves.

- Remove any leaves that will sit below the waterline.

- Recut 2–3 centimetres from the stem ends. Cut on an angle.

- Place into water. Preservative is essential.

COMMERCIAL HANDLING

- There should be no need to place these flowers in the cool room.

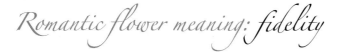

Romantic flower meaning: fidelity

324

VERTICORDIA

(vur-ti-kor-dee-ua) Common names: *Golden Morrison;*
Feather Flower BOTANICAL VARIETIES Verticordia grandis (red), Verticordia nitens (yellow) and Verticordia grandiflora (white) FAMILY Myrtaceae
NATURAL SEASON Spring COLOUR AVAILABILITY Gold, red, yellow, pink, white CUT FLOWER LIFE SPAN 5–7 days

CARE AND HANDLING

- Cut or purchase when the leaves look fresh and the flower centres look tight.

- Separate the bunch and check for flower drop.

- Remove any leaves that will sit below the waterline.

- Recut 2–3 centimetres from the stem ends. Cut on an angle.

- Use bleach or preservative in the water.

- Do not mist.

- Verticordia is sensitive to ethylene gas so keep it away from cigarette smoke and ripening fruit.

COMMERCIAL HANDLING

- Do not place in the cool room as this may cause fungal infection.

GENERAL USE

Verticordia is pretty vase flower. The Golden Morrison variety is very popular. The flowers outlast the foliage. These flowers can be used in floral foam but remove the foliage as it will dry out.

Do not use in office decorations as the flowers will dry out in airconditioned or heated environments.

GROWING CONDITIONS

Verticordia is not easy to grow. It likes well-drained soil, low humidity, sandy, rich soil and plenty of sun.

HISTORY

Verticordia is native to Western Australia. Its name is Latin for 'to turn the heart'. Approximately 100 species of Verticordias are found in Australia, with all but three found in the south west of Western Australia.

VIOLA

(vee-yoh-la) Common names: Violet; Pansy

BOTANICAL VARIETIES Viola hortensis (tricolour), Viola hederacea (Australian Native Violet), Viola x wittrockiana (Pansy), Viola odorata **FAMILY** Violaceae **NATURAL SEASON** Winter and early spring (Violets), spring and summer (Pansies) **COLOUR AVAILABILITY** White, mauve, pink, purple, tricolour **CUT FLOWER LIFE SPAN** 3–5 days

GENERAL USE

Viola odorata (Violets) are highly perfumed when fresh. When sold commercially, they are usually presented with 40–50 florets to a bunch, constructed as a tied posy with leaves surrounding the flowers. The consumer can split the bunches and reorganise the flowers into smaller bunches or clusters, with two or three leaves around each bunch.

For funeral work, especially wreaths, the stems can be angled upwards and wired so that they sit upright at the back of the little posy cluster. This is a traditional English design method. They can also be worn this way as a shoulder corsage.

Pansies make a pretty vase flower and were once very popular as a 'topping' flower on wreaths. They were wired individually and then several were wired onto a wooden pick (often called pegs). This was placed into a wreath base and the pansies were arranged in a semi-circular design.

Do not use Violets or Pansies in corporate designs.

WEDDING USE

Violets can be used in wedding bouquets but they will spot (look black) in photographs, especially when teamed with light coloured flowers, and they can only be used in cool weather. They should only be used in wired bouquets (as opposed to other bouquets). Use the pierce and mount wiring method and air seal the stems with binding tape.

Pansies are rarely used in wedding work.

GROWING CONDITIONS

Violet requires a moist leaf layer and rich soil. It enjoys a semi-sheltered position and will spread quickly through a garden. Violets will self-seed.

CARE AND HANDLING

- Cut or purchase when the florets are at least half open.

- Violets drink through their heads as well as their stems. They should be constantly misted but do not plunge the heads into water as they will lose their perfume.

- Do not place in direct sunlight.

- Violets and Pansies like cold water. Additives in the water are optional.

COMMERCIAL HANDLING

- They dislike refrigeration and will dry out on removal.

Romantic flower meaning: consideration (Pansy);
faithful devotion (Violet Blue); modesty (Violet Sweet)

HISTORY

Violet is native to Europe. Viola hederacea is native to Australia. There are many stories incorporating the Violet in Greek mythology. In Germany, finding the first spring Violet was celebrated with dancing. Napoleon Bonaparte gave Violets to Josephine and later used the flower on his political emblem. The edible Violet flower is a good source of vitamins A and C.

VRIESEA (vree-see-ya) Common names: Flaming Sword; Painted Feather

BOTANICAL VARIETIES Vriesea carinata (Painted Feather), Vriesea splendens (Flaming Sword) FAMILY Bromeliaceae NATURAL SEASON Summer

COLOUR AVAILABILITY Pink, yellow and red, green and orange/red CUT FLOWER LIFE SPAN Up to 4 weeks

GENERAL USE

Vriesea flowers are very striking in floral design work, due to their colours and shape. They are dramatic in modern wedding design.

CORPORATE USE

These flowers are visually dramatic, but if placed in airconditioned environments their tips will brown and they will only last for around five days. In ideal conditions they can last up to four weeks.

GROWING CONDITIONS

Vriesea need lots of shade, humidity, and temperatures above 16 degrees Celsius.

HISTORY

Vriesea is native to Central and South America. It was named after a Dutch botanist, W H De Vriese. It is a very similar flower to the Tillandsia.

CARE AND HANDLING

- Cut or purchase when the flower colours are strong and vibrant.

- Brown tips are a sign of age or refrigeration. Avoid these.

- Recut the stems and place into water with preservative.

- Mist lightly, as the flower will absorb moisture through its petals.

- Vriesea is mildly sensitive to ethylene, so keep it away from cigarette smoke and ripening fruit.

CARE AND HANDLING

- Cut or purchase when the base flowers are half open and the buds are showing colour.

- Open the bunches to allow for air flow around the flowers.

- Remove the sword shaped leaves that will sit below the waterline.

- Recut the stem ends and place into deep water with bleach or preservative added.

- Keep them cool for maximum life span.

- Watsonia is sensitive to ethylene. Remove the base florets when they are spent to prevent their ethylene emissions affecting the other flowers.

COMMERCIAL HANDLING

- Watsonia can be kept in the cool room at temperatures of 6–8 degrees Celsius.

GENERAL USE

Watsonia flowers can be used in the vase at home, in floral foam or in bouquets. They have a wide use and can also be cut in half and used to base a wreath. They are considered 'active flowers' as they point upwards.

Watsonias can be used in church arrangements as well as gift items. They give a strong outline to designs, especially natural designs.

WEDDING USE

These flowers can be used in hand-tied, natural stemmed bouquets or in bouquet holders.

CORPORATE USE

Watsonias can be used in corporate designs if the lower base florets are in half bud form and the upper florets are still in bud. Check them mid-week, as the spent lower blooms may need to be removed.

GROWING CONDITIONS

Watsonia will grow in almost any soil conditions, although a loamy soil is the best choice. It will bloom three years from the time of planting seeds. It multiplies from seed quite easily.

HISTORY

Watsonia is native to South Africa. The genus is named after Sir William Watson, a British botanist.

ZANTEDESCHIA

(zan-tee-desh-ee-ya) Common names: Arum Lily; Lily of the Nile; Calla Lily BOTANICAL VARIETIES Zantedeschia aethiopica (Lily of the Nile or Arum Lily, its hybrid is Green Goddess with white tipped green spathes), Zantedeschia rehmannii (pink Calla Lily), Zantedeschia elliottiana (Golden Calla lily), Zantedeschia oculata (lime to yellow with a black/purple base) FAMILY Araceae NATURAL SEASON Spring and summer COLOUR AVAILABILITY Pink, white, green/cream, gold/yellow CUT FLOWER LIFE SPAN Up to 3 weeks

GENERAL USE

Technically speaking, Zantedeschias (Arum Lilies) are not Lilies, despite their common name reference.

Some varieties have cream/silver variegations through the leaves. A vase of these beautiful flowers with their own leaves looks elegant in any home. They can be used in bouquets and they look striking in modern design work. Sometimes they are internally wired for floral foam work.

Floral designers should place these flowers carefully as the spadix and spathe give a directional flow in a design. The spathe is actually part of the foliage. The spadix has the tiny flowers attached. If these flowers are left out of water for two to three hours, you will be able to flex the stem for linear designs, to curl or contort.

There is a superstition that Arum Lilies are also known as the Death Lily and are therefore unlucky. They were a popular funeral flower in Victorian times. Arum Lilies are often featured on bereavement cards. There are mixed emotions about this superstition today depending on the generation.

WEDDING USE

Zantedeschias are fabulous for arm sheaves. Squeeze out the stem sap before use to prevent it leaking onto the bride's gown. If the arrangements are made up the day before the wedding, the stems will seal overnight, or they can be sealed with cold glue.

These flowers can also be used in hand-tied or fully wired bouquets. Some of the flowers will need to be internally wired.

Zantedeschia stems are generally too thick to use in bouquet holders.

CARE AND HANDLING

- Cut or purchase when the flowers are half open and the spathe is unmarked. The foliage should be firm to touch. The stems should be firm and the stem ends should not be white or splitting upwards.

- There should be no sign of pollination on the spadix (centre of the bloom).

- Check that the spathe is not curling under at the tip as this is a sign of age.

- If purchased commercially remove immediately from plastic sleeves.

- Wash the stems to remove particles of dirt.

- Recut 2–3 centimetres from the stem ends, using a knife. Cut on an angle.

- Place into clean water. Preservative is optional.

- These flowers are sensitive to ethylene, so keep them away from cigarette smoke and ripening fruit.

- Zantedeschias hold a lot of sap, which needs to be eased out before the flowers are used. To do so, squeeze the stem and run your hand downwards. The sap will come out.

Romantic flower meaning:
ardour (Arum Lily)

CORPORATE USE

These flowers (and foliage) will last in corporate designs, but make sure there is no visible sign of pollen in the centre of the flower as this indicates age. Their stems can be bent into angles and will stay on the angle created.

GROWING CONDITIONS

Zantedeschia can be grown under water. It makes a striking pond flower. The easiest variety to grow this way is Zantedeschia aethiopica. Grown from bulb, this plant will flower for months.

HISTORY

Zantedeschia is native to South Africa. It has undergone many name changes; from Arum to Callas to Richardias. It is now named after the Italian botanist, Giovanni Zantedeschia.

In South Africa this flower is known as 'Pig Lily'. When early settlers to South Africa observed porcupines eating the roots of this wild growing plant, they dubbed it the 'Pig Lily', as porcupines were then referred to as 'pigs'.

ZEPHYRANTHES

(zef-a-ran-thas) Common names: Zephyr Lily; Storm Pink Lily; Autumn Crocus; Rain Lily BOTANICAL VARIETIES Zephyranthes grandiflora (Storm Pink Lily), Zephyranthes citrina (yellow Rain Lily), Zephyranthes atamasco (pink and white) FAMILY Amaryllidaceae NATURAL SEASON Late summer and autumn COLOUR AVAILABILITY White, yellow, red, pink CUT FLOWER LIFE SPAN 14 days

GENERAL USE

The Zephyranthes grandiflora is the most popular of this genus and these lovely pink Lilies last quite well as cut flowers. The anthers can be removed to prevent staining on the petals, but doing this will slightly shorten the flower's life span.

WEDDING USE

Zephyranthes (Zephyr Lilies) are popular flowers and a good size for wedding work. They are suited to all forms of wedding designs, including wired bouquets or natural stemmed bouquets. Always remove the anthers from the stamens as the pollen can stain clothing.

CORPORATE USE

These flowers are suited to corporate decorating and will last well in office conditions. Always remove the anthers before use.

GROWING CONDITIONS

Zephyranthes grows from a bulb in well-drained soil. It can be planted at any time if it is kept relatively dry for three months and then moist before planting. Zephyranthes will flower throughout the year. Offsets from the bulbs can be divided in spring.

HISTORY

Zephyranthes is native to America. The Zephyranthes derives its common name of 'Rain Lily' from the fact that it always flowers directly after a rainfall that follows a dry period.

CARE AND HANDLING

- Cut or purchase when the buds are half open and foliage is glossy green.

- There should be no sign of pollination in the centre of the flower. If there is, this means the flower is older and should be avoided.

- Remove from the sleeve and separate the bunches as soon as possible.

- Remove any foliage that will sit below the waterline.

- Use a sharp knife to remove the white section from the base of the stem (if it is present), as this section does not uptake water well as a cut flower.

- Change the water and recut the stems regularly.

- Zephyranthes is mildly sensitive to ethylene gas so keep it away from cigarette smoke and ripening fruit.

COMMERCIAL HANDLING

- Zephyranthes can be kept in the cool room at temperatures of 6–8 degrees Celsius.

ZINGIBER

(zin-gee-ber) Common names: Ginger; Beehive

BOTANICAL VARIETIES Zingiber species, Zingiber spectabile, Zingiber zerumbet FAMILY Ingiberaceae NATURAL SEASON Summer

COLOUR AVAILABILITY Yellow/orange and red CUT FLOWER LIFE SPAN 3 weeks

CARE AND HANDLING

- Select glossy cones that are fully coloured.
- Avoid any cones with brown/black marks.
- Remove the small flowers that protrude from the cones.
- Recut 3–4 centimetres from the stem ends. Cut on a sharp angle.
- Preservative is optional.
- Replace the vase water every three days.
- If the stems wilt they can be bathed to revive them.

COMMERCIAL HANDLING

- Do not place in the cool room.

GENERAL USE

Zingiber flowers are dramatic in modern work as well as in display arrangements. They are too large to use in bridal designs.

CORPORATE USE

These flowers will dry out in airconditioning, but will last a week in corporate designs.

GROWING CONDITIONS

Zingiber requires well-drained soil and a warm, moist climate. It only grows well in the tropics or in glasshouses. The flowers are produced on separate spikes from the leaves.

HISTORY

Zingiber is native to Asia. Its spice, Ginger, appears to be one of the first spices known. Ginger possesses aromatic, fleshy rootstocks that are rich in volatile oils. In the 16th century, King Henry VIII of England recommended Ginger as a medicine to treat sufferers of the plague.

Today, Ginger's rich oil is extracted for medicinal purposes and is also used to impart an oriental flavour to some perfumes. Dried or powdered, it is used in cakes and in Ginger Beer.

ZINNIA *(zin-nee-ya)* Common names: *Little Star; Youth and Age*

BOTANICAL VARIETIES Zinnia elegans FAMILY Asteraceae NATURAL SEASON Summer and early autumn COLOUR AVAILABILITY Red, yellow, light pink, dark pink, mauve, purple, white CUT FLOWER LIFE SPAN 5–7 days

GENERAL USE

Zinnias can be used in all forms of floral design. They are very colourful and always look bright and cheery. There are also miniature Zinnias and these can be used in posies or nosegays.

The stems of Zinnia are brittle and can crease. In floral foam it is best to wire them internally for support. This will have a minor effect on their life span.

WEDDING USE

These flowers come in a range of sizes and colours. They can be used in hand-tied, natural stemmed bouquets (use an internal wire support) as well as bouquet holders, or fully wired bouquets. In bouquet holders they are internally wired, and for wired bouquets it is best to wire using the pierce and mount method.

Avoid refrigeration as this can cause the petal edges to burn.

CORPORATE USE

Zinnias are risky in corporate work. They can brown on the edges and may need a mid-week check. They will foul the vase water so use bleach as well as preservative to prevent this.

GROWING CONDITIONS

Zinnia is best sown in early spring. It is a frost-tender annual and does best when it positioned in full sun.

HISTORY

Zinnia is native to Mexico. It was planted in the garden of Montezuma, the last Aztec emperor, and it was here that it first attracted attention. The flowers were named after the German botany professor, Johann Gottfried Zinn (1727–1759).

CARE AND HANDLING

- Cut or purchase when the flowers are open, but the centres look very tight.

- Avoid them if the centres show any sign of pollination.

- When purchasing, check that the stem ends are free of any discolouration or slime.

- Open the bunches and separate the flowers.

- Recut 2–3 centimetres from the stem ends. Cut on a sharp angle.

- Remove all foliage that will sit below the waterline.

- Place in shallow water if preservative added.

COMMERCIAL HANDLING

- Zinnia can be kept in the cool room at temperatures of 6–8 degrees Celsius.

Romantic flower meaning: thoughtful recollections

COMMON NAME INDEX
Common flower names

This index lists all the flower varieties in the A–Z directory of cut flowers (Chapter 6). In this index the flowers are listed alphabetically by their common names. Some flowers have more than one common name, and in this instance all names have been included. Some flowers are known simply by their botanical name (with no known common name) and in this instance the botanical name is included here, as well as in the Botanical name index.

Note that some flowers share their common names with other flowers, i.e. Gerbera and Lonas are both commonly known as African Daisy.

BOTANICAL NAME INDEX

Botanical flower names

This index lists all the flower varieties in the A–Z directory of cut flowers (Chapter 6). In this index the flowers are listed alphabetically by their botanical names.

Image credits

All images © **iStockphoto**, except:

Main cover image, title page i, pp. 43, 44 (both), 45, 54 (all), 55 (both) © **Hayden Golder**; pp. 37, 51 (right) © **Marjorie Milner College**; p. 309 © **C.Baral**; pp. 85, 94 (both images), 103, 114, 116, 117, 134, 141, 154, 156 (middle and right), 178, 180, 191, 193, 194 (both images), 230, 255, 256 (left), 261 (both images), 266, 285, 290, 296, 319, 320 (left and middle), 329, 334 © **Country Farm & Garden**; pp. 115, 144 (right), 151, 195 (right) 218, 224 (both images), 226, 231, 236, 325 (both images), 333 © **M. Fagg, Australian National Botanic Gardens**; p. 321 left and right © **Ken Gilliland**; pp. 10 (both images), 14 (top), 173 (left) © **Lauren Milner**; pp. iv-v, 41, 46, 76 (right), 112 (middle), 124, 144 (left), 173 (right), 264 (right), 295, 326 (right) © **James Milner**; p. 48 © **Nicole Gibson**, p. 307 © **Julie Oertel**; pp. 12, 14 (bottom), 17, 19, 22, 33, 34, 50 (both images), 51 (left), 53 © **Rob Ryan**; pp. 28, 276 © **Shutterstock**.

Floral design credits

Thank you to the following for their inspirational arrangements:

Cover image: **Gregory Milner and Nicole Gibson**

Title page i: **Nicole Gibson**

Page 37 (top): **Nicole Gibson**

Page 37 (bottom): **Gregory Milner**

Page 41: **Gregory Milner**

Page 43: **Gregory Milner**

Page 44 (both): **Nicole Gibson and Gregory Milner**

Page 45: **Nicole Gibson and Gregory Milner**

Page 46 (all): **Gregory Milner**

Page 50 (both): **Nicole Gibson**

Page 51 (left): **Nicole Gibson**

Page 51 (both): **Gregory Milner and Nicole Gibson**

Page 54 (top two): **Kathryn Amor**

Page 54 (bottom two): **Nicole Gibson**

Page 55 (top): **Gregory Milner**

Page 55 (bottom): **Nicole Gibson**

Page 56: **Gregory Milner**

Page 63: **Nicole Gibson**